Watching Daytime Soap Operas

Opening shot, *The Young and the Restless,* November 27, 1981

Watching Daytime Soap Operas

THE POWER OF PLEASURE

Louise Spence

WESLEYAN UNIVERSITY PRESS Middletown, Connecticut

Published by Wesleyan University Press, Middletown, CT 06459

www.wesleyan.edu/wespress

Printed in the United States of America

5 4 3 2 1

LIBRARY OF CONGRESS CATALOGING-IN-PUBLICATION DATA

Spence, Louise, 1945–
Watching daytime soap operas : the power of pleasure / Louise Spence.
p. cm.
Includes bibliographical references and index.
ISBN 0-8195-6764-7 (cloth : alk. paper) — ISBN 0-8195-6765-5 (pbk. : alk. paper)
1. Soap operas—Social aspects—United States.
2. Soap operas—United States—History and criticism. I. Title.
PN1992.8.S4S64 2005
791.45'6—dc22 2005006651

Contents

Watching Daytime Soap Operas

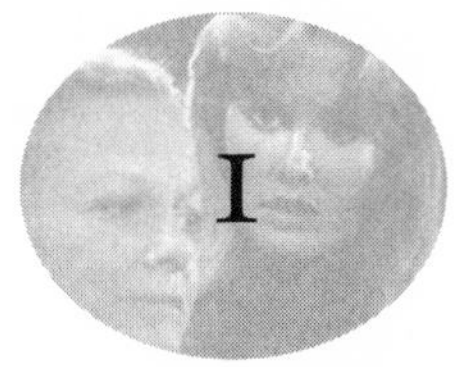

I

My mother says when I get older my dusty hair will settle and my blouse will learn to stay clean, but I have decided not to grow up tame like the others who lay their necks on the threshold waiting for the ball and chain.
—Sandra Cisneros

Life's Little Problems . . . and Pleasures; or, Why Study Soaps?

This book began one crisp autumn afternoon in 1980 with a graduate student ensconced in a sofabed, a box of tissues and a bottle of antibiotics nearby, watching soap operas on television. I was that student. And I still recall the warm feeling that came over me: although I hadn't watched soaps in nearly thirty years, the comfort of the familiar assaulted me with the poignancy of Proust's madeleine. Memories of watching them when I was small—literally at my mother's feet, as she sat and looked at *Search for Tomorrow* and *Love of Life* on a snowy, black-and-white TV while feeding my infant sister—came back in an instant.

But the sense of familiarity that I perceived carried with it a sense of loss as well: a connection to family, to women. This book is rooted in a strong interest in women who are at home during the day, a curiosity about the pleasures afforded by American networks' daytime soap operas, and a desire to learn more about the appeal and the resonance of this pastime.[1] It has moved slowly toward a suggestion of how one might study pleasure ("the most obscure and inaccessible region of the mind," according to Sigmund Freud[2]), using soap operas as both an example and a case study.

Twenty years after that autumn afternoon, while packing away some World War II–era magazines, I discovered a "complete novelette" by Irna Phillips and Janet Huckins in a 1942 *Movie-Radio Guide*. Titled "Lonely Women," it was a promotional piece for NBC's radio daytime dramatic serial of the same name ("Read this stirring novelette . . . and then listen to 'Lonely Women' over NBC Monday through Friday at 2:15 EWT [Eastern

War Time] . . . under the sponsorship of General Mills for Gold Medal Flour").[3] The novelette was centered on single women, "women who have to live alone" in a residential hotel, The Towers. "Yes, The Towers is dedicated to women living alone. But it is much more than that . . . a symbol, perhaps, of the loneliness of all people . . . all of us who are shut up within the prison of self" (p. 19).

Irna Phillips's name will be familiar to those who know their soap opera history as the creator and writer of numerous radio and television daytime serials. William J. Bell, who worked with Phillips as a dialogue writer on *The Guiding Light* (in 1956) and co-wrote *As the World Turns* with her (from 1957 to 1966), described Phillips herself as lonesome.[4] And Phillips, in a 1965 article in *McCall's,* discussing some of the "essential hopes and fears" women have in common, wrote, "None of us is a stranger to . . . the need to be loved, the struggle to communicate with another human being, a corroding sense of loneliness."[5]

But why are the young working women in the novelette lonely? They are, Phillips seems to suggest, lonely because their secret passions and secret shames have isolated them from their families and prevented them from beginning a family of their own. Unattached women are frequently unsettling, but these women seem to be threatening, not because of some assumed moral turpitude, but because of their independence in a world where the traditional family is seen as the bulwark against a yawning emptiness.

In the *McCall's* article, Phillips explained the origin of *Lonely Women.* Writing about herself in the third person, she tells of having shared a bedroom with her mother until her mother's death at age eighty. Phillips then left Chicago and moved to New York. There, "[s]he sat alone among the blank-faced women in hotel lobbies. After a year, she fled back to Chicago. . . . She was thirty-eight years old and making a quarter of a million dollars a year. She had everything in the world except a family of her own" (p. 117).

Loneliness. Do we need to be reminded? Loneliness is not surprising; the surprise is that so many "lonely" women live productive, sometimes deliciously imaginative, lives.

The same year that "Lonely Women" appeared in *Movie-Radio Guide,* Herta Herzog wrote a scholarly article about women who listened to radio serials. Formerly associate director of the Office of Radio Research (a part of Paul Lazarsfeld's Bureau of Applied Social Research at Columbia University), she was, at the time, in charge of the Program Analyzer Department at the advertising agency McCann-Erickson, Inc. After conducting a review of several academic studies of the characteristics of regular soap opera listeners, the effects of their listening, and the major types of gratification listeners reported,[6] she suggested that the serials may "provide the more naive individual with a much-desired, though vicarious, contact with human affairs which the more sophisticated person obtains at first hand through her wider range of experiences" (pp. 11–12). Herzog wrote of soap operas as "opportunities for wishful thinking . . . [filling] in the gaps in [the listeners'] own lives . . . [compensating] for their own failures . . ." (p. 24). In 1956, Donald Horton and R. Richard Wohl, in the journal *Psychiatry,* discussed the way the media, especially television, create parasocial relations, the illusion of face-to-face exchanges between viewer and performer, the simulacrum of conversation.[7] "All you have to do is turn that dial," says the television salesman in the 1955 film *All That Heaven Allows,* "and you have all the company you want—right there on the screen."

This idea of the homemaker's loneliness as the cause of her being easily affected by TV has persisted. A key 1978 book on television and human behavior argues that because of homebound women's "psychological and social isolation," they are "particularly susceptible to influence by television."[8] Eight years later, Robert Cathcart discussed narrowing networks of kinship, high mobility, and intense individualism as factors reducing emotional involvement with neighbors and relatives and suggested that soap operas, like the parasocial interaction that Horton and Wohl describe, can and do "provide a surrogate means of meeting these emotional interpersonal needs."[9] Seeing an attraction to soap operas as compensating for the lack of emotional involvement with others, Cathcart, like Herzog before him, declares that soaps afford psychically impressionable female viewers "an opportunity to try out a wide range of responses and emotions." "You can get close to characters, study their reactions, and imagine yourself in their position without embarrassment or fear of disapproval" (p. 218). Ruth Rosen in "Soap Operas: Search for Yesterday" (1986) also perceives soap opera viewing as a substitute for face-to-face interaction[10] and claims that viewers "care at least as much about soap opera characters as about people they know" (p. 42). And Jib Fowles, in 1992, speaks of loneliness and claims that soap operas "are ways of extending and peopling a sparse social universe," and that many fans "genuinely experience soap opera characters as perfectly real," indivisibly attached to their sense of real life.[11] What an impoverished emotional life they project onto viewers!

Some researchers actually measure interest in soaps by the viewer's refusal to be distracted by other activities that are assumed to be more worthwhile or beneficial—in particular, "real" social interaction.[12]

This picture has a certain tedious familiarity. There is a sense in all these studies that soap operas are harming innocents (the childish, the weak, and the powerless), and that viewers are self-indulgent, mindless, emotionally feeble, unable to cope. With this construction of the soap opera viewer, it is understandable that critics worried about their perceptions of social reality. But perhaps these critics are also securing their own prestige through a differential relation to these women. It may be that they need something or someone whom they see as lowly or underdeveloped against whom to define themselves. By doing so, they solidify their own position of respectability, for authority and legitimacy are partially dependent on that which is denigrated in others.[13] Likewise, in disparaging the suspect pleasures (or tastes or preferences) of others, by distinguishing themselves so clearly from someone supposedly so different, they draw symbolic boundaries, acceptable limits that people "like us" are supposed to occupy.[14] Distinctions and boundaries, as Sharon Crowley notes, are never disinterested.[15]

By admonishing women for letting soaps compensate for what their lives lack, these researchers call up images of the socially inept, the rejected, those with low self-worth or an incomplete identity: the psychologically needy. It is assumed that their lives are otherwise uneventful, unrewarding, or insufficient. But there is also the implication that these TV relations inadequately imitate "normal" social relations, or that they spoil one's appetite for real life. And the victim is blamed for her own isolation. She is hopelessly captured by the evils of banality, and her lonesome (and marginal) existence is brought about by her soap opera "addiction." If she had only sought out more meaningful social intercourse!

The notion of "addiction" itself explains little. After all, many viewers do stop watching soaps. And continuing the habit may imply a commitment to finding some satisfaction or reward. Perhaps the ongoing nature of soaps, their seriality, the delightful anxiety of anticipation, can tell us something about the conflicting nature of the pleasures they provide. For most of the women I spoke to, watching soap operas might be aptly described as a habit (like a hobby), a practice that requires some repetition. In fact, as we shall see in Chapter 2, the repetitive and therefore predictable attention (or at least, attendance) of the audience is a vital part of television's commercial basis. It is difficult to talk about watching soap operas if the activity is conceptualized as an isolated viewing event.

The notion of "addiction," however, can be reassuring to the networks in an era when the remote control, VCR, and personal video recorder services (such as TiVo, ReplayTV, or DishPVR) encourage us to treat programs as interchangeable options.[16] And the image of a timid female viewer, vulnerable to psychic manipulation and lured by "human" contact, implies that she may also be susceptible to the promises of the products advertised: the perfect consumer. This is a happy situation for the advertiser (and for the commercial broadcast industry, which frequently funded early audience studies).

Along with the psychological and social concerns projected onto these belittled viewers, these studies of soap opera audiences reflect larger concerns about technology and modern life. There seems to be a major apprehension that, along with technological progress, modernity has created ever more isolated, lethargic, and anonymous individuals. Could it be that technical achievements, together with material advances, bring spiritual deprivation, and social, moral, and cultural decay? Fearing that distant, impersonal, and mediated contact with strangers would substitute for face-to-face relationships with family and friends, many critics have seen the increasing power of the mass media as producing atomized and alienated individuals and as threatening "community."[17]

It seems to me that this nostalgia for community is a romantic longing (rooted more in desire than in memory) for a time and place where personal growth and self-fulfillment were found not in individual autonomy but in interpersonal intimacy. Perhaps society uses "community," or more exactly, the feminine aspects of community—responsiveness and connection to others[18]—as a defense against the individualism and aggressiveness of modern public life. It may be that a housewife's unselfish devotion is all that remains today of the tradition of reciprocal caring and of work that contributes to the common good. This idea of community offering intimacy, mutuality, and sharing as a defense against the individualism and achievement-orientation of the public realm is not so far removed from the mid-nineteenth-century ideals of true womanhood, where the wife's domesticity, along with her piety, purity, and submission, compensated for (and allowed for) her husband's ruthlessness and brutal competitiveness in the business world.[19]

It is obvious that behind all this scrutiny of women's viewing behavior[20] lies an unacknowledged disdain for that audience. But the concern for the welfare of women also belies a profound anxiety over their potential power, the instability of the investment in their domestication, and the threat that their rebellion poses to family life. Clearly a cultural anxiety about domesticity coexists with an equal fascination with transgressions against domestic life and violations of the social strictures concerning the home. What happens when we do not wish to grow up tame? When we don't want to trade our dreams for the ordinary? Soaps titillate—and threaten—precisely because they prick those fragile psychic balances. When the frequent swirls of virtue and evil, the secrets and the seductions, the hyperbolic acts and extravagant expression, the stories of betrayal and revenge, the staging of sexuality and treachery, and the acting out of moral identifications take on philosophic significance and cultural value, what will become of the quotidian?

Is the fact that many women like soap operas an indication of their loneliness and heart-fluttering gullibility? Or do soaps speak, with some material urgency, to their concerns? These shows are opportunities for heightened attention and feeling, for the refusal of subtlety, censorship, and accommodation. The critics' self-serving moral landscapes conceptualizing the fan as desperate and dysfunctional suggest that these women should be "explained" and restored to "normalcy."[21] What is often repressed or not expressed, and certainly not interrogated, are the criteria that go into such judgments. These critics celebrate reality over fantasy, reason over imagination, and without exception, cognition trumps emotion.

But are the mind and feeling necessarily incompatible? Is intellectual pleasure necessarily in conflict with emotional life? Perhaps feeling and thinking cannot be separated except by doing great damage to the truth of experience. One reason the idea of women watching soaps may be so disturbing is that it asks us to reformulate the frameworks through which women's experience and pleasure have been understood. It shows us that the emotional and the rational are not mutually exclusive realms at all, that the distinctions between reality and fantasy, reason and imagination, are not so precise. If fantasy and reality, fiction and truth, can exist simultaneously and intersect, each essential to the other's existence, then the assumed dichotomies between them are really false. Perhaps the subjective and the imaginative are not irrational at all. We will revisit this, with specific examples, at various points in the chapters ahead.

But many women *are* embarrassed by soaps. It may seem to them that damaged women, their most outrageous acts, and their vulgar lack of restraint are getting inordinate screen time. These non-watching women are almost puritanical in their complaint that the operatic excesses of many of the storylines and performances are unrealistic. (They are not the truth, and are, therefore, lies and immoral.) Hyperbole, like irony and other departures from literal truth, is liable to be understood by inexperienced viewers as false. The unlikely coincidences and sudden plot reversals may seem unbelievable. And all those instances of girls falling in love with their long-lost half brothers strain credulity. The tethers of family propriety have been so internalized, become so much a part of the modern self, that images of families out of control can be more than slightly unnerving. No wonder women enjoying soaps is a little upsetting!

Until the recent spate of feminist studies, both fans and academics alike remarked on how critics have denied credibility to an entertainment form that is loved by millions. They invariably listed some of the wonderful—or anomalous—people who watch soaps (wonderful or anomalous because they are not housewives: a supreme court judge, an avant-garde artist, a former governor, movie stars, professional athletes, or college students).[22] Yet it is precisely the people deemed hardly worth mentioning whom the shows are made for—the nonexceptional women who are at home during the day: women with an appetite for wonder and the responsibility for purchasing the health, beauty, food, and cleaning products that are advertised twenty-seven to thirty-five times an hour. It seems to me that it is because the shows are so important to these women that soap operas are worth studying.

Another reason may be even simpler: We are justified in taking soaps seriously because the people who watch them do. The shows are a significant, often intensely visceral, part of their lives.

Daytime soap operas have not produced many cultural heroes or heroines. Characters seldom become household names (as have Cinderella, James Bond, or Robin Hood). Yet the generic form itself sometimes does. One does not have to have watched soaps to know what the *New York Times* means when it says that Claus von Bülow's life is like a soap opera. Or when the presiding judge at the Bess Meyerson/Carl A. Capasso/Hortense W. Gabel bribery trial sustains a defense objection and instructs the prosecution not to turn the case into a soap opera. Or when the headline of a book review about the Henry Ward Beecher–Elizabeth Tilton scandal reads, "True Soap Opera." Those references need no elaboration. Soap operas and the *activity* of watching soaps have taken on cultural meaning—and it is not very pretty. Isabel Allende describes her grandfather retiring to the family's large, rundown beach house: "When grandfather had made the last repairs on the house, and tired of fighting the ineluctable erosion on the hill and the plagues of ants, roaches, and mice, a year had gone by and solitude had embittered him. As a last desperate measure against boredom, he began to watch soap operas and without realizing it became ensnared in that vice; before long the fates of those cardboard characters became more important to him than those of his own family." A touch of jealousy here? "He used to follow several at one time, and gradually the story lines blended together and he ended up lost in a labyrinth of vicarious passions." But worry not, dear reader, this feminized gentleman was cured: "That was when he realized that the moment had come to return to civilization."[23]

Television in general, as Ellen Seiter has pointed out, is both widely accessible and widely deprecated.[24] But the ambiguous social status of those who watch soap operas seems to have attracted paternalistic concern about social alienation and social impairment. And, as Dorothy Hobson argues in her book about the British serial *Crossroads,* the social status of soap fans may have influenced the critics' evaluation of the aesthetic status of soaps themselves.[25]

I once noticed a woman on a crosstown bus who was trying to tune in a television-band radio and was making an enormous racket with the static. She apologized for the noise, explaining that she was trying to "watch" her soap opera and was missing a crucial scene on *As the World Turns.* When I told her that I was studying soap opera viewers and asked if we could talk sometime, she immediately asked if it was for one of the networks. After assuring her that this was an independent scholarly project, she replied, "They think we're a bunch of idiots, but I find it relaxing." A neighbor of mine, with whom I have been speaking about soaps for quite a while, grumbled about the contrived nature of one of the shows she had been watching. "Every once in a while I get so angry at it. I feel, why am I watching, why am I such an idiot? I get angry at the people who make it, that they think so little of the people who watch." One viewer discussing an article in a fan magazine about the "new breed" of "professionals" watching soaps commented on an electronic bulletin board, "I was bothered by the implication that 'typical' viewers (homemakers) can be stereotyped and that anyone who wears a suit and watches a soap on his/her VCR at night is by definition a more intelligent viewer than someone who watches while doing ironing."[26] These attitudes reflect not only a certain conflict over watching soaps, but also a wholesome lack of self-patronization and a concomitant disrespect for those who they feel think little of them.

And they are right to be wary. Like academic researchers, many broadcast industry executives do seem to have small regard for the ordinary housewife. In a 1969 interview in the Toronto *Globe and Mail,* for instance, Robert Aaron, then head of NBC television's daytime programming, described soap operas as giving the housewife assurance that "her lower-middle-class values are fine, that giving up what she thought of as a career in favor of marriage is fine, that life's little problems are the ones that really count."[27] And Harding Lemay, in his early days as head writer of *Another World,* was told by Irna Phillips that he was creating "fantasy lives for millions of people who longed for emotional involvement their own lives could not provide."[28]

Whether we are revolted or enticed, surely we can agree that soaps must offer, along with life's little problems, some pleasures. These pleasures are what interest me. As we have seen, the idea of studying media audiences has a long history. Yet there has not been much discussion of pleasure. And until the mid–1980s, there has been even less systematic critique of how the "audiences" of these studies have been constructed (and of the theoretical and political assumptions underlying those constructions). The origin of this project was partially my dissatisfaction with early cinema and television studies' conceptions of "audience," studies whose formulations of audience were generally based on unreflective presuppositions about the nature of the individual and his or her cultural life. Often describing the audience as if it were an undifferentiated collective or as hypothetical individuals motivated by wholly rational-conscious processes, the studies reduced socio-historically specific audiences to the utilitarian concept of quasi-individuals, and abstractions were invested with sweeping explanatory power. And few of the studies have taken the contradictions and complications of pleasure and displeasure as subjects of inquiry. This book should probably be seen as an essay in method that attempts to overcome these problems with empirical research.[29] Of course, along the way my investigation generated new problems and new questions. So I soon realized that my goal shouldn't be to offer final truths or an authoritative analysis, as much as to grapple with the different sensuous ways in which we might explore experience. The book is, then, at once an analysis of popular culture, a theoretical exercise in the study of pleasure, and an ode to soaps.

I was curious about how and why women who are home during the day watch soap operas, and what their feelings are about their viewing practice. It seemed to me that there was much that could be learned about soap operas and how they are interpreted, and also much that could be learned from soaps about the culture, desires, and pleasures of the homemaker and caregiver. My study investigates audience discourses and mechanisms of interpretation, what people say about soaps and how they make sense of them. I also explore a socio-historic-specific audience and query audience members about their activity. I consider the social uses of the media and the domestic context of the viewing experience as well, since meanings and pleasures are not derived solely from the sounds and images that come from the screen.

My report is based on my discussions over a period of fifteen years with more than twenty-five viewers who watch soaps on a regular basis in New York City and in several other locales outside the metropolitan area. The exchanges ranged from informal conversations to more formal, lengthy audio-taped interviews in the viewer's home. In some cases, we had several discussions over the years, sometimes watching television together. But I have not attempted to construct a quantitatively typical viewer or a quantifiably representative experience. Nor do I attempt to generalize or categorize by age, race, or class. Rather, this is a saturation of viewings, a polyphony of voices that is, like soaps, inherently incomplete. I haven't aimed for "absolute truths," for in order to reflect on or illuminate experience, it is often important to retain and savor ambiguities and a variety of meanings. Though it was sometimes tempting, I have tried not to transform the viewers' experiences into a coherence.[30] The material may sometimes seem unmanageable, unintegrated; however, I wanted to respect the complexity, the contradictions, and the paradoxes.

In order to develop an adequate means of approaching this experience, it was essential for me to engage with (and question) some of the traditional needs, assumptions, and procedures of cultural analysis. My own training was in cinema studies where I had been taught to pay close attention to the formal properties of the text itself. However, there was also a long tradition of television scholars in communications studies who had taken a more sociological orientation, discussing the context of viewing and the audience's social and historical determinations. This was frequently coupled with a behaviorist attitude toward the viewing activity, seeing television as directly influencing viewers. The media were seen as transparent bearers of meaning, and the audience was generally seen as passive.[31]

Most television or communications scholars either ignored the shows or analyzed the content of the shows as if the meaning were quite evident. Cinema scholars, on the other hand, with their roots in literary traditions, generally concentrated on the meaning of the text and how the meaning is produced. They emphasized the means of representation (the mise-en-scène, camera work, editing, and sound) and the narrative conventions that are specific to film or television (or to a type of film or television show). They generally saw the viewer as a function of the text, or "inscribed" in the text and positioned (or constituted as a viewer) by textual maneuvers. This approach was seldom attentive to viewers' historical circumstances, personal differences, or material situations.[32]

Annette Kuhn, in her mid-1980s article that analyzed studies of women's genres and gendered audiences, has distinguished between social audiences and spectators.[33] The social audience is engaged in a social practice, and as such can be surveyed and categorized (p. 23). The spectator, on the other hand, is a hypothetical subject "constituted in signification, interpellated by the film or TV text" (p. 23). Most television studies discussed social audiences; most cinema studies discussed spectators. This distinction reflects the different conceptual frameworks of the various academic disciplines. The conception of social audiences in television studies seldom took into account the complexity of the individual or saw the individual in a specific context. Cinema scholars generally explored the relationship of "ideal" viewers to the text from a theoretical point of view. Psychoanalytic and feminist studies speculated on the power of the cinematic apparatus and its fascination (the experience of seeing films in a darkened room, the relation of the spectator to the view of the camera, and so on).

However, until recently, there had been few studies of specific audiences and fewer still that saw viewers as both socially and psychologically structured.[34] This study will be working toward a theory of viewing that includes "pleasure" and sees viewers interacting dialectically with what they watch. It is an approach that is more attentive to the viewing experience and examines that experience in, and as part of, a wider social and cultural context.

The methods I used were borrowed from the social sciences, especially ethnographic studies that see their efforts as intersubjective engagements. It is empirical research that is aware of and problematizes the *relation* between the scholar and those who are being studied. As a modern and politicized approach to popular culture, my method is cognizant of how my own tastes and concerns are coded into my analyses. I do not claim neutrality. There is no such thing as a view from nowhere, as Susan Bordo makes clear.[35] Research is always historically and socially located. The areas we choose to explore, the very questions we choose to ask, and the manner we communicate our observations are informed by the place and moment we inhabit. But however much our personal autobiography inflects the research, we can't assume that it corresponds in any real way with the experiences of our subjects.[36] Feminist solidarity (or empathy) is not a method; and in academic research it may be a somewhat romantic ideal. This work is based on the understanding that the researcher is involved in interpretation (not explanation) and in a struggle that must be both self-conscious and dialogical.[37] It offers a "symptomatic" reading: one that is sensitive to the conceptual structures that inform the thinking of both the researcher and the women being studied. It attempts to uncover hidden levels of meaning, a reading not just for facts and opinions but, as Louis Althusser puts it, for "insights" and "oversights."[38] Such questions about method relate to some of the larger political and epistemological debates on representation and authority that have been discussed in the arts as well as in the social and natural sciences.[39]

On rereading my work, I have noticed an abundance of qualifiers and subordinate clauses. These are probably indicative of soaps' resistance to being tied down (and of the commercial necessity for soaps to display some variation). They also expose a certain tendency on my part to want to elaborate shades of thought. In some parts of the book, certain linguistic structures, academic language, and abstractions have been difficult to avoid; in others, the effusive sensitivity, affection, and indignation expressed remind us that experience is often unruly and elastic. I propose we take this kind of experience into consideration and look at watching soap operas as a social process that involves contradictions and private as well as collective fantasies and joys. The spectator is active (rather than passive) and the meaning of the soap opera is the product (not the object) of interpretation.[40] But I am getting ahead of myself. We will look at this further in the next chapter, but for the moment we should note that the program and the viewer intersect and interpenetrate one another in elaborate and subtle ways; they exist in an interdiscursive and mutually constituting space, with viewers utilizing both shared cultural conventions and personal histories each time they watch.

At the same time, however, soap operas are produced with an institutionalized audience in mind. Their means of representation are organized and structured for this specific audience, an audience that is thought to share certain viewing habits and cultural codes (as well as buying needs). The audience then, at least in some ideal form, can be seen as both source and receiver of commercial television, and consumption can be seen as a moment in the production process.[41]

The similarities and variations among and within soap operas play a part in organizing our expectations and understandings. It is difficult to analyze one text without considering how it relates to other texts of a similar nature. The relation of these "intertextual encrustations"[42] to the sounds and images of the daily episodes can be very complex. Yet, ironically, the sounds and images seem so unambiguous. If questioned while viewing, anyone would reply that "the meaning" is obvious, so clear, so easy to grasp. There appears to be little need or room for interpretation or negotiation.

In this conception, meaning is a social and cultural phenomenon. Meaning is not *in* the program itself but is inferred by individual viewers (on the basis of unconscious, preconscious, and conscious processes) from the means of representation and narrative strategies of the program, and from the wealth of experience that the viewer carries into the viewing situation. While watching soaps, the viewer brings private associations to the specific sounds and images being broadcast. Knowledge of past episodes, other soap operas, publicity, promotion, conversations with friends, or real-life events can all contribute to the construct we think of as "the story."[43] Watching television is a multidimensional activity. And when we investigate the activities of viewers and see the variety of contexts and modes of viewing, we realize, as Charlotte Brunsdon has insisted, that the television text can never be a simple, self-evident object for analysis.[44]

Therefore, I have tried to avoid the ideas of consumer and cultural artifact and to think of television as a lived practice, as a part of a social process.[45] The emphasis is on soap operas as the women whom I have been speaking with have experienced them, and yet this cannot be separated from the ways I myself have experienced them.

In retelling some of their stories, I regret that I have lost the orality of the originals: the inflections, timbre, volume, and rhythm of women speaking. It has also not been possible to convey most of the gestures and postures of our conversations, the waved arms, shudders, downcast eyes, raised eyebrows, pursed lips, faces that dissolved into troubled wrinkles or self-conscious blushes. I have tried to include references to pauses, intonation, giggles, velocity of the speech, and so forth, where they appear on the tape recordings; however, much of the richness of the nonverbal communications has vanished. Body movements and laughter often accentuated the emotional content of what was said. The written representation misses many nuances of the live encounter. However, it is not simply this lack of resonance that worries me. Movement and laughter might also have expressed an attitude toward the material, perhaps an attitude that the speaker might not have been able (or willing) to express otherwise. Sheila

Rowbotham has commented that we sometimes giggle (and, I might add, wiggle) at the moment of taboo. It is a way, frequently unconscious, of both making a point and avoiding an issue.[46] A smile or a nod can sometimes indicate the recognition of discrepancies or possibly modify a complaint in a way that recognizes the necessity to contain it. It might also be an indication of a shared understanding and help make sense of both the fan's experience and our mutual dialogues.

It is also difficult, in a written account, to include the gaps and silences. What is not said might be, at times, more expressive than what is. I raise these issues not as a question about the purity of the transcriptions or representations, but because it is a point of theoretical importance, a question of interpretation: the way the speaker and her narrative has affected me. It would be wrong not to acknowledge both the fascination of confessional revelation and the pull of theoretical argument.

Through the interviews (and observing "talk" in letters to the editors of fan magazines and in Internet chat rooms, newsgroups, bulletin boards, and other public communication channels), I try to examine some of the different discourses embedded in the viewing experience, the systems of pleasure and power that inflect the experience, and the varied ways women are able to recognize and acknowledge themselves as "soap opera fans." It is an approach that does not presuppose a rigid opposition between necessity and freedom, family service and individuality, duty and desire. Rather, it is an approach that sees that duty, service, and necessity are often met with ambiguity and creativity from—or even within—individuals. It proposes that there is diversity and contradiction in how we see ourselves; fulfillment and despair in our desire. Therefore, I have tried to be sensitive to differences both among viewers and within viewers (sometimes even a conflicting self). And while I tried to be careful not to reduce viewers' multiple relations with soap operas to a single statistic or set of statistics, or reduce the audience to a lifestyle or value system, if there *are* shared interpretative strategies or a sense of community, this might be a way to describe them. Therefore, besides being responsive to psychological and social factors (such as class, gender, and age) that affect individual viewers, I have also attempted to be sensitive to shared concerns.

A soap opera can be an invitation to enter into a specific social world. And upon entering, the viewer is implicitly obliged to respond. Many viewers converse with each other with a sincere and lively interest about the characters and their narrative situations. But talking back to soaps is also not uncommon. The cases that immediately come to mind include a ferociously unladylike young woman with a somewhat ironic stance who vocally encourages characters she approves of and criticizes those she thinks are foolish. (She particularly dislikes those who act "like wimps.") Another, a much older woman, has a more maternal attitude and warns or advises characters she cares for or feels are about to act foolishly. Neither believes that she can affect the characters or their actions, but that does not keep her from expressing her opinions. Of course, in practical everyday life there are social constraints that inhibit staring at, eavesdropping on, or talking back to the real people who share our physical space. The hazards, liabilities, and risks are fewer with fictional people. Indiscretion doesn't penetrate the iridescent screen, and soap opera characters never gaze back at us. Bell hooks, in her essay on back talk, writes of having been brought up in the "old school," where she was meant to be seen and not heard, and where the act of expressing herself was daring, an act of courage.

Hooks writes of the socially imposed silences that break our spirit and of talk that is not only the expression of creative power, but also an act of resistance, "a political gesture that challenges the politics of domination that would render us nameless and voiceless."[47] And she decries the silences, the unheard voices of those wounded, tortured individuals who do not speak or write. Graham Greene, in one of his autobiographical works, *Ways of Escape,* describes his own experiences regarding the despair of ordinary existence and the need for expression: "Sometimes I ask myself how all those who cannot write, compose, or paint are capable of escaping the absurdity, the sadness, and the panic fear which characterizes the human condition."[48] In a life of isolation, alienation, and frequent monotony, those who do not (or have been denied the time to) write, compose, or paint, those who have been silenced, those who wish to escape the absurdity, sadness, and panic fear, might delight in and find expression through distractions and fantasies with books, dreams, movies—and television. Although there may be no one to talk with, there *is* someone to listen in on.

In the beginning of 1987, ABC initiated "Soap Talk," a 900 (pay-per-minute) telephone number that viewers could call to listen to a tape of a soap opera character discussing his or her life and hinting about upcoming plot complications. The network reported that the line received five million calls in the first eleven weeks.[49] Around the same time, the fan magazine *Daytime TV* advertised 900 numbers that you could call to join a party-line group conversation or hear and leave a personal message for a soap opera performer. *Soap Opera Digest* has run a classified section for viewers requesting pen pals and local contacts with people who watch a specific soap or admire a particular character or performer.[50] Commercial luncheons, where viewers can meet each other as well as two or three performers, are held in larger metropolitan areas. Special events, such as *Days of Our Lives*'s annual Memorial Day weekend fan festival in California or ABC's autumn Super Soap Weekend at the Disney–MGM Studio in Orlando, are opportunities to "get up close and personal with your favorite stars" (to quote the ABC Daytime and Colgate Total ad) and get acquainted with other fans.

"Soap Talk" changed to a format in which the caller can express her opinion on her soap (at ninety-five cents a minute in 1996), with specific numbers for each ABC soap opera, "Tell us what you think of the people in Port Charles. You give us your opinion and we'll give you a sneak preview." In 1991, *Another World* asked fans to telephone a 900 number and participate in a survey to decide which of the five backup bands they were featuring on the program should be selected for the character Dean Frame's new music video.[51] And, in another 900 enterprise, *Days of Our Lives* offered viewers the chance to choose a name for Jack and Jennifer's new baby (1992).[52] *Soap Opera Now!* gave *As the World Turns*'s viewers the opportunity to submit a conclusion to the 1992 Carolyn Crawford murder mystery and printed the responses.[53] Recently, this sort of input has moved to the Internet. In the spring of 2000, *All My Children* queried viewers about which wedding dress Hayley should choose: "cast your vote at ABC.com." In August their website offered a contest for a free trip for four to the fifth annual Super Soap Weekend, with the winner given a chance to "star in a scene with an ABC soap star." *Soap Opera Digest* now conducts polls via e-mail.

Viewers who watch the same show sometimes have their own dialogue, talking about and comparing inferences, pondering possibilities and consequences, sharing deductions. Though watching soap operas is probably one of a housewife's more solitary and individual experiences and is often savored as something private and her own (women often refer to soap operas in the first person singular possessive, "my stories," for instance, or "my soap," or "my show"), many also discuss their stories among friends and family members, in the neighborhood, at work, or, since the mid-1990s, on the Internet. And it's fun! Mary Ellen Brown notes that the groups she observed discussing soaps often enjoyed a carnivalesque playfulness, full of laughter that she argues can be "an affective response" and "a transgressive act."[54] Brown admits that she herself began watching *Days of Our Lives* because that was the soap most of her friends favored, and she looked forward to talking to them about it (p. x). Elayne Rapping writes about weekly phone conversations with her daughter Alison about *The Guiding Light* and laughing over the characters' "often ridiculously implausible lives."[55] Alisa Holen told me that she never watched soaps ("What a waste of time!") until she moved to a small town and started working at J. C. Penney's ("It's all women, you know").[56] During their fifteen-minute breaks, the employees would watch *The Young and the Restless* in the lounge, and then talk about it all day long. She started a betting pool, "Whether or not Victoria had AIDS . . . If Victor was going to propose to Nikki . . . How long so-and-so would be pregnant . . . They're so slow, this made it more exciting." In graduate school now (the only woman in her program), and no longer at Penney's, she doesn't follow the stories anymore. "I just don't watch it at all alone; it's no fun." One informant, in a study of soap opera viewers in western Oregon, sometimes watches *All My Children* while on the telephone with a friend: "I'll call Christie . . . and we'll sit on the phone and watch it together and talk about everything as it's happening."[57]

Soaps can be a springboard for creative play. Solidarity and support with other women are fortified, despite the fact that an important part of their viewing enjoyment may be carving out a private cultural space and time for their own pleasure.

Christine Geraghty, writing about British soap operas, says that because the pleasures of soaps are so bound up with speculation and analysis they almost demand that the experience be shared.[58] Prediction is an important part of the appeal in all formulaic fiction,[59] but the ongoing nature of soaps actively encourages the sharing of these predictions. Talking about a soap is, for some, a kind of "social obligation," a way to relate to a community. R. L. Barton's study of elderly viewers found that soap operas provided them with common ground for discussion. Viewing is "the result of, and perhaps the reason for, the viewers' interaction with others in the real world."[60] For many of the women I spoke with, speculation on possible story outcomes is a regular part of their talks.

These days, networks sponsor electronic message boards for their soaps and the commercial servers marketed to residential customers (America Online, Prodigy, etc.) draw subscribers with their bulletin boards and chat rooms. Even *Soap Opera Digest* sponsors a chat room now. Those with a computer at home, at school, or on the job can participate, initiating friendships on-line, and joining new groups for discussion, speculation, analysis, and interpretation. Do these groups exist solely for the transmission of information and opinion? Or are the participants drawn together through fellowship and commonality?[61] Maybe participation itself is a transaction that draws people in.

As had been the case with film, radio, and then television, the rhetoric surrounding the information superhighway includes its wondrous potential for the democratization of information and a renewed sense of community. But is this community forged by its participating individuals, or merely chosen from a menu of what's available?[62] Is it a new social formation (a counterpublic sphere where counterdiscourses and counterinterpretations are invented) or a recasting of the old, with social hierarchies and conventional discourses intact? How does an individual's gender, status, social role, and/or character influence his or her social use of computer-mediated communication? Who *are* we when we are on-line?[63]

While some revel in the anonymity, other electronic discussion group participants know each other from face-to-face encounters—such as colleagues in the same office or former college roommates who communicate on-line—and in some cases they know each other from their participation in other electronic-mediated communication: other bulletin boards or chat rooms. Some members of one group have extended their electronic relationship to face-to-face communication, arranging regional meetings on a regular basis[64] or occasionally coming together to meet a visiting out-of-towner.[65]

Annual reunions, complete with yearbooks chronicling the soap's storylines and the members' fan activities, are becoming more common for electronic discussion groups. The members of one bulletin board arranged a visit to the CBS production studio;[66] others coordinate attendance at performers' personal appearances. For some people, the opportunity for participation in such a group may actually be an incentive to watch a soap. And of course, as Barton observed with elderly viewers, such interaction may enhance the enjoyment of soap opera involvement.

However, because anyone can read a posting and participate, the interaction is fundamentally multiparty and public. People never know who all the readers of their messages are.[67] The public aspect of the interactions often encourages a bravura display of ego (sometimes high spirited and sardonic) and/or knowledge. There is frequently a sensitivity to commonly shared meanings and collectively accepted references and a willingness to engage with anything and everything. For many, the common bank of references and the potential for anonymity break down social inhibitions and allow the discussion and negotiation of private feeling that would be more difficult in face-to-face interactions. They grant an expressive freedom that one can seldom enjoy in the workplace or while working alone at home.

The anonymity of the Internet permits all participants potentially equal status. However, although it is possible to be anonymous, soap opera posters almost always create identifiable personae, often playful or exaggerated or negotiated versions of their own identities, so that they are seldom indistinguishable from one another. Mocking or boldly announcing one's body size or other markers is frequently a part of one's screen name: "liljamie-rose" or "big-gay-allan." Much of the humor in the postings involves poking fun at the show itself and displays a certain mastery over the commercial product. A posting Lauren Rabinowitz observed on America Online's *All My Children* board in 1994 is a good example of both this and the distinctive personality a message can evoke: "Writer alert: The writers are getting feistier. I loved it today when among Anton's otherwise boring, monotonous lines he said, 'I have better things to do with my life than kiss up to archaic Eurotrash!'"[68] Fans "annoyed" at Victor Newman's manipulative domineering on *The Young and the Restless* called him "Victurd" in their on-line discussions.[69] And *All My Children*'s naive, dimwitted Dixie was nicknamed "Ditsie." The carnivalesque excess that Brown saw in the discussion groups, and others have seen on the Internet, celebrates—to borrow from Mikhail Bakhtin—"temporary liberation from the prevailing truth and from the established order."[70]

Rec.arts.tv.soaps.abc (r.a.t.s.a.) is a Usenet computer network newsgroup, which functions like an Internet bulletin board, on which ABC soaps are discussed. Although unmoderated, the group has established its own behavior norms and forms of expression. A popular site, in 1993 it was estimated that in its precursor, r.a.t.s. (the group has since divided into the ABC and a CBS group), there were approximately 150 new messages posted every weekday (much less traffic is generated on weekends), with several hundred participants writing each month, and over forty thousand readers logging on to "lurk" (reading without contributing) at least once a month.[71] Yet in this potentially anonymous terrain, r.a.t.s.a. posters, mostly women, generally use their own names or, if they create nicknames, use their own names in the headers or signature files.[72]

Identity within the group is sometimes established by other means of self-disclosure, for instance, discussing the poster's own experiences with some of the issues being explored in the storylines.[73] According to Nancy K. Baym, "creating friendly relationships [is] one of the emergent purposes of the group."[74] Even though "flaming"—personal attacks or argumentative rudeness—is officially discouraged on r.a.t.s.a., I found many playful insults and talking back. A degree of banter, dissent, and free play appear to be perfectly permissible. The *All My Children* messages are also marked by many complicated in-jokes, a high degree of self-reflexivity, and irony.[75] Although user etiquette (or "netiquette," as it is called on-line) includes prohibitions about not spoiling the viewing experience for others, r.a.t.s.a. postings, as well as those on other boards, generally take advantage of the backstage information they have heard or read to express pleasure—or discontent—about what they see as possible future storylines. On Yahoo!'s *All My Children* board, for example, in the spring of 2000, "marcia rb" posted, "Word is that Bianca is on her way back to P[ine] V[alley] as a 16 or 17 year old. Will Erica finally have to grow up then?"

Besides familiarity with the soap's characters and locale (Bianca is Erica Kane's daughter, born in 1988, and Pine Valley is the home site of the show), the posting refers to the soap opera convention of children (especially on the shows taped in New York City, where child-labor laws make it very costly to have school-age children perform regularly) being written out of the story during their middle years and, often soon after, returning as sexually active teens played by young adult performers. It also refers to Erica's personality (her mischievous, brazenly adventurous and obstinate disposition, and her childish, egotistical attitude toward responsibility) and, of course, would resonate with readers who know her foibles and have followed her most recent machinations. Using their knowledge of the serial's history to update others, sharing information on contract renewals, discussing hunches and insights, teasing other participants, posters certainly seem to assume a common understanding of the storylines, communal definitions, collectively accepted referents, and a shared culture. There must be solace and sweet delight in this sense of kinship. Although hardly a town meeting, it might be helpful to look at these discussion sites as public plazas at the strip mall of television.[76]

But besides sharing an interest in a particular soap (and the Internet system that links them), *are* there many commonalities? Can we expect a sense of agreement when diverse people are stating opinions on emotional and moral dilemmas? There certainly is no automatic connection between women because of their gender, and it may be an illusion to think that we have a common sensibility, set of values, or even interests simply because we are women, or because we watch soaps or a particular show. If there is a consensus, it needs to be built rather than assumed or asserted. And this can be a difficult project. Like "family," "community," is both a symbol and a slogan in the late twentieth and early twenty-first centuries. And the relation of the writing self, or viewing self, to other experiences of self is a complex, often contradictory, relation that needs to be explored in its many voices. The shifting roles and identities we take up on the Internet, as Sherry Turkle points out, are indicative of the multiple roles and identities we experience in our daily lives.[77]

What I have seen on the boards *is* a complex performance of identity and difference. Responding to "marcia rb's" posting, "jimiphil" took the opportunity to comment on Erica's wardrobe: "why do they keep putting erica in sleeveless outfits with those skinny arms/not only is it not a good look for her/but it keeps those eatting disorder rumours going" (spelling, capitalization, and punctuation thus in original). Others responded with stories of how important carbon monoxide detectors are, the pros and cons of different medications for their children's Attention Deficit Disorder, and "BTW [by the way] little jamie is having her exploratory surgery today." Such tangents are so common that r.a.t.s.a. insists they be marked "TAN" on the subject line. One woman told me that she was more comfortable "venting" about her husband with her *One Life to Live* on-line group than she would with someone she knew personally.

The seemingly spontaneous, untutored quality of on-line writing is closer to conversation than to literature. (Although often very articulate and humorous, there doesn't appear to be much rewriting or involvement with craft. There are frequent apologies for linguistic failings: "I just don't express myself very well in print," wrote an *All My Children* enthusiast.) And there seems to be not only social engagement, but also a sense of discovery. Such communication can be a way of finding out how one feels about something and a way of preserving sensations. Having someone "to talk to" also means having the input that allows us to experience and appreciate our own perceptions. We often, as Barbara Herrnstein Smith puts it, "come into possession of an idea or feeling precisely through the expression of it, the process required to make it intelligible to others."[78] The fear of becoming bored and lonely and thus alienated, unresponsive, and torpid is a real fear of many homebound women and those who work alone or whose lives are rigidly structured by repetitive, task-oriented work. As the proliferation of these Internet discussion groups indicate, people are crying out for the chance to express themselves. Loneliness is—among other things—the unavailability of listeners, an audience, someone we can affect. Anyone who types a message in a chat room and hits "send" is calling for a response.

Laura Stempel Mumford and Sean Griffith (Mumford lurking on AOL's ABC board and Griffith contributing to r.a.t.s.a.) have studied many of the postings around a particular *All My Children* storyline: the fall 1995 introduction of a gay high school history teacher to Pine Valley. The postings on r.a.t.s.a. included discussion of the appropriateness and impact of gay representations on soaps, the definitions and meanings of homophobia in our culture, and conjecture about what the writers might do with the story. "Soaps are about romance. . . . A gay character could have a good initial storyline in which he fights for acceptance, but then what? If he's to have any good screen time at all, he has to be paired up with someone. Since every present major character is clearly straight, there has to be someone brought in. But after they pair the two up, then what? The writers have a real hard time keeping a married . . . [and] happy couple interesting."[79] Many posters confided their own coming-out stories. When a boyfriend was introduced on the show, there was glorious debate about whether they would ever show any physical affection. Although Mumford found some resistance on the AOL board,[80] Griffith reported that r.a.s.t.a. participants enthusiastically projected possible adventures. Disappointed when the gay story appeared to be disappearing (it did fade away in the spring of 1996), many participants (Griffith included) began creating a parallel story, an alternative online narrative, where a gay character could have more compelling storylines.[81] "Because popular narratives often fail to satisfy," Henry Jenkins writes, "fans must struggle with them. . . . Because the texts continue to fascinate, fans cannot dismiss them from their attention but rather must try to find ways to salvage them for their interests."[82]

As Jenkins points out, fan writing translates personal responses into social expression. In chat rooms and bulletin boards, a love for feeling and emotion, a highly subjective experience, is translated into talk that provides others with expressions and information that are meant to dispose them to act in ways that serve our interests. Such dialogue is a transaction, sometimes altruistic, more often selfish, generally designed to secure encouragement, gratitude, or possibly simply a reaction. "This is much better than yelling at the television!" exclaimed one board participant.[83]

Posters freely offer their own perspectives, but often mark them as such. "IMO" (in my opinion) or "IMHO" (in my humble opinion) are frequently appended to an interpretation, so that they leave room for—or at least imply that they are open to—others' impressions. Often disclaiming authority, both in their comments on, and evaluations of, the soap and in their tangential messages, most postings seem to be meant to provoke replies. Many ask someone to fill them in on the backstory or to give their view on something, or ask for information in areas of extranarrative expertise, "Does anyone know how the law defines bigamy?" Some habitually end their message with, "Am I right about this?"

Although responses range from rapturous enthusiasm to an almost languid appraisal of the nuances and subtleties of argument, most of the daily postings do seem designed to counter something that had been previously said and are not always about the soap. They pester each other about the best fast-food restaurants, comment on Tom Selleck's body, and debate the effectiveness of "tough love." One of Baym's informants responded to her questionnaire on r.a.t.s. participation with, "I find the subjects brought up as tangents almost as interesting as the soaps . . . for example, the cross section of rats who are cat lovers, star trekkers, etc. some of us have shared our birthdays, our taste in beer and our butt size. . . . We know who has read GWTW. . . . We know who has PMS."[84] As this poster's references to butt size, *Gone With the Wind,* and premenstrual syndrome suggest, postings are often gendered. They are also generally supportive, frequently telling each other how funny they are. Humor is clearly valued on-line and the acronyms LOL (laughing out loud), LMAO (laughing my ass off), and ROTFL (rolling on the floor laughing) appear in many responses.[85] Thanking each other for providing information is also common.

Posters certainly seem to be individuals using the Internet as social encounter, as the occasion for an affective response to the ideas, the sentiments, and the preoccupations of others. Even if they do not feel they can affect the television show itself (in the sense of being able to influence the direction taken by the writers, producers, or characters),[86] by nurturing and directing the flow of on-line communication they can affect each other. The chat rooms, bulletin boards, and newsgroups may be spaces without places, but they *are* socially produced spaces, and the creation of a new social space can be an act of faith as well as an act of hope. Participants often post from work sites, stealing time from their employee personae for intimate talk, fantasy, conjecture, enjoyment, and affective interaction.[87] Is this an act of resistance to the regimentation of the workplace? Or does it, like soaps, anchor the sameness of the everyday? In a time when work is seldom a calling and when few of us find a sense of who we are in public participation as citizens,[88] such social networks, fragile and shallow though they often are, can fulfill an important identity function. But can this "community" forge an interconnected sense of the world? Can it become the basis for turning frustration and disappointment into social or political engagement?

Reading these sites, one can detect both what people are enjoying—and some of their dissatisfactions. But perhaps the dissatisfactions can be pleasurable themselves when they inspire a particularly witty posting, an angry diatribe, or a new turn in an alternative on-line narrative. There might even be a perverse pleasure in seeing the professionals, "the powers that be" (or "TPTB," as they are called on-line), get it all wrong. What is the nature and meaning of such acts of creativity and resistance? Is it simply intellectual game playing or does it have the potential of radical intervention? An oppositional reading certainly can be enjoyable. As John Fiske points out, for many, the construction of representations is in itself a joy.[89] Does partaking in such activities actually encourage resistant or oppositional interpretations? Does it facilitate preferred readings of the network show? I wonder, can an alternative on-line narrative ever achieve enough legitimacy to incite a network response? Be far-reaching or confrontational enough to challenge the commercial media system or dominant culture? Be controversial enough to provoke a counterreading? A new on-line narrative? You see, it *is* a complicated business.

But now researchers say that the Internet causes loneliness. A front-page article in the *New York Times* reported that a Stanford University study found that the "more hours people use the Internet, the less time they spend with people."[90] Once again, researchers are troubled by the use of new technology, worried about social isolation, and valorizing interpersonal interaction. Although the article's accompanying graph most forcefully demonstrated that 59 percent of those who are on-line five hours or more a week spend less time watching television, the article itself stresses the 13 percent who spend less time with family and friends.

With articles like this in the popular press, and the general way that soap operas and women's talk are devalued in the popular imagination, it is not surprising that some of us may feel conflicted about soaps, chat rooms, and fandom. We may also feel uncomfortable about our pleasures. We may even find that we really enjoy some things to which we are politically opposed. One of the soap opera viewers with whom I have been speaking, a well-educated woman, mused, "What is interesting to me is why I continue to watch *The Bold and the Beautiful* when I don't approve of the way they portray women. I think that the women on that show are basically, except for Stephanie, victims." Feminist television scholar Laura Stempel Mumford took her own struggle to reconcile her pleasure in watching soaps with her belief that the genre has repressive sexual politics as the stimulus for her book.[91] Both pleasure and displeasure can be sites of multiple, complex, and potentially contradictory sets of experiences and a matter of considerable flux.

However difficult it may be to acknowledge the ambivalence around pleasures and displeasures, shame and desire, these are important areas to explore. If we are careful not to reduce the complexities and contradictions to simplistic needs or immediate satisfactions, and if we refuse to censor out "unacceptable" feelings, it may be that women can build strength by recognizing and understanding both our pleasures and our vulnerabilities.[92]

A woman I interviewed, Ann Weinstock, whose children are off at college, confessed to having periodic longings to stay in bed all day with some minor ailment or when it's raining hard or very cold outside: "Okay, this is my day and I'm not going to do anything except read and watch the soaps. If you start out at twelve o'clock by the time four comes you're depressed, pokey, you haven't really enjoyed it. It's something that's more appealing in the contemplation than in the execution. I found that if I did that for a day, it was a real downer and very depressing, even though I had made up all kinds of excuses and reasons and wasn't feeling guilty that I had taken a day to do this."

Another of my informants described her nighttime ritual almost as though it were a transgression. She told me that she watches her taped soap opera before she goes to sleep, sitting on the edge of the bed ("I don't want to lie down because sometimes it would put me right to sleep in the middle of it!"). She waits until her husband goes to sleep, because, "I think it's psychological, I think he's interested in it to the extent that he doesn't want to admit that he's interested in it and it irritates him so when I put it . . . , 'You have all day to watch that' [she imitated his angry voice], so I kind of wait, he falls asleep within ten seconds, and the thing goes on."

Although there must certainly be some thrill in the violation of taboos, confronting transgression can also be profoundly disturbing. Soaps are not merely depictions of conflicts fought out in the domestic terrain; they are themselves a material part of these struggles. One woman who heard about my work volunteered that she and her husband watched their soap on tape before going to bed weeknights, "Pitiful that it is, it's our quality time together." Soaps charm, yet are seldom understood or represented as unequivocally positive.

A housewife in a wealthy suburb named a friend who watches soaps, then paused, questioning whether she should be disclosing such information. "I just don't know how [she] feels about divulging . . . It's something that's fraught with shame, right? It's sort of like you're coming out of the closet." Later, she told me about one of her husband's clients, a woman she described as "so bright, she writes and is always going back to school. . . . She's a very smart woman. And lo and behold, one day her sister told me that she watched *General Hospital* and I found myself taping—they have many homes and go abroad for the summer—and I would end up taping three months' worth of *General Hospital* [for her]." Her voice quickened, "So, I mean, a lot of us who thought that only the masses of stupid people watch these shows—it's not something that we're so ashamed of." Then, in the classic statement of postfeminism, "You know it's different for women now, we don't all have to be ashamed of the fact that we don't work, either."

It is possible that the concern about women's "free time," coupled with the many derisive comments, parodies, and jokes about soap operas, have not only helped to sustain soaps as gendered discourse in the popular imagination, but may also have helped to "politicize" them. That is, the interplay of antagonisms may have actually turned soaps into a "resistant" discourse when no overt oppositional element was necessarily present before. For some, this may even make watching soaps an important source of resilience. If our life is the result of both free choice and oppressive circumstances, women have to look at the ways we try to push out of and beyond the constraints, and how our illusions of independence are nourished.

However, we should also look at the effects of these constraints. Perhaps when we don't have what we want, we begin to need or to want what we have. If so, then, to paraphrase Delmore Schwartz, in dreams begin possibilities. Fantasy can structure our expectations. It is not, in any literal way, the representation of desire; it is its setting.[93] It can be our own "Street of Crocodiles," where, as Bruno Schulz's short story describes, "nowhere as much as there do we feel threatened by possibilities, shaken by the nearness of fulfillment, pale and faint with the delightful rigidity of realization. And that is as far as it goes."[94] Fantasy can be an act that creates the space that makes survival (or a rational order) possible.

If we think of them in this way, soaps can be, and often are, simultaneously transgressive (of "respectable" domestic values) and reactionary (stimulating and reinforcing, rather than transforming, those same values). Maybe these small transgressions are a sort of makeshift inventiveness, one of our ways of "making do": the dissidence or disorder that order needs to prove itself. Irna Phillips, in her *McCall's* article, wrote, "We show people *adjusting* to situations rather than changing them, which is the only path to contentment I know."[95] This may be similar to what Claude Levi-Strauss refers to as *bricolage* in mythical thought, the adept drawing on whatever means at hand, economically including collected odds and ends and reused old materials when there is nothing else at one's disposal. Levi-Strauss discusses how an engineer maneuvers his way out of limitations, while a *bricoleur,* the improviser, by inclination or necessity, always ends up remaining within them.[96]

Meeting with me for the second time, a woman began by stating that her husband thinks it's foolish for someone who's so intelligent to watch so much television. But she added that she is not ashamed. Later, she spoke lovingly of her husband's good nature and emotional strength and mentioned that television is the only thing that they disagree about. When she was traveling in Europe one summer, she didn't want to miss her soaps. "I have this friend who's really—she's a very intelligent person. In spite of what she might think of me [laughing], I asked her to tape it!" After a walk in a local park and a long discussion about *As the World Turns,* we returned toward her apartment building and she summarized by justifying her viewing, "I mean, when you think about it, it really *is* a waste of time. But on the other hand, it's also entertaining and [slowly, hesitantly, but with emphasis] I want to be entertained a little bit!" That was that. It was almost dusk; we both needed to fix our evening meals.

Back at home, I realized that there was something missing. And without it, we would never be entirely free of guesswork, of speculation, of conjecture. Why do we want—or need—to be entertained? This is a challenging question in a cultural context in which the domestic is the natural, the given, the unquestionable, but also a potential ideological battleground.

"The domestic" is a discursive construct, produced by the junction and disjunction of symbolic domains. As an analytic concept, it can never be evaluated "in itself." But for many women it is the site where they most experience oppression. Terry Eagleton, while discussing Samuel Richardson's *Clarissa,* calls the family "the central apparatus of patriarchal society."[97] If the family and domesticity are defined as the negation of fantasy, if a strict duality is constructed with the family and domesticity valorized and fantasy relegated to a subordinate position, then perhaps the outlandishness of soap operas' excesses reinforces (antithetically) the status of the domestic. In order for the middle-class family to construct itself (however unsuccessfully) as the site of respectability and emotional security, it must construct danger, excitement, and thrill as degraded otherness. It may be that this act of exclusion encourages us to produce an "other domestic" out of the outrageousness of soap operas, an identity-in-difference that is nothing other than a negative symbiosis with that which we reject in our social practices.

Along with such resourcefulness, however, we also have to consider the element of surrender. One woman told me with some amusement (and a hint of agreement) that her husband calls watching soaps "closet pornography." "It's okay to watch it, but you shouldn't talk about it." Lee Meltz excitedly volunteered to be interviewed for my study. "Eighteen years of watching *All My Children* should be good for something!"

Many critics do think of soaps as girl-porn. But unlike porn, which, as Laura Kipnes demonstrates, flaunts its contempt for all proprieties,[98] soaps are more selective: it is the authority of the family that is seemingly under attack. The family, and the psychology and culture of femininity, are crucial to defining domestic duties. Our identities are strongly bound up in these often unspoken, but very powerful, dictates. But because of the seemingly conflicting images of necessity and freedom, family service and individuality, duty and desire, the bonds of family and the home can also make "femininity" socially and psychologically insecure. For women in the home, the lines of ideologically approved feminine behavior are difficult to draw precisely because these values are presumed to be rigidly opposed. But are they? And do real women actually live up to cultural expectations of what it means to be "feminine"? Are we really servants of the broad pragmatic day? Or do we live our lives with a little more creativity—and ambiguity—than the model would have us believe?

We may need to acknowledge the difficulty in accounting for the areas of likeness and separateness that arise between soaps and daily life. What might we learn from this dissonance, from these oscillations between similarity and difference, recognition and disavowal? We need to recognize that the limits we feel are necessary to the social formation can be simultaneously, at the level of our imagination, an impetus to fantasy; but we must also admit that there can be interference between the manifest and the imaginary, the here and there. This may be similar to the reverberations that Jean-Louis Comolli writes about in historical films in which a well-known performer plays a well-known historical figure, when the spectator's "I know very well" irresistibly calls forth a "but all the same."[99]

A psychoanalytically inflected theory of fantasy and the pleasures and displeasures of watching soaps would have to encompass both the theatrics of transgression and the intricacies of unfulfillable longing. If, as Freud claimed, unsatisfied wishes are the driving power behind fantasies; if every separate fantasy contains the fulfillment of a wish and improves upon unsatisfactory reality,[100] then perhaps soap operas' romances take up and improve upon (but ultimately manage) dissatisfaction, wishes rooted in fundamental desires, fears, anxieties, and needs (shaped by dependency and frustration). If women are brought up to express a minimum of ambition and erotic desire, soaps maximize that minimum. We often accommodate social expectations by concealing our power (doing what is expected). When difference is perceived, do we perceive it as implausible? As sick? As dangerous?

Though the idea of watching soap operas as "escape" grossly simplifies the complex pleasures we get from watching and the complex reasons for our pleasures, when women tell me why they think they watch soap operas they often mention that they feel the need for a break, a fantasy, imaginary solutions, some excitement, relaxation, or a moment "for themselves." NBC, in the summer of 1987, ran a campaign of relatively expensively produced comic spots for their daytime serials[101] that played on the popular image of the harried housewife watching soap operas as a respite from family responsibilities, household chores, and her own emotional and intellectual poverty. One spot depicted a woman's frustrations with her husband, her son, and her mother-in-law, ending with an image of the exasperated woman watching television and an off-screen male voice saying, "It's time to escape to *Another World,* a world of excitement and ecstasy," or alternately, "It's time for you to get away to *Santa Barbara,* where romance, passion, and excitement await you."

Another spot showed a woman plagued by various domestic disasters (curiously animating household appliances as though they were members of the family), "The vacuum cleaner turned on you at nine A.M., the blender threw a temper tantrum at ten A.M., and the washing machine tried to clean the whole house at eleven A.M. Some days you really need *Days of Our Lives,* a daytime drama you can count on." A two-thirds page print ad that ran in the July 11, 1987, issue of *TV Guide* featured the word ESCAPE in large-type bold caps followed by, "You've started communicating in baby talk; You can't fit into your old jeans; Someone finished off the last pint of chocolate chocolate chip; It's time to escape to DAYS OF OUR LIVES."

Some of the products advertised on soap operas also address this image while attempting to sell their goods as a necessary indulgence: Hershey marketed its new low-fat chocolate candy bar, Sweet Escapes, on soaps. "Do I have to be a mom today?" asks the waking-up woman in the soap commercial, before coming "alive with Coast," and several frenzied housewives have asked Calgon bath products to "take them away."

Interestingly, the frequent disclaimers I heard that soaps are "just escapist," reflect the moralism of their families and the popular press: watching soaps shouldn't be taken seriously because soap operas aren't worthy of serious attention. Such an evaluation, like value itself, is produced discursively. It is rooted in a process of exchange and reflects not only sensitivity to the standards of dominant aesthetic discourses, but also consciousness of the viewer's position as consumer.[102] A fan from Green Bay, Wisconsin, writing to *Soap Opera Digest,* expressed a genuine market-consciousness when she wrote that she felt such prime-time television serials as *A Year in the Life, St. Elsewhere,* and *L.A. Law* shouldn't be considered soap operas and covered in the magazine because they "deal with real life . . . people who die on these shows don't come back to life." Soap operas, on the other hand, "are a sort of fantasy you watch to forget your troubles."[103]

While it is sometimes tempting to accept a tidy fit between the frustrations and spiritual impoverishment of our daily lives and our escapist diversions, that would not explain the forms our pleasures take, the content of our reveries, or the sorts of emotional impulses and longings that need nourishment. Nor could it explain why certain types of entertainment are especially privileged in this way. And it cannot account for the struggles of ideology within our pleasures. For however much we may desire to escape (physically, mentally, and/or emotionally) or to relax, we also form ourselves in part through these diversions, through our fictions and our thrills. Our attention may be captured and distracted from the ordinariness of ordinary existence, but the activity cannot help but exert some force on our lives and become a part of the way we see our worlds and ourselves. Since the acts of response and interpretation we perform are an inextricable part of our identity, it would be best to acknowledge the crucial place this type of pleasure has in our mental life. Fantasy, if seen as a process rather than a particular scenario, is part of what defines us as human subjects.[104]

Rather than simply an escape from social reality (deflecting our attention), soaps and fan activities might be seen as sites for fantasies: fantasies that serve to celebrate, and possibly even perpetuate, certain emotions, values, and needs of family life even while giving noise to complaints about that very situation. The lifestyles soaps deliver may be far from normative, and they may sully many of the social mores we live by, but even while suggesting alternatives to the existing order, the exceptional always implies the ordinary. By naturalizing and valorizing the domestic and personal life, the desperate dreams of soap operas—and their commercials—can still serve to reinforce the existing situation.

However, perhaps it is in such fictional adventures—such fantasies—that we are able to imagine (even explore) the desires that exceed our social possibilities or exceed what we think socially acceptable.[105] And perhaps it is in imagining such fictional adventures that many of our desires are produced. An analysis of reception should be based on a conception of response that is both interactive and transformative—dialectical—and acknowledge that there are, as Julia Kristeva reminds us, political implications inherent in the very act of interpretation, in the desire to give meaning.[106]

Sure, soaps help to sell cake mixes, detergent, and deodorant. But maybe they are also, like love songs, the narrative of our lives: the ways in which we engage in and realize fantasies, furtive lessons in the vocabulary of desire.[107] And perhaps they remind us of how necessary such pleasures are to those productive, sometimes deliciously imaginative, lives we piece together.

Women like to sit down with trouble as if it were knitting.

—Ellen Glasgow

The Theoretical Matrix; or, How to Study Soaps

Women savoring trouble . . . What does that mean? In Ellen Glasgow's 1932 novel, *The Sheltered Life,* the observation is one that the grandfather makes when he sees some of his women kinfolk sitting around gossiping about their neighbors' problems. R. W. Stedman uses the quote as an epigraph for one of his chapters on radio serials.[1] I have used it to begin a chapter that discusses television soap opera audiences. The emphasis is once again on women—women, not simply as an aggregate of individuals, but as a group, "the audience." But "the audience" can be a surprisingly slippery concept. It may seem intuitively obvious, yet what we think of as the audience and what we think of as the audience's activity are different for different researchers, depending on their aims and what they want to know. The audience constructed by the television institution (broadcasters and advertisers) is not necessarily the same as that constructed by legal and regulatory bodies, scholars, or reform groups. We might say that "the audience" is a discursive construct; that is, it is formed by the attitudes and ideas that various examiners bring to bear on the subject. We would do well, then, to look at what attitudes and ideas contribute to differing conceptualizations of the soap opera audience, of viewers, and of the viewing activity. I propose that watching soap operas is a complex signifying process engaged in by a viewing subject, the soap opera fan, who is not monolithic but contains multitudes, so that diversity and contradiction, pleasure and displeasure, can be seen as a part of the variety of often contending ways we experience soaps.

But first let's look in more detail at some of those academic and industry discourses and how they have been employed to construct the audience and describe the audience's activities. As I have suggested in the previous chapter, many of these discourses have construed soap opera audiences as easily manipulated, passive women with limited horizons. Robert C. Allen tells us about Max Wylie, a radio writer who, defending himself (and his job) against contemporary criticisms of manipulation, wrote in a 1942 *Harper's* article: "Women of the daytime audiences are having physical and psychic problems that they themselves cannot understand, that they themselves cannot solve. Being physical, they feel the thrust of these problems. Being poor, they cannot buy remedies in the form of doctors, new clothes or deciduous coiffures; being unanalytical, they cannot figure out what is really the matter with them; and being inarticulate, they cannot explain their problem even if they know what it is. . . . [The soap] takes them into their own problems or into the problems worse than their own (which is the same thing only better). Or it takes them away from their problems. It gives listeners two constant and frequent simultaneous choices—participation or escape. Both work."[2]

Using language only slightly less patronizing than Wylie's and associations probably more appealing to the sponsors, Irna Phillips, in a 1944 public address to academics and the press, said that the soap opera listener "is without realizing it learning how to cope with reality—something that you couldn't begin to teach her by lecturing. She also feels, for having listened, a sense of satisfaction and returns to her job knowing it's the greatest and most worthwhile career in the world, because she has seen reflected her own life and her problems—yes, and had many times found a solution for those problems."[3] Phillips claimed, in a 1945 press conference, that she and NBC felt that soaps were a "vehicle that can not only entertain, but educate, and that has been what we have attempted to do . . . for 15 years."[4] And a Benton & Bowles 1943 policy statement called radio soap operas "a powerful force for setting behavior patterns."[5]

And this way of thinking continues. Robert E. Short, who had been manager of daytime programs for Procter & Gamble since the early 1960s, in a congenial 1981 interview with Thomas Skill and Mary Cassata of the State University of New York in Buffalo, declared entertainment to be the soaps' "primary reason for being" (adroitly ignoring any commercial benefits), but said he felt strongly that they also served a "useful function" because "they carry a lot of good information . . . to a lot of people."[6] And Agnes Nixon, a protégée and close friend of Phillips, in a series of public seminars at the Museum of Broadcasting in 1988, was still using the same stance as she discussed *One Life to Live*'s and *All My Children*'s "socially relevant" subjects, and "proving to the powers-that-be that people could learn and be entertained even while learning."[7]

This discourse of learning (which tacitly implies that fans are susceptible to persuasion) persists to this day in press releases, in fan magazines, and, most importantly, in the commercials. Many products (cleaning agents and over-the-counter drugs, for example) are advertised with pseudoscientific spots, often with graphs, surveys, and "authorities" in lab coats. Others seem to be offering us more motherly advice, with "characters" addressing "our problems" with information from their own experience. Notions of the consumer as someone in need of improvement, and commodities as the path to personal growth and self-realization date from the early twentieth century when the "therapeutic roots of consumer culture," as T. J. Jackson Lears put it, took hold among the educated strata of Western capitalist nations and when consumption became associated with individual fulfillment.[8] These ads give viewers reassurance that they are on the track to betterment, even while the ads tap into their insecurities.[9]

In order to justify their viewing or to validate soap opera storylines, audience members also frequently use this discourse of learning. An anonymous writer to *Soap Opera Digest,* for example, was very upset with *All My Children*'s "copping out" on the interracial marriage of Cliff and Angie: "This story line could have served as a tool to educate people about race relations."[10] And several women whom I spoke with mentioned social issues that they felt they had learned more about through their viewing. Likewise, many net habitués praise their chat rooms for heightening their awareness of social issues. I find that they often defend the time they spend on-line by mentioning that the diversity of the participants introduces them to various opinions—not only about their soap, but also about the outside world—that they may not have considered otherwise. By confirming viewers' sense of themselves as intelligent and broadminded individuals willing to be expanded and challenged, for some, watching and talking about soaps have become devices for providing education and the comforts of topical truths.[11]

The characterization of the soap opera listener or viewer as impressionable and in need of, or desiring, advice or improvement, and of soap operas as more than merely entertaining, is a useful and redeeming defense for the industry. The idea that soaps may reconcile the audience member to her role in the home is also reassuring to advertisers whose interests are best served when viewers find homemaking valuable enough to repay their efforts. The uplifting informational posture of both the soaps and the commercials makes the homemaker's role seem important, modern, progressive, and challenging.[12] Such a pose may even provide evidence that viewers are, indeed, *productive* beings (generally considered a moral good in American society).

Some supposedly liberal academic studies have also supported this informational posture. Herta Herzog's 1942 study, for example, suggested that the radio serials were "a major form of entertainment for the less-educated segment of American women,"[13] and concluded from her quantitative analysis of women's own reports of their listening experiences that soap operas functioned as "sources of advice," explaining things and teaching "appropriate patterns of behavior" (p. 25). The "concrete experiences" listeners reported ranged from learning English, refinement, and self-expression to learning how to comfort themselves when they were worried, how to handle their husbands, how to bring up their children (p. 27).

Herzog did question the adequacy of the advice, the extent of its influence, and how the hypothetical or fantasy situations were applied to the mastery of real personal problems. She also noted that the stories seemed to teach "how to take it" and a Panglossian doctrine that "things come out all right" (p. 30). However, rather than question the implications for the listeners, she pointed out the "social responsibility of those engaged in the writing of daytime serials . . . who must live up to the obligations to which the influence of their creation, however unintended, commits them" (pp. 31–32).

By suggesting that any social advance might come through a change in the writers' attitudes, that is, from given individuals, rather than at the social level, Herzog was calling for social responsibility and education *within* the existing social structure (thus implicitly supporting that structure). A radical break with the idea of psychically malleable listeners would have been a threat to (or called into question) the authority of the program and the media. This would have been anathema to Herzog's funding source, the McCann-Erickson advertising agency. Women can choose and use, but an attitude of resistance or negotiation, or even of irony, would have suggested a failure on the part of the program—and its commercials.[14]

Herzog's measuring of the effects of the program assumed a certain effectiveness that was, of course, very flattering to the industry. She clearly saw radio as an important social instrument. This was compatible with her agency's claims to influence people. It was also consistent with both the nation's wartime needs[15] and Paul Lazarsfeld's Bureau of Applied Social Research's "administrative approach." The Bureau, Herzog's employer before McCann-Erickson, received its major funding from CBS and the Rockefeller Foundation and it depended on the commercial broadcast industries for much of its data. As Todd Gitlin points out, there was a powerful convergence of commitments among the administrative mentality of the Bureau, the corporate interests of their funders, and the positivist mode of postwar American social science.[16]

In 1975, more than thirty years after Herzog's study, Sari Thomas, at the University of Pennsylvania, conducted forty "open-ended" interviews with television soap opera viewers.[17] She used Herzog's directed interview methods with women who watch *The Young and the Restless* or *All My Children*, two midday soap operas. She divided her sample by age and education and coded and quantified the answers to her interview questions in an attempt to draw some conclusions about the purposes served by the women's viewing; whether the women treated the show as real or fictional; whether there was a relation between the viewers' uses and gratifications and their treating the show as real or fictional; and whether or not the viewer's age and education levels were systematically associated in the patterns (p. 8). The meaning of the soaps to individual viewers is not problematized; it is how the meaning is used and what gratifications are offered that interests Thomas. As in Herzog's model, meaning is still situated in the content and flows from the producers to the viewers, filtered through the individual's needs and experiences (in order to maximize her gratifications). The study of uses and gratifications—itself a reaction against mass-communication studies that emphasized the powerful effects of the media—reconceptualized the audience as active and involved (and the media, therefore, as less directly determinate).

Thomas's formulation of the audience is remedial, more optimistic and less deterministic than the direct-influence model that Herzog used in 1942. The audience is portrayed as rational, capable of acting, of resisting influence, of reporting about itself, and able to choose and purposively use the media to find satisfaction or to gratify needs. In many ways, Thomas is still concerned about control. However, the media are not seen as all-powerful molders of desire with society at their mercy. And action and motivations are not reducible to a stimulus/response model of behaviorist psychology. Soap opera viewing in this approach is still treated in isolation from other viewing and is abstracted from any social environment. Thomas specifically chose lunch-hour shows so she could include working women and college students in her sample, but she reduced their social life to statistics of age and education. As Philip Elliott has remarked, however, "[p]eople are not simple objects available for study"; they exist within a social structure, and their descriptions draw upon social meanings.[18] By giving priority to a person's behavior, Thomas implies that the viewer is an autonomous individual who does what she will with what she chooses to view. By relying on their informants' self-defined intentions, both Herzog and Thomas place (or misplace) the locus of behavior with the sentient individual. But it is important to recognize that our needs are always mediated by psychological and social factors and are only accessible in interpreted form.

I began my own study not too long after Thomas's. Several impulses propelled my quest for methods. I felt that it was imperative to find a model that saw the viewer in a larger social context, reacting to and constructing not only the text under question, but that larger social context, as well. This would allow me to explore not only individuality but also the conventionality of so many of our social meanings. It might even see imagination as culturally, as well as psychologically, formed, and help in my search for the wider significance of people's needs.

It seemed to me at the time that I was beginning my research that any evidence that women's choice and satisfaction are selective is valuable to the industry in programming for specific audiences. (It explains what audiences choose to view.) But the media can also use audience selectivity as a defense and an exoneration: the uses and gratifications approach makes the media seem functional. It makes the research itself seem functional, too, because it helps to determine people's needs so the media can satisfy them. The research demonstrates the reasons why people are gratified by what the media give them. We "fashion" the media for our own use within and for our own values, interests, social roles, and the like. Since such an approach does not consider how the media mediate those same values, interests, and roles (or the extent to which the media create the values, needs, and interests they supposedly satisfy), the research can easily be used by the media to defend the status quo: the media (as is) are giving the people what they want. This is a comfortable view for the media industries, as it takes the blame for harmful effects as well as the burden for change away from themselves (thus implicitly seeing their role as more benign) and places it on the users. One might even say that this approach is essentially conservative: it confirms that media use is a functional means of adjustment.[19]

Later studies in the uses and gratifications of audience members have considered more subjective motives and individual uses of the media, but as communications scholar Carl Bybee puts it, "The history of mass communication effects research in the United States is the history of a relentless, empirical search, first for direct, powerful, short-term attitudinal effects, and later for intervening variables which could be regarded as either facilitative or obstructive of those effects."[20]

I was encouraged by new changes in the image of the audience that had been coming from American scholars trained in the humanities, especially literary theory, and from British social scientists who were attempting to renew the field with qualitative studies infused by methods learned from European semiotics and post-Freudian psychoanalysis.

Although Tania Modleski's influential late-1970s study of American daytime soap operas is more of a textual analysis than an audience study, there is an idea of audience implicit in her work, and she raises some important theoretical questions about pleasure and reception.[21] Responding to a broader trend to re-evaluate what has been important in women's lives, Modleski came to her study with a specific interest in women's mass-produced entertainments and how they relate to women's lives. She notes the double critical standard applied toward these genres because of what she sees as a "pervasive scorn for all things feminine . . ." (p. 13). In fact, as we have seen, in many of the earlier studies of soap operas, there had been an uneasy implication that since soaps are watched by women—similar to mass culture aimed at children—they need special attention and perhaps even a guardian eye. Modleski observes that the narrative structure of soaps is diametrically opposed to the individual protagonist and the movement toward closure of Hollywood film.[22] She suggests that the difference might have a subversive potential. For Modleski, soap operas offer uniquely "feminine" pleasures that are attuned to the rhythms of women's life in the home and are an alternative to the "masculine" pleasures analyzed by film theorist Laura Mulvey and others. Thus soaps might be *used* for a radical intervention (p. 87).

Arguing from the ideas of Fredric Jameson, Hans Magnus Enzenberger, Louis Althusser, and Richard Dyer, Modleski sees mass culture as necessarily addressing at least some aspects of our material experiences and longings, and therefore possessing many specific criticisms of everyday life. Quoting Jameson, she reminds us that mass culture texts perform "transformational work on [real] social and political anxieties and fantasies" (p. 27), and, in her own words, satisfy "*real* needs and desires, even while they may distort them" (p. 108). For Modleski, soaps function "in a highly contradictory manner: while appearing to be merely escapist, such art simultaneously challenges and reaffirms traditional values, behavior, and attitudes" (p. 112). After the immobilizing pessimism of the Frankfurt School's "false pleasure" and Mulvey's wail against pleasure, some radical scholars found attractive the idea that viewers might adapt messages for their own purposes, thereby reappropriating domestic space and subverting the idea of the mass media's ideological control. Modleski's remarks seemed not only to justify pleasure, but also to show how women's social and cultural specificity and sensitivities might be used to undermine the existing patriarchal order.

Modleski argues that soaps, by including numerous characters and multiple storylines, necessitate multiple identifications on the part of the spectator and position the viewer "as a sort of ideal mother" having diffused interests, but divested of power "[f]or the spectator is never permitted to identify with a character completing an entire action" (p. 91). Modleski sees the narratives speaking to the domestic situation of the viewer, inscribing her as "a person who possesses greater wisdom than all her children, whose sympathy is large enough to encompass the claims of all her family . . . and who has no demands of her own" (p. 92). Because soaps "convey a structure of feeling appropriate to the experience of the women in the home" (p. 111), she suggests that feminists might consider incorporating the features of the genre—or at least the pleasures they offer—into their own artistic practices (pp. 104, 111).

While at first this doesn't seem compatible with the idea that mass-produced texts—serials more than most—also displace, defer, or deflect the satisfaction of the very needs to which they are responding, at least one feminist television project has taken up the suggestion. *Two in Twenty,* a lesbian soap opera that aired over a community-access cable station in Somerville, Massachusetts, in 1986, employed the seriality and basic narrative conventions of network soap operas while introducing characters who have personal and social characteristics more in tune with the show's political aims. For example, lesbian lovers, equal and autonomous individuals, deal with family problems, restlessness, doubts about their lover's feelings, and so on. The press release for the serial's 1988 screening at The Kitchen in New York City said that the producers, Laurel Chiten and Cheryl Qamar, chose the format for practical and artistic reasons, but above all because of soap opera's accessibility. Minimal transformations allowed them to use a form that appeals to a large number of women, and introduce them to more "politically correct" characters who, as the press release put it, "grapple with real issues."[23]

But does the genre offer a collective context in which women might act to change the institutional and familial structures that frustrate and limit? How can pleasure—or displeasure—be channeled into productive social action? What is the relation of the "feminine" inscribed in the soap and feminist social concerns? If soap operas inscribe a particular idea of femininity, the viewer, besides being conditioned by such representations, is already conditioned for them.[24] Tania Modleski seems to be suggesting that there is metaphorical association between a type of femininity and a form of social and political oppression. But is the relation between the two as direct as her language implies? What are the points of consonance and dissonance between the femaleness of the social audience and their femininity?

What are the points of continuity and discontinuity between the social audience and the text? What are the points of contact between a specific spectator and the assumed audience? Between the individual viewer and the text? How is this related to the historical viewer (Tania Modleski here) who is describing the structures of soap operas for us? Can the viewing practices that Modleski alludes to be demonstrated empirically? It may be that we have to distinguish between gender as an analytical category, and gender as historical agency. As Charlotte Brunsdon points out in another context, to take description for explanation can lead to a theoretical short circuit.[25]

Brunsdon, working at the University of Birmingham's Centre for Contemporary Cultural Studies, published an interesting short essay on the British serial *Crossroads*.[26] Her analysis extends Tania Modleski's to include a wider cultural context. Brunsdon's "social subject" (who almost seems to be a hybrid of Modleski's "ideal mother," whom she sees as a function of the text, and the historical viewer) offers more of a balance between text and context, or, as Annette Kuhn suggests, perhaps even a reconciliation between the two.[27] Brunsdon distinguishes between subject positions proposed by the text and the social subject, that is, individual audience members, who may or may not assume these positions (p. 32). For Brunsdon, the viewer addressed by *Crossroads* is constituted not only by that text, but also by a whole range of other cultural discourses; therefore, it does not necessarily follow that any individual viewer will unproblematically take up the position proposed (loc. cit.). Indeed, she argues that the viewer is required to bring to the viewing experience "an extra-textual familiarity" with certain generic knowledge, knowledge specific to the serial, as well as knowledge of the "socially acceptable codes and conventions for the conduct of personal life" (p. 36). Thus the show "textually implies a feminine viewer to the extent that its textual discontinuities require a viewer competent within the ideological and moral frameworks, the rules, of romance, marriage and family life" (p. 37). She suggests that because they are "feminine," these skills and discourses are often taken for granted.[28]

But even more than Charlotte Brunsdon's study, what attracted me to the efforts of the Centre for Contemporary Cultural Studies was that some

of the social scientists there were using ethnographic methods as a tool of sociological investigation.[29] By starting from concrete cases so that the media and other leisure activities are grounded in specific contexts, these interdisciplinary studies avoid abstracting ideas from the social complexities that produced them.[30] Marked by a reflexive epistemology (looking at their own moral and political assumptions and commitments), they consider the mass media, as James Carey put it, "as a *site* (not a subject or a discipline) on which to engage the general question of social theory,"[31] and see culture as the product of multiple social practices. In many ways a reaction to the for malist and apolitical aspects of structuralism, cultural studies is meant to b a political-intellectual stance that confronts social possibilities.[32] Rath than narrowly concentrating on the effects of the media, cultural studi scholars are more interested in how the wider social order is created, mai tained, and modified. Antonio Gramsci provides them with a theoreti construct for relating the specifics of pleasure to the larger and more gen problem of consent. They also draw on Bertolt Brecht and Roland Bart especially on their ideas of the popular and the pleasurable. The focus i the way that popular culture handles and manages the contradictio everyday life and the manner and effect of the media's intervention i popular structures that tend to go unquestioned.[33]

Rejecting the conception of media audiences as undifferentiate passive, the cultural studies theorists have moved toward a concep an audience as heterogeneous and active. They refuse behaviorist of direct influence in favor of an approach that stresses the role media in the circulation of society's dominant ideological definiti representations. Learning from feminism and working-class strug tural studies looks at such social issues as power, subjectivity, co ness, and pleasure in an almost pragmatic political sense.[34]

When it comes to TV, these theorists seem less interested in t sion text than in larger social practices, including the social use and its more general significance in different communities. The is seen as a site of struggles over meaning. By moving beyond texts as transparent bearers of meaning, they are able to examir plexity of the signifying practice. The "message" is not natural c is the result of a discursive practice. The meaning of a "messa mined in the reception (or decoding) process and is not fixed is a "structured polysemy," so it has many possible senses. The ing process is problematized so that it is not assumed to be th viewers; nor is there necessarily a "fit" between the encoding

and the decoding in reception.[35] However, the text is structured so that certain readings are proposed (and preferred) over others.

In an influential 1973 paper, Stuart Hall itemized three theoretical positions from which a television text can be decoded: a *preferred* reading, a decoding that complies with dominant ideological definitions (that is fully adaptive to the "naturalized" hegemonic position); a *negotiated* reading, a decoding that partly shares dominant definitions (that contains a mixture of adaptive and oppositional elements); and an *oppositional* reading, a decoding that is contrary to dominant definitions (that uses an alternative framework to understand the text).[36]

David Morley has explored Hall's hypothetical positions in two important empirical studies. In the first, *The 'Nationwide' Audience* (1980), Morley attempts what he has called an "ethnographic" investigation of the decoding process and the multiplicity of discourses, ideas and information, at play among different groups of students (each group rather homogeneous in class and gender) watching the British television news-magazine program, *Nationwide,* together in the classroom.[37] He is particularly interested in the structuring of discourses and the frameworks of interpretation at work in decoding, the ways that understandings (or "readings") of *Nationwide* stem from various class positions (p. 31).

The project was an auspicious beginning, but admittedly left many methodological questions unresolved (p. 22). The fact that the subjects were extracted from their natural viewing environment is, in itself, contrary to ethnographic methods; however, that Morley was able to conduct his study in such an artificial environment points to one of the limitations of the cultural studies approach during the late 1970s and early 1980s. It was, after all, meaning, not the viewing experience, that Morley was interested in. But can the relations of viewers to the text, the social relations of the television viewing situation, be separated from the concrete social situation of the viewer? This may even include relations to other viewers (family members, for instance). Such aspects of the experience as use, pleasure, interpretation, and meaning are complicated and dynamic.

Watching television is a social practice and, as such, has the potential to be an experience of tension and struggle that would influence any decoding process. Morley's decoder existed only for the text. There is a residual bit of direct-effects approach in Morley's *Nationwide* study (perhaps that is why he is able to isolate his audience): class is, for him, a *mediator* between the textual structure and its inscribed subjects, but the direction is still one-way. This is a fairly passive notion of subjectivity where the subject is

interpellated by the discourses that constitute that person. As in Sari Thomas's study, social activity gets reduced to statistics, in this case, of class, race, and education.[38]

Morley's second study, *Family Television: Cultural Power and Domestic Leisure,* from the mid-1980s, acknowledges what he calls the "Althusserian drift" of the *Nationwide* study and looks further at the encoding/decoding model. This time entering people's homes, he considers questions of both the social use of television and the behavior of viewers.[39] This study has an admirable sensitivity to notions of difference and diversity, and to situations of power within the family. Although Morley seldom isolates or comments on soap opera viewers specifically, *Family Television* does have a chapter on gender in which he discusses the different positioning of men and women within the home and, in addition to his own interviews with eighteen white working-class families living in the Battersea section of South London, draws on the very interesting research of Ann Gray (women's use of videocassette recorders) and the theoretical work of Charlotte Brunsdon (women watching television in the domestic sphere).[40] Morley looks at gender differences in such facets of viewing as control over program choice and the VCR, program preference, styles of viewing, amounts of viewing, and television-related talk. One section, entitled "'Solo' viewing and guilty pleasures," (pp. 159–62) is entirely devoted to women watching—generally "a nice weepie" or their favorite serial—when the rest of the family is asleep or not at home.

However, in *Family Television,* Morley seems to lose track of both the specifics of texts and any critique of institutional formations. He aims "to generate insights into the criteria used by viewers in making [program] choices and in responding (positively or negatively) to different types of programming and scheduling" (p. 51). Seeing his work as a useful complement to institutional surveys of what people are watching, Morley examines the "why," so to speak, to their "what" (loc. cit.). Like the "uses and gratifications" approach, this study seems potentially helpful to the industry in planning programs and predicting audiences. While he extends his first study by looking at the power dynamic in the living room, there is no attempt to analyze the power of the broadcast institutions.[41]

Dorothy Hobson, at the time of her research also a member of the Centre, has published a book-length study of the British serial *Crossroads* in which she interrogated the broadcasting authorities and the show's production team, as well as the program's critics and its fans.[42] Hobson interviewed and directly observed the *Crossroads'* executives, cast, crew, and some working-class female viewers. Her conceptualization of the audience and the audience's activity, although less theoretically opaque than Brunsdon's, seems quite similar. Viewers are firmly imbedded in a social and cultural life, and they employ that context, as well as their history with the program and the genre, while viewing.

In the chapter that reports on her interviews with viewers and her analysis of their viewing, Hobson discusses the audience as active and the program's "message" as not solely in the text but can be "worked on" and "augmented" by the audience as they add their own experience and opinions to formulate their interpretations of the program (pp. 106 and 135–36). Although she admits the difficulty in determining what *Crossroads* means to its audience, "for there is no single Crossroads, there are as many different Crossroads as there are viewers (p. 136)," she does nonetheless describe "the audience's," "audiences'," and "viewers'" reactions to the show.

Since she doesn't write about her research plan at length, it is difficult to know whether she found a consensus or whether she generalized the reaction of some of her informants to the audience at large. But can an audience that sees so many *Crossroads* be so homogeneous? And perhaps even more importantly, does she see the individual viewer as homogeneous? Are viewers and their viewing habits ever so stable or unambiguous as Hobson's report seems to imply? In celebrating the integrity of the experience, must we make it appear coherent (even though that might make it easier to describe)? Isn't watching television a dynamic experience, a social practice, and a cultural process, and, as such, necessarily contradictory and unruly?[43]

Hobson's research is based on a respectful and modern view of the people she interviews and observes as subjects, not "objects"; she observes them in their natural environments (the workplace and the home); and there is no pretense of passivity or impartiality on her part. But with such interview questions as "And do you think that's realistic?" (p. 133) and "What do you think about the way that the programme sometimes brings in subjects that are a bit difficult?" (p. 134), I wondered how much she was projecting her research categories onto the viewers. Are *they* concerned with "realism" or "difficult" subjects? It may be inevitable that, by aiming for some narrative closure, researchers ultimately demonstrate their own assumptions. Does the need to report in an orderly fashion become a part of how we understand surprises? Perhaps it is impossible ever to reach knowledge not prefigured in our theoretical paradigm.[44]

Ien Ang's study of *Dallas* watchers in Holland allows for "disorder": she questions her own interpretations and ambivalences, and delights in areas that remain obscure to the researcher.[45] Intrigued by the heated debate over the extraordinary popularity of *Dallas* in Holland, Ang placed an advertisement in a Dutch women's magazine requesting that readers respond with letters about why they like or dislike watching the show. She was hoping to find out what happened in the process of watching *Dallas* that made people's experiences pleasurable or displeasurable (p. 10). As a study of concrete viewers, her work has limitations; however, as a work that confronts the limits of knowledge and creative uncertainty, it is extremely valuable. The study is admittedly influenced by the work that was being done at the University of Birmingham (p. vii), but it also seems to be in tune with what Clifford Geertz described in the early 1980s as a recent tendency to blur the boundaries between the humanities and the social sciences and to move from exploring general explanatory laws toward case studies and interpretation.[46] As a social scientist, Ang focuses on an unconventional object for analysis (pleasure). As a feminist and a fan of *Dallas,* she had to redefine the position of the analyst and the language of analysis, challenging the once-dominant ideal of a detached observer using neutral language to describe "brute facts," demystifying the idea of any strict separation of theory and data.[47] Her efforts remind us that researchers are neither innocent nor omniscient. Indeed, I found myself intrigued that Ang's "findings" may not be generalizable.[48]

Although Ang is interested in contradictions, her chosen method of inquiry may have made it difficult to explore the density, unevenness, flexibility, and richness of a viewer or a viewing experience. Although she offers a "symptomatic" reading of the letters, searching "for what is behind the explicitly written, for the presuppositions and accepted attitudes concealed within them" (p. 11), Ang, as Robert C. Allen points out, analyzes texts not subjects.[49] Because of this, she is not able to examine the tensions between what is said and what is done, between what the letters seem to say and what is experienced.[50] Or the dialectical relationship, the reciprocating effects, of experience and interpretation. But it may be very audacious even to attempt this. If we have to question if a subject is ever really knowable to himself or herself, how can we hope that he or she would be knowable to a researcher? Can an epistemological and political self-consciousness overcome this? On another level, aren't we always analyzing texts? Textualizing subjects? Decoding, then re-encoding? The question is, how can we acknowledge and use this social dynamic?

Ang's study seemed, and still seems, to me exemplary in that it does not merely illustrate a theory, but uses empirical data to develop and to test theoretical suppositions. Her reflexivity engages the researcher's subjectivity, challenging presumptions and charting out fresh terrains of inquiry.

Janice A. Radway's *Reading the Romance: Women, Patriarchy and Popular Literature* (1984) also attempts to explore the contradictory positions that women seem to occupy in relation to their pleasures.[51] Written about the same time as Ang's *Dallas* study, *Reading the Romance* investigates the mass-produced paperback romance industry and a small group of romance readers (composed largely of middle-aged, middle-class, homebound mothers) who regularly sought the advice of a particularly knowledgeable bookstore employee in an American midwestern town. While romance novels' textual concerns are different than the visual media, Radway's methodology interested me. She combines social science research methods (ethnographic) and the critical methods of the humanities (primarily literary narrative and reception theories) with psychoanalytic theory to discuss differing incentives for reading romances, the ideology of the texts themselves, and the use of reading as a strategy to secure and justify leisure time. But as she admitted in a 1994 article, her research plan was still motivated by the "assumption that someone ought to worry responsibly about the effect of fantasy on women readers."[52]

Radway's post-Freudian subject is not fully sufficient unto herself, but is constructed and functions within and against a specific social context. The reader-response critique of literary formalism provides Radway with a model for both the reader/text interaction and for a plurality of interpretations. Although reader-response critics are far from unified in approach, and accord differing degrees of power to the reader, they do tend to agree that the reader is active, that (at least some) meaning is made in the interaction between the reader and the text, and that different interpretations are not only possible, but probable.[53]

This idea of multiple reading positions and interpretations has been attractive to those analysts who would like to think of audience members using the media in variable ways, those who would like to think of the mass media having at least some potential as an empowering tool, and those who would like to think that they (and those like them), at least, can resist the conservative nature of the mass media. Radway, in a 1986 article that reflects on both the difficulty and the necessity of synthesizing contextual and psychoanalytic analysis, calls the strategy of reading against the grain "therapeutic," and sees the possibility, the "hope," that these oppositional interpretations might be transformed "into the active resistance of alternative speech."[54] That is, like Tania Modleski, Radway sees the possibility for women's genres being used as a site for political intervention. Since reading is an active process "that is at least partially controlled by the readers themselves, opportunities still exist within the mass communications process for individuals to resist, alter, and reappropriate the materials designed elsewhere for their purchase" (p. 17).

This is similar to Michel deCerteau's argument that marginal peoples insinuate themselves into a system imposed upon them by establishing a degree of plurality and inventiveness within that system.[55] In the 1986 article Radway writes, "If . . . the patriarchal surface of these texts conceals a womanly subtext . . . female audiences are capable of interpreting these forms against the grain."[56] But is such interpretation necessarily an act of subversion or emancipation? And is there latent in this position the idea that texts *themselves* are meaningful and then twisted or perverted in some way by the counterculture reading?

Of the studies described so far, however, Radway's seems the most "ethnographic": she studied an organically composed community of avid readers, one that was "another culture" from her own.[57] She observed them in their "native" environment and, although their culture may not have been too discrete, it was complex enough to sustain extensive analysis. She connected the significance of their reading to specific details of their lives. The study is a sensitive interplay between making the familiar strange and making the strange quotidian (without normalizing the practice of reading romances by implying it is repeated in the same manner by everyone in the group or by all readers). Like Ang's, Radway's object, language, and moral position reflect a rethinking of social science methods and their potential for social analysis. And like Ang's, the work is at once a map of past investigations and a program for future research.

Robert C. Allen also draws on literary reception theory in his 1985 book, *Speaking of Soap Operas*.[58] Like Tania Modleski, he notes the double critical standard applied toward women's mass-produced entertainment. But whereas Modleski attacks it from a feminist point of view, Allen approaches it from the point of view of the academy and its prejudice toward "art." In a useful review, he interrogates the traditional aesthetic and empiricist social science reception of soap operas and shows how these analysts' philosophical principles and procedures function to predetermine and limit their "findings." He looks at how soap operas and their audiences have been and might be studied—a goal that is admittedly polemical (p. 5). Surveying a wide range of theoretical literature, he seems to be addressing a broad readership: American mass communications scholars (especially those working in quantitative analysis), as well as American and European cinema studies and British media studies scholars (especially those who embrace an anti-empiricist position), and perhaps even scholars from the alternative perspectives he proposes: "poetics" (mainly semiotics) and "reader-response" or "audience-oriented" literary criticism. However, he is not aiming for a synthesis, but an engagement that allows various scholars, as Thomas Kuhn puts it, to "recognize each other as members of different language communities and then become translators" (quoted in Allen, p. 7).

For Allen, the viewer is neither passive nor pacified and soap operas are complex narrative systems. The reader-oriented poetics that he proposes draws heavily on the theories of Wolfgang Iser and Hans Robert Jauss. Their construction of ideal readers would seem incompatible with research on actual readers or viewers, such as Radway's, Ang's, or Hobson's. Iser and Jauss are, however, very helpful to Allen's historiographic orientation toward soap opera reception. It is really audience, not viewers, that Allen is studying, and that audience is historically predominantly female (with pleasures different from a male audience) and is able to produce a range of "actualizations" of the text.[59] In the final chapter in his book, Allen charts a project that attempts to historicize the listener or viewer/text relationship by constructing the "interpretative horizon" (the dominant cultural and social context) within which soaps have been experienced. The sketch is not too class specific and admittedly is not able to suggest how actual listeners and viewers have understood soaps (p. 132); however, it maps out the terms by which an audience might be identified and contextualized, and how one might inquire into the way audience members may have experienced soap operas. It also looks at changes in the narrative discourses of the shows themselves.[60] Allen's epilogue calls for the empirical study of concrete viewers.

Although he doesn't seem to be aware of Dorothy Hobson's British study, and at the time of his writing Ien Ang's book on *Dallas* viewers had not yet been translated, Allen cites with guarded admiration Janice Radway's recently published study and David Morley's observations of the *Nationwide* audiences as models for the joining of textual and audience analysis. Laying out the enormity and some of the potential problems of such a project, he recognizes the need to reconceptualize many of the research paradigms that have determined the way that mass communications has been studied in the past.

The book that you have before you was stimulated by many of the same questions that inspired Allen's work. Others have also responded in a similar spirit to my own enterprise. Ellen Seiter's 1981 dissertation included a semiotic inquiry into the signification of soap operas in the abstract, outside of their socio-historical conditions of existence and removed from the processes and practices of reception. Nevertheless, she argues that soap operas allow for the possibility of alternative readings not necessarily intended by their producers.[61] Then, working with a team of researchers in the late 1980s, around the time that I was interviewing, she talked to viewers of both prime-time and daytime soaps in the western Oregon area. Addressing many of the issues Modleski asserted from a textual and psychoanalytic point of view, the interviewers directed questions at actual viewers and later asked them to fill in a questionnaire. These "ethnographic interviews" consisted of groups of two to nine participants, mainly working-class women (but nearly half of the groups also included men), who had responded to a newspaper advertisement.[62] Around the same time, Mary Ellen Brown was also speaking to soap opera viewers, and she was particularly interested in the oral networks that exist around soaps and the possibility that talk about soaps might generate a "resistive feminine discourse."[63] Her final study was much broader than my own, encompassing fans of daytime and evening soaps—Americans, Britons, and Australians, mature women, young adults, and teens—using a questionnaire as well as discussion groups.[64] And Seiter has recently published a book reporting on her empirical research on television and new media audiences. This book discusses soap operas very little, but includes a helpful review of qualitative audience research and recent ethnographic studies of television audiences.[65] In all of these studies, viewers are seen as active, struggling over the meaning of "polysemic" texts.[66]

Any attempt to describe the viewer/text interaction is loaded with methodological challenges. Dana Polan has characterized *Watching Dallas* as two books: one a theoretical celebration of the actual diversity of viewer positions and practices, the other, Ang's univocal interpretation of *Dallas* and its position in the "ideology of mass culture."[67] Must our descriptions use the writer's interpretation as a prototype[68] or suggest a representative or typical interpretation (from quantification, an inferred consensus, or creative deduction)? Is it possible to communicate an event without putting it under interpretation? The point is not that the scholar is uniquely qualified to make these interpretations but that the text can only be known through the eyes, ears, and opinions of a viewer. Is that viewer to be the academic analyst? Or a prototype/consensus constructed by the analyst? Or an unexamined and arbitrary, an uninterpreted and unorganized listing of the opinions of nonacademic viewers? It may be that any representation is inescapably univocal.

However much we may aspire to a more democratic mode of explication, to giving people the opportunity to speak about their experiences in their own voices with their own understanding of their lives, what we get are not unmediated testimonies or records, but imaginative constructions, interpretations that conform to the structures, codes, and literary customs of a discipline. Letters to the editor of fan magazines tend to resemble the discourses and expressive conventions of the editorial articles. Indeed, the authority of any report may well reside in its manner of storytelling—its rhetorical performance. As scholars, reading and writing, we are always dealing with the structures of expectation, negotiation, and improvisation that are as much a part of exposition as they are of ordinary interactions.

But how can we observe and report responsibly? How can we observe and represent the complexity of cultural realities? Clifford Geertz suggests a "continuous dialectical tacking" between the specific and the general, between local detail and global structures, between "the whole conceived through the parts that actualize it and the parts conceived through the whole that motivates them."[69] He suggests a restlessness, "a sort of intellectual perpetual motion," that turns interpretations of other people's points of view into explications of one another.[70] One doesn't simply describe a text (be it a soap opera or a cultural practice or an informant's consciousness of an experience), one unavoidably offers an interpretation (in effect, "producing" a text via discourse), and Geertz is suggesting an investigative process that exposes the dialogic aspects of interpretation, the discursive aspects of cultural representations. This may be the difference between a formalist analysis of texts and an ethnographic one.

In order for empirical research not to be empiricist, it is important to establish (as part of one's theoretical construct) a case for research that is not premised on a separation of subject and object, that is cognizant of and problematizes the relation between the subject and object; that is admittedly an *act* of research.[71] The subjectivity/objectivity split, a positivist perspective, may be in itself a mystification, obscuring the dialectical process from which understanding arises.[72] What we should be aiming for is an intersubjective dialogue. If scientific criticism claims to have purged itself of the subjective, feminist critics have been struggling to reclaim the authority of experience.[73] I consider this a strength, though it also makes the researcher more vulnerable (especially where professional taboos against self-revelation are very strong).[74] For me, an adequate theory of practice must deny a neat split between subject and object, us and them, and also reflect critically on the tight interweaving of our thoughts and our feelings.

Therefore, the possibility of historical or cultural dissonance (or even an ethnocentric, class, or gender bias) must be recognized as participating in any such intersubjective dialogue—and in the formulation of knowledge. This may seem rather paradoxically to be calling for a self-centered point of view; however, it is meant to draw attention and suspicion to motives, rather than legitimating them. It is also meant to invite a modern skepticism concerning the possibility of texts referring to actual events and to celebrate the distinction between interpretation and truth. If ideology often makes our consciousness appear natural, we should look for a mode of analysis to reverse the process.[75]

But we also have to question what kinds of knowledge are suppressed by the convention of coherence, by a discipline's modes of inquiry and norms of exposition. Can't we frustrate coherence deliberately? Use incompleteness, digression, and fragmentation as political and rhetorical strategies? Shouldn't we employ an expressive mode that produces gaps even as it fills them in? That undermines the whole idea of "completeness" and appreciates an inherently imperfect mode of knowledge?[76] A montage, rather than a linear argument?[77] Just as we have to struggle to find a way to describe without hopelessly impoverishing the complexity of experience, we have also to confront the probability that any attempt to analyze experience or consciousness will be thwarted by the fluency that is the very essence of the phenomena. Experience and consciousness are active processes (not static products), thoughts and feelings that are related, held in tension, always emerging.[78] Perhaps subjects perceive their practices differently from academic analysts precisely because they do not see them as completed events. It may be that this fluency cannot be frozen for analytical inspection, that it may, ironically, resist objectification.

Although my theoretical perspective has been informed by an ethnographic sensibility, I would not claim that this is an ethnographic study. And since I am not making any sociological arguments, sampling did not concern me very much. There was no attempt, for example, to get a statistically representative sample. However, my intense curiosity about fans' habits and pleasures led me to speak to a range of women: a few inner-city welfare mothers, some mothers from a wealthy suburb whose children were away at college, a retiree in a sunbelt retirement complex, and a retired clerical worker who stayed in the same New York City apartment where she had lived for the many years she worked, a few middle-class city dwellers. A couple of my informants were currently working outside the home and taped their shows. The majority, however, were working-class women who stayed at home during the day. You have already met some of them in the previous chapter.

I approached them mainly through word of mouth; many volunteered after someone told them about my project. For a while I even began to think of myself as "the soap opera lady." The formal interviews were each tape recorded, generally in the viewer's home; they averaged around two hours and the questions tended to be general and open-ended with minimal direction. If conversation did not begin naturally when I turned on the tape recorder, I would say something relatively open, like "Do you remember when you began watching soap operas?" or, if there was a lull, I might ask, "Are there any characters or stories that you particularly like or dislike?"

These interviews are not evidence; they are opportunities for discursive analysis and interpretation. I tried to be attentive to what was not said as well as to what was, and to how it was said. As Ray L. Birdwhistell has noted: "The report of an informant about his [or her] behavior is itself behavior."[79] The interviews have been treated as narratives, as performances, and as special events. Of course, the informants didn't speak in the abstract but *to* the researcher and *with* the researcher and inasmuch as the information is disseminated *through* the researcher, it is essential to analyze the dynamics (and the politics) that produce these special events. A great deal of power—and accountability—lies in the hand of the researcher and writer. Reconciling the trust these women gave me with my power to analyze their words and actions is a complex task.

A conception of research as just a conversation with fans about matters of interest may be as naive as the notion of "capturing" attitudes and beliefs without the informants being aware. The informant's tales were, after all, created to answer the questions I was curious about. In some cases, the informant may not have thought much about the issues discussed until presented with the interview situation. So, in a large measure the informant's views can be seen as a response to my views. The questions I asked or did not ask helped to form the structure of the interview and were grounded in my consciousness of the subject and the event, as much as in the informant's answers to the previous questions (or the informant's consciousness of the subject and the event).[80] My informants' thoughts weren't necessarily pre-existent and communicated to me; rather they may have actually taken form when presented with the opportunity to articulate them.

Yet sometimes I would arrive at an interview and would be greeted with a barrage of questions about which my informant seemed to want a "scholarly" opinion. Sometimes I would be asked one or two thoughtful questions that had obviously been troubling the viewer for some time. And certainly my own ideas were crystallized through my talks with the viewers. The interview dynamic, then, must include the relationship between the informant and the interviewer/interpreter; it also includes, however, the relationship of the informant with her consciousness and the researcher with her own. Elizabeth Bird contrasts ethnographic research seen as "an objective scientific exercise" with a more modern approach in which research is seen as "an interpretative, humanistic enterprise, in which the subjectivity of the researcher is crucial in both fieldwork and writing, and in which the ethnographer's claim to speak in the name of the other is increasingly brought into question."[81] This is a good description of what I have called above "intersubjective dialogue," and what I will call below, "dialogic interdependence."

Because the experiences that viewers have communicated to me are the result of very complicated processes of identity, interaction, and interpretation, we should factor in the fact that for some people, especially those with many household responsibilities, watching soap operas has not attained the same respectability that writing about soaps has in academic circles.[82] For many viewers soap opera watching involves complex emotions, and what they choose to talk about and how they converse about themselves and their activities often involve feelings of guilt, boasting, justification, and/or apology. For example, a retired schoolteacher who had moved to a condominium complex in a new state explained that her habit of watching an entire afternoon of soaps followed a failure at her attempt to learn to play bridge (and thus a withdrawal from a social environment in which she felt inadequate). Many of her comments seemed to be an effort toward justifying her viewership, proving it worthwhile by conforming to academic interests and fitting her acts and talk into an intellectual framework. When we parted, she thanked me for talking to her. One new mother told me that she began watching soaps to have something to talk about with the other mothers in her neighborhood playground. Yet it seemed that she still had a desire for encouragement, the need for me to justify her activity as worthwhile, or to tell her to go ahead and not mind what critics might think.

Another woman, who told me that her husband had blamed the breakup of their marriage on the values and attitudes she got from soap operas, seemed to be seeking absolution. I wondered if she, unable to forgive herself for the failure, was so frank in the interview because she treated it as a confessional: recounting her sins, abasing herself before me, and thereby earning forgiveness from the feminist scholar who considers her experience worthy of attention.

A few of the women who I had heard watched regularly and whom I approached to speak with disavowed that soaps were important to them, but seemed nonetheless excited to speak about their experiences. Some seemed motivated by a need to apologize for deviating from what they thought of as the accepted moral/ethical way to spend the afternoon or from feminist standards. When I approached Anne van der Does in our apartment complex's laundry room and told her that I had heard that she watched soap operas, she giggled and denied it. Later, still laughing, she admitted that she watched "only one." She told me that she began watching *Days of Our Lives* seven years earlier when the elder of her two daughters started kindergarten. The four-year-old arrived home tired and the two of them would sit down to relax and watch the one-hour soap together.[83] When I asked her about the possibility of an interview, she said that she didn't know what she could tell me and seemed uncomfortable, so I didn't pursue it. When I asked her if she knew anyone else who watched, she replied, "I don't know anyone who has time for such nonsense!" When I said, "I do!" she was speechless. A few weeks later, I saw her on the street and she stopped to inquire about my work. The following week we spoke for over an hour and a half in her home, her declarations punctuated with such questions as, "Is that stupid?" and "Isn't it silly?" She even expressed admiration for her mother who after a couple of months abroad had weaned herself from watching her soap.

On the other hand, some of the fans I interviewed seemed to be bragging about their independence (from "acceptable" behavior or household chores), their willingness to indulge themselves, and perhaps even their daring. (But even these women didn't claim the activity was intellectually stimulating or morally uplifting.)

Many I spoke to volunteered that their mates do not think very much of their watching soaps or don't feel that soaps were very interesting. Yet the first time I met Candy Lampropoulos she happily boasted that every man she has been with has ended up watching soaps with her. I wondered if she was imputing power to herself, expressing pride in the sensitivity of the men, or bolstering what she thought of as a maligned genre by claiming that it had an appeal to a less-maligned gender. She also told me of the usefulness that soaps had served when she worked as a social worker, as a means of breaking the ice with tough pregnant teenagers and as a stimulus to discussion in a colleague's group therapy sessions. Another woman, who had been watching *All My Children* since it began to air eighteen years before, told me, with some embarrassment, that until she began discussing it with me, she had never let anyone know that she watched a soap opera.

I don't wish to imply that soap opera viewers are riddled with guilt or that all are ambivalent about their activity; that is clearly not the case.[84] Although there are many prescriptions for valuable ways for a homemaker to spend her "free" time (such as crafts, physical exercise, and civic or charitable activities), watching soap operas has seldom been described to me as either a duty or a serious wrongdoing. But ethical concerns over worthwhile conduct and leisure time are not always tied to particular prohibitions or interdictions. And the apparent freedom women have in the home places a burden on their own individual choices. Moral solicitude, as Michel Foucault has pointed out, is often strongest precisely where there is no obligation or prohibition.[85]

Motivations for answering an interviewer's questions are complicated, and the answers should be seen as politically and metaphorically complex. I realized that it was important to see informants as social analysts themselves, not simply as my "raw material." How viewers morally problematize their time, how they acknowledge the relation between watching soap operas and their household responsibilities, and how they feel their viewing experiences have a practical relevance to their material and social situation are also politically and metaphorically complex. Do they see watching soap operas as a form of political resistance? (Do we want to consider "coping" a form of resistance? Are fantasies a helpful way of working through conflicts?) Or do they see the act of watching soap operas functioning more to derail political resistance, normalizing the social situation by containing the contradictions and oppositions? Or perhaps watching soap operas functions more like psychoanalytic resistance, stabilizing the familiar by denying contradictions and oppositions, discouraging any significant transformation of present conditions. Do they perceive the pleasures involved as growing out of a more basic and systemic *dis*pleasure with daily life? Suppressing guilt about being unhappy? To some, my respondents' cooperation, forthrightness, and sometimes even pleasure in the interview situation might be interpreted as another indication of their loneliness and powerlessness. To others, it will seem like tangible evidence of their freedom, that they are mistresses of their fate. It may be their secret vice, talking about soaps, but it is also a small act of self-affirmation.

I didn't think of the visits to viewers' homes as attempts at participant observation because it seemed to me that the presence of the researcher in the home is too intrusive, creating a situation not at all similar to ordinary viewing (especially where the viewer usually watches alone).[86] Rather, I treated them as opportunities for dialogic interplay and discursive analysis. The presence of the researcher provoked and effected a new situation (an *extra*-ordinary situation) because it precipitated discussions about the soap opera, descriptions of characters, recounting old plots: stories about the stories. In other words, rather than deny it, I wanted to *use* the interaction between the researcher and the informant, while remaining cognizant of my own role as an interested (in both senses of the word) partner. We were actively collaborating on versions of reality.

I have often wondered about the appropriateness or adequacy of the term "informant." Perhaps "collaborator" *would* be better, but that doesn't really recognize the lack of equality between researcher and the person being interviewed. The ideal of a transcendence of disparity is a happy fiction that seldom exists in real life. Not that the relationships are static. They continually shift with many coexisting elements and there is often cacophony and disorder in the interactions. Informants impose certain role expectations on the researcher (which the researcher may or may not adopt); and the researcher, consciously or not, transfers reciprocal preconceptions and expectations onto the informant (which the informants may or may not adopt). And though responding to the instigating force of the researcher, any dialogical research is also partially directed and/or circumscribed by the informants. Yet the uses of the research—and its purpose—are generally decided by the researcher (in this she may have the tacit support of an academic community) and are generally for the benefit of the researcher (or her career or status).

My personal engagement with soaps and with the women who watch will be evident in many places. I don't approach them as a disinterested critic, but as someone examining my own pleasures, my own desires. I enjoyed speaking about soaps and they were so much a part of my life that it would have been silly for me to try to discuss them from the traditional distance of academic "objectivity." To put it bluntly, I am a character in this book. The use of my autobiography, subjectivity, familiarity, and situated knowledge seems to me more honest than assuming detachment, or attempting to translate experience into abstract discourses.

However, research conceived as conversations about shared convictions is a utopian ideal. Although our common experiences contributed to the ambiance, in many ways, the interview rests on an artificial sense of intimacy. The bonding between us as women, or as women with an allegiance and enthusiasm for soaps, implicitly carries with it a generally unspoken nervous tension about our differences. We must examine our dissonance because, in some senses, as intellectuals, we are always traitors.[87] As Pierre Bourdieu has pointed out, the social scientist's "objectivity" may be simply making a virtue out of necessity, the conversion of a *de facto* exclusion into a choice of method.[88] It is possible, however, that *recognition* of the dialogic interdependency of the interaction can be a bridge to greater understanding. And although a tradition grounded in detachment, abstraction, and coherence may seem more legitimate then one that honors partiality, fissures, and lacunae, if we reject a positivist perspective, as Steven Webster has stressed, existential gaps can be the foundation of knowledge, not its subversion.[89]

Besides the ethnographic, my approach also borrows from both the sociological and the psychoanalytic, not as master doctrines or explanatory systems, but as interpretative frameworks that illuminate elements of the viewing experience. To me, soap opera viewing is both institutionalized and conventionalized, but it is also a personal experience involving private fantasies and recompense. The viewing subject constitutes the text (in this way, I am differing from the sociological-behavioral model), but that viewing subject is already in social practice. That is, the viewers are subjects in history, living in material social formations, not merely subjects of a single text (in this way, I am differing from the psychoanalytic model). And the meaning of the text is produced in the context of interpretation. Jonathan Culler, writing about literature, says, "To speak of the meaning of the work is to tell a story of reading."[90] And as Michel deCerteau, from a sociological perspective reminds us, "consumption" can be a form of production as our ways of using representations, regulations, and rituals, what we make of them, can be quite different from what the originators had in mind.[91] We will be looking at this other production—how soap operas are enunciated (to use an analogy from linguistics)—as a dynamic and complex social practice.

By rejecting the simplistic and linear sender-message-receiver of the sociological-behaviorist approach, I am rejecting traditional content analysis, as well.[92] Marlene G. Fine, for example, has discussed the conversations in twenty randomly selected broadcasts in "Soap Opera Conversation: The Talk That Binds."[93] Like most communications scholars who analyze television content, Fine (a longtime viewer) did not find the meaning of soap opera conversation (or "what they are about") particularly problematic. Therefore, she was able to isolate conversations, categorize them into types, quantify them, and then compare them to sociological studies of real life.

The complexity of my model makes it difficult to isolate, measure, or even describe a "message." Messages are not self-contained units. They are products of interpretation, not objects of it.[94] As Roland Barthes has written, "[A] text's unity lies not in its origin but in its destination."[95] This model appeals to me because it makes it impossible to look at elements outside of the social relations and practices that produce them. The act of watching soap operas, then, becomes at the same time a *use of* television and an operation *performed on* it.

"The audience" is, as Arthur Kroker and David Cook argue, an abstract and empty quanta of attention that is sold to advertisers.[96] It does not exist in any social form.[97] It is individual viewers and the viewing interaction that I wanted to study. Soap operas are aimed at housewives; and while the idea of "housewife" has a number of different ideological inflections, it is also a body of people that can be located socially and historically.

Housewives can also be located physically; they are women who spend much of their day in their homes. Gaston Bachelard gives the house a privileged position in his poetics of space. He writes that our house is "our corner of the world," "our first universe, a real cosmos in every sense of the word."[98] It is a "psychic state" of intimacy and protection, resonant in both memories and daydreams, the realm of comfort and imagination.[99]

For women, it is also a place of work. And housework is not much fun. It is generally mindless and emotionless, fragmented and unfulfilling.[100] It has a repetitive and compulsive nature, and even well-managed chores are cyclical and infinite. The relentless toil is almost serial, always being undone (food gets eaten, clothes get dirtied), needing to be done again. The day-to-day, like soaps themselves, as we shall see presently, is constituted by repetition. An accomplished task still remains to be repeated again the next day, the next week, or the next season. Simone de Beauvoir wrote of the Manichaean struggle against dirt, where we never sense the "conquest of a positive Good, but rather an indefinite struggle against negative Evil." Or as the narrator in Helena María Viramontes's short story, "Snapshots," puts it, "How can people believe that for years I've fought against motes of dust or dirt-attracting floors or bleaching white sheets to perfection when a few hours later the motes, the dirt, the stains return to remind me of the uselessness of it all?"[101]

While in their home, women are continually confronted with the potential for work. No wonder they are susceptible to distant and "dangerous" dreams!

There is also little compulsion—and little chance—for women to discuss all the small things in everyday life that are so important precisely *because* they are experienced over and over again.[102] Despite the enormous time and energy expended, homebound women see most of their lives as "ordinary." I found it difficult to get my informants to believe in the importance of the insignificant, that I was very interested in "the everyday." Some of our most common feelings and experiences, because they are assumed to be common, have been relegated to silence.

Ann-Sargent Wooster's 1982 video, *House,* uses a voice-over commentary about housework and child rearing interspersed with the sounds of street noises, children playing and crying, and daytime television, over very close shots of hands housekeeping, cooking, caring for a doll, and pretending with child-sized housework toys. She plays the visual and aural chaos of daily work (the noise of the eggbeater drowns out the sound of the soap opera) against a romanticized and nostalgic remembrance of her own mother and her own childhood. The profusion of image and sound, without the inclusion of the housewife, reminds us that along with the relative autonomy and independence of household work often comes both fragmentation and isolation—a lifetime of ordinary days and frightening regularity. A Sunlight dishwashing detergent commercial begins with a slow pan of a sink full of dirty dishes while the sound of soap operas is heard from off-screen.

To many women, housework and child care must seem like miniscule chores within an endless maze of routines. Or, in the words of the housewife recovering from a breakdown in the 1986 Canadian film, *Dancing in the Dark,* "Instead of larger purpose I saw the tiny tasks." It can be overwhelming. Is there no place or way to escape from unfinished work? As one of the young mothers I spoke to put it, "Sometimes I feel that everyone asks me everyday for everything, even if they can do it themselves. Like it's 'Mommy get me a glass.'" Or another, "I feel like you're always waiting . . .'til they need you next. Which is hard sometimes; it really is."

Yet for many, the home offers independence and leisure along with responsibilities—both freedoms and constraints. Indeed, the fact that they have no "boss" may be a welcome relief to those who have experienced the supervisions of the workplace or an authoritarian family life. However, many women do create inflexible, self-imposed schedules to give structure and meaning to their job in the home. Ann Oakley's early 1970s study of English housewives noted the frequency with which her informants rigidly adhered to standards and routines. It is partially because they are without formal supervision that they, in Oakley's words, "devised rules which give the work the kind of structure most employed workers automatically find in their job situation. Having defined the rules, they then attempt to adhere to them, and to derive reward from carrying them out."[103]

Although this way of coping with the profusion of work probably adds to the monotony of the job, a sense of organizing one's day does create goals and a set of values that, once met, help to define a job well done, despite the indifference and apathy of others. Oakley goes on to say that "since housework is not paid and husbands are by and large uncritical appraisers of their wives' work in the home, self-reward for housework activity is virtually the only kind housewives can hope to experience."[104] As one mother told me, "There's not too much positive feedback." When asked if she found mothering more rewarding or frustrating, she hesitated, then began slowly, "It's rewarding, but . . . The rewards, you don't know when they're coming; there's no paycheck. The job satisfaction—you don't get a pat on the back. My daughter, I definitely get positive feedback from her, you know there *are* good times, but just sometimes it's hard to see that when I get so caught up in the everyday and all that that goes on." If it is, as Irna Phillips put it, "the greatest and most worthwhile career in the world," where do homemakers find their appreciation, respect, status, and exhilaration?

Though most women seem to enjoy child rearing and find it pleasurable and rewarding—or say they do—there is still a certain tension and sometimes ambivalence: it was the responsibilities associated with child rearing that made them into "housewives" and contributed to a more sedentary lifestyle and lack of leisure outside the home. Julie Pars Cadenhead, while a New York City college student who described herself as a feminist, looked back twelve years to earlier days when she was a young mother fresh from the Midwest, "motherhood can be about isolation. Soap operas were a welcome friend—adult company. . . . This was not an act of escapism. I loved being home with my child and enjoyed my situation. The reality, however, was that my mobility was now limited and I did not know any new mothers in my neighborhood."

Another woman described her daily routine and how much being a good homemaker and mother means to her. She brings her children to school each weekday and then works for four hours, either at free-lance photography or housework, and then "takes a break" to watch a soap opera from 1:00 P.M. to 2:00 P.M. While she watches she generally sews (she makes all the clothes for the family of four). After that is over she does her daily grocery shopping. She then picks the children up at school and spends the rest of the afternoon with them, helping them with their homework, taking them to music lessons, orchestra rehearsal, or other afterschool events. When I commented on how busy she was, she replied, "That's why I have to have something that's stupid and doesn't mean anything, so I can just tune out work." She was talking about her soap opera viewing. (I understood; I would sometimes tape several hours of soaps on Thursday and Friday so that I would have something to watch over the weekend when I needed a break from my writing.) Later, she expressed some dissatisfaction with the show she was following and asked me to recommend another that was "romantic" and not full of "those tough kids with long hair." When I told her about one on another channel which begins at 12:30 P.M., she immediately replied that that was much too early for her to quit working. This woman was not one for unearned enjoyment.

I saw her the morning before Thanksgiving Day on her way back from walking her children to school. She greeted me with a cheery, "Good morning." When I asked her how she was, she replied, with equal good humor, that she had four things to bake and seven rooms to clean before noon. Later, walking back from the market together, she asked me if I had baking to do. I told her that I had my sister's eight-month-old and three-year-old sons for the day, so I thought I would limit my cooking to mashing turnips. In a tone that sounded part wistful and part censorious, she responded that it would be nice if someone would take her kids for the day.

It seemed to me that no matter how cheerfully and efficiently she managed her day, there was a desperate need for recognition, wholeness, and rewards. I thought back to the day when we had spoken at her apartment. We had been comparing daily schedules, the long hours that we both work, how we manage certain tasks when we were too tired to do others. At one point she asked me if I had a husband or children. Then, with a hard edge to her generally soft and sweet voice, "But it's only for you that you're working! You don't have any other people in the house that you're responsible for."

One woman said that her three-year-old is "too demanding" and so she tapes her shows and watches them after her daughter has gone to bed. Awilda Valles told me that when she watches her shows she wants complete concentration. Her brother watches some of the same soaps, but he talks too much, so she insists that he watch in the other room and she usually convinces him to take her infant daughter with him.

Marilyn Morales claimed that watching *All My Children* wasn't all that important to her and she doesn't watch too often; yet when she does watch, she has trained her son to play by himself for an hour. "I'll get angry if I miss something important. Since I'm not really into it as much, I want to know what's going on when I'm watching it, *while* I'm watching it, so you don't want a little kid [mimicking a child's voice], 'Mommy this, Mommy that.'" But if a storyline she's not too interested in comes on, "I'll leave the volume up high and go into the kitchen or go do whatever else I have to do," and listen for something more exciting to come on.

William Boddy tells us that early television producers did worry about integrating television viewing into housewives' daily responsibilities. As with radio, television was counting on sales of receivers to families for use in the home and commercial advertising to pay for the programs. With women as the target audience of the commercial appeals, success depended upon, as one Philco executive put it in 1944, "the degree to which housewives would drop their housework to watch television during the daytime."[105] A CBS monograph the following year noted that daytime radio broadcasting had served as background activity to daily chores. While noting television's special demands they nonetheless argued that "television daytime programs . . . can be constructed so that full attention will not be necessary for their enjoyment. Programs requiring full attention of eye and ear should be scheduled for evening hours when viewers feel entitled to entertainment and relaxation."[106]

In a 1948 letter to Procter & Gamble, Irna Phillips herself suggested that daytime TV should develop techniques whereby the "auditory could be followed without constant attention to the visual."[107] DuMont planned its daytime schedule that year with shows that could "be appreciated just as much from listening to them as from watching them."[108] In 1955, *Variety* referred to daytime TV as "tailored for the ears alone."[109]

Mary Beth Haralovich quotes a 1957 editorial in *Industrial Design* magazine that begins by summarizing how household design has contributed to increased leisure, making things easier for people, freeing them. It then goes on to note that "automatic ranges and one-step washer-dryers leave the housewife with a precious ingredient: Time. This has come to be regarded as both her bonus and her right, but not everyone regards it with unqualified enthusiasm. Critics belonging to the women's-place-is-at-the-sink school ask cynically what she is free *for*. The bridge table? Afternoon TV? The lonely togetherness of telephone gossip? The analyst's couch?"[110]

But the idea that work and leisure in the home are separate, divided entities is probably false. The two areas flow together, repeating and reinforcing each other.[111] A 1947–1948 study of American housewives and their leisure time, which seems rather silly today, somewhat arbitrarily included sewing as housework and knitting as leisure. It also considered listening to the radio, knitting, and crocheting as discrete activities.[112] Lynn Spigel's chronicle of the impact of television on postwar American households tells of 1952 advertisements for an ensemble appliance that addressed the problem of women's labor and leisure in the home with a television set built into the wall above the washer/dryer and, another, for a TV screen above the oven window.[113] Back in the mid-nineteenth century, a critic in a literary quarterly discussing serialized fiction hit the nail on the head: "now our dreams are mingled with our daily business."[114]

More recent studies suggest that women do not watch television in their home the same way that men do; they are more distracted.[115] This should be seen in the context of their household responsibilities. For most men, the home is not a place of production; it is associated with leisure and generally with comfort and relaxation. Many of the women whom I spoke with told me that they often perform chores while viewing. (I, myself, watching television as part of my professional practice, seldom sit down to view without getting up during commercials to straighten things up or dust off the TV set.)

One woman told me that, besides caring for the home and her daughter, she is responsible for much of the family business's paperwork. When I asked her when she finds time to do it she laughed and said that after her daughter goes to bed she sometimes sits down, but if her husband is home, he gets angry. "It's like, 'pay attention to me'. . . . So I do stuff late at night after they've both gone to sleep. Sometime I'll be sitting here and I'll turn [the tape of] *One Life to Live* on and I'll do my work." A woman whose children are grown and away from home and whose husband comes home from work later than she likes to eat, tapes *The Bold and the Beautiful* and *Loving* and watches them while she has her dinner. During our conversation, she seemed quite knowledgeable about *One Life to Live* also. When I asked her about it, she said that twice a month, when she pays her bills, she would listen to that show.[116]

While some argue that the audio track and narrative structures of today's nighttime television are also based on an assumption of distracted viewing,[117] the typical network daytime (the hours when children are at school) schedule has historically been made up of game shows, talk shows, courtroom trials, hosted variety shows, and soap operas, all dialogue-centered genres that are composed of short segments that can be easily missed without losing much understanding. They are genres that can be experienced in bits and pieces. The extreme conventionality of the weekly evening series means that we can generally foretell how any one episode will end; however, they are still, at least nominally, based on some idea of closure, and much of the satisfaction seems to be in seeing the expected ending. Game shows, talk shows, soap operas, and, to a certain extent, courtroom shows and variety programs, on the other hand, are all serial in composition. Some guests or characters might depart but the game, talk, or story goes on. The episode may be over in a half-hour or an hour, but there's more to come the next weekday and the episode's "end" is mediated by a sense of "so far."[118]

The rhythms of housework should not be seen as inevitable or even self-generating. The way we conceptualize our work, our time, our pleasure—and our gender—is intricately linked to our cultural environment and must be interpreted in relation to the social contexts in which these conceptualizations occur. Daytime television helps to create or sustain that rhythm as much as it reflects it. In this sense, it might be seen as domesticating.

Family life is not the cause of economic or emotional failure or success; but for homebound women, the family is where they experience economic and emotional life. It may be through isolation that women most experience oppression. The isolation and the oppression are real enough; they exist. The task for us should be to explore how and why women can survive under such difficult conditions. And paradoxically, how and why, under such conditions, many are able to live vigorous, textured, and sometimes lyrical lives. However, many do not. They express restlessness, rebellion; for some, even rage and refusals. Others are overwhelmed by the lack of spontaneity and of a sense of self—and by loneliness.

In Sari Thomas's study, media consumption is a logical and sequential process of need satisfaction. She assumes that this relationship is conscious, predictable, and noncontradictory. But is it? What are the differences between reported behavior and actual behavior? Explaining one's tastes and behavior is extremely complicated and difficult. Are we aware of all of our needs? Can we identify the sources of our satisfaction? Or is the analyst inferring this from other questions—or from stereotypes? In thinking about a general orientation to watching soap operas, we might ask if the habit is considered an acceptable, even potentially rewarding, activity.

To what extent is the activity scheduled? And what are the attitudes toward the flexibility of the schedule? To what extent are soap operas discussed with other viewers? Does that affect responsibilities toward scheduling and the viewing experience? Is the viewer embarrassed to think of herself as a soap opera fan? How has her idea of fandom been affected by my interest?

When we talk about "different" audience members are we necessarily talking about different people or "difference" within individual viewers? The same woman who gets involved in the story and cares what happens next stirs the stew during breaks and knows she needs a rest. Or a woman who feels that soap operas are politically regressive may enjoy watching them. There may be a certain ambivalent (and perhaps even ironic) disjunction between our multiple identities. (Soap opera commercials often exploit these tensions. Sunlight dishwashing liquid's, "Sometimes the dishes have to sit until life's little tragedies are over," is probably the least subtle, but others play on the homemaker's family and household responsibilities and her need for the "relief" that the housekeeping or personal care product offers, or on her professional responsibilities outside the home and her tender concern for her family, which is identified with the "care" the product provides.)

John Fiske's (and other scholars') celebration of television as "cultural democracy" may be an overreaction to the Frankfurt School–type of leftist criticism that sees the people as lured into reactionary attitudes or homogenized into an unthinking mass by the drug of popular culture.[119] Although Fiske's populism and autonomy is a joyful remedy to this kind of passive accommodation, I wonder if his romanticization of the media as a site of positive struggle, of individual freedom, and of a rosy plurality of interpretations, doesn't ignore how exercises of power (in the personal as well as the political realm) always generate, as Foucault reminds us, both some acquiescence and some resistance on the part of those who are the objects of the exercise.[120] We also must be careful not use "resistance" or "oppositional" reading as an ecstatic endpoint without looking into consequences of the stance. What difference does it make? Can it help us to question whether life has to be this way? To imagine how it might be or might have been? As Todd Gitlin and others point out, pleasure may be streaked with politics, but to think of it as a form of political engagement can slide into a pious celebration of marginality.[121]

Taste poses a ticklish problem as it is tied to issues of social class and class distinctions.[122] Henry Jenkins points out that "fans speak of 'artists' whereas others see only commercial hacks, of transcendent meanings where others find only banalities, of 'quality and innovation' where others see only formula and convention."[123] The popular image of soap opera fans as devoid of intelligence, rationality, and emotional stability may indicate just how much critics need soap fans as someone against whom to define themselves. However, being endlessly surrounded by embarrassment and shame makes it hard for viewers to declare that soaps have many redeeming values or to think of oneself as having much aesthetic competence. And while scholars need to try to understand popularity (that is, how the popular connects to the lives and desires of consumers), we should be careful not to glorify popular taste uncritically simply *because* it is popular. As Judith Williamson has pointed out, potentially radical desires and drives often take the forms offered by the existing order, but that doesn't make the forms themselves radical. Although how we are constrained to live can be made to yield enjoyment, that doesn't make it liberating or even radical.[124]

Television itself and alone is not what forms us as viewers. The textual strategies and discourses may not even be the most significant determinants; the social use and social experience of television may be as, if not more, important. Lawrence Grossberg (in an approach more in concert with my own) has suggested the term "nomadic subjectivity" to stress the changing, shifting, and "contradictory partial relations" of television viewing.[125] He thinks of this as a posthumanist theory of the subject. "Rejecting the existential subject who has a single unified identity that somehow exists in the same way in every practice, [the theory] proposes a subject that is constantly remade, reshaped as a mobilely situated set of vectors in a fluid context." He also rejects a poststructuralist deconstruction of the subject, proposing that "it does matter who is acting and from where, that the subject is a site of struggle, an ongoing site of articulations with its own history."[126] It seems to me that it is important to think of subjectivity and identity as processes, not fixities. Subjectivity and identity, like soaps themselves, are perpetually in the process of becoming. That is why representations are so important; they are a part of how we form our consciousness of our gender, class, race—of ourselves.[127] In part, we *do* see our selves as others see us.

As Jerome Bruner tells us, we are constantly constructing and reconstructing our selves to meet the needs of a situation, and we do so with the guidance of our memories of the past and our hopes and fears for the future. Stories are an important way we both know and tell who and what we are.[128] So people who watch soap operas all afternoon or every weekday or over years are formed in part by this practice, and this practice also contributes to their interpretations, desires, and pleasures. Our experience with television is part of what forms us as people, and all the other social and cultural experiences we have and have had are part of what forms us as television viewers. In other words, both the text and the viewing subject are constituted in an interdiscursive space and, along with shared cultural conventions, different viewers bring different discourses to bear on the text (different knowledge, prejudices, reveries, delusions). The complexity of this situation, as Jim Collins puts it, "necessitates a notion of the television subject that is . . . both decentered and recentered, neither completely absorbed by all programming, nor entirely detached from all of it, a subject that is a construct acted upon by any number of discursive formations, but who also *acts* in making distinctions within the glut of those very same formations."[129]

But we cannot forget those shared cultural conventions. The production of meaning is not totally individualistic or totally a matter of independent choice. The production of meaning must be seen in its social and historical context and within a specific social and historical tradition. People are not independent entities (who make totally autonomous, idiosyncratic interpretations). We are social beings and we construct our interpretations, in part, from our beliefs and assumptions (some held in common with others in the community or communities to which we belong and of which we are a function) and from the shifting social and material experiences that make up our life practices, including exposure to the media. Our interpretative operations are constrained not only by the narrative strategies, but also by the systems of intelligibility, the norms, and the values of the interpretative community.[130]

Some consensus of interpretations and pleasures is quite likely, not only because the viewers have watched the same show (and been affected in some degree by its narrative strategies), but also because norms and beliefs are partially communal and conventional. Interpretative communities, however, are not always in agreement, inflexible, closed, or complete, and the viewing experience can, in practice, reveal incoherence, instabilities, and unexpected divergence.[131]

Part of the reason for this is that soaps do not call for passive obedience on the viewer's part. For example, dialogue is often a trap. To believe the face value is to misunderstand it. The "right" understanding consists in rejecting and refuting what is said and inferring another meaning (from knowledge derived from previous episodes, from the mise-en-scène, the camera work, music, from our experience with daily life, and so on). Often calling for an ironic interpretation, soaps are not impermeable. I watched an episode of *General Hospital* with Diana Ortiz. Knowing that I don't follow that show, every time the music swelled or there was a prolonged reaction shot, she generously kept me aware of what was *really* going on. The electronic bulletin board debates over *All My Children*'s 1995 gay high school teacher include much speculation about the camera pausing on the teen, Kevin, whenever the teacher was mentioned. Viewers aware of the conventions realized that Kevin was also gay long before he came out.[132]

A soap opera or a daily broadcast is not a thing of meaning in itself that is variously understood or explained.[133] So-called "aberrant" interpretations, then, are interpretations that are different from conventional interpretations, not misinterpretations or interpretations that propose meanings that are different from meanings inherent in the soap. Even resistant or oppositional readings are learned (which is not to say that they are wholly conscious or totally cognitive) and part of a larger social and political practice: a practice that is informed by class, race, gender, and sexual orientation, as well as knowledge of the conventional narrative requirements of the genre (such as, "virtue must win"). We should also consider the connections that mass culture has to people's emotional experience and their lives. It is probably best to think of watching soaps as a dialectic of interpretation and experience. For some gay viewers, Kevin's elder brother's homophobia caused speculation that he, too, was gay. "Jason reminded me of how I pretended to be a homophobic back in high school," wrote S. A. L., "because I was afraid to face my own homosexual feelings."[134]

We must learn from individual viewers, individual viewers in specific social and historical circumstances. How do they use texts? What do those texts mean? How do they see the connections between the sounds and images they experience and the meanings they come away with? Any narrative is a social transaction, "a medium of exchange," according to Roland Barthes.[135] More than structures, they are acts. If we admit that any act of viewing is an act of interpretation as well, we must also admit that our insights and perceptions are produced, in part, from the sounds and images coming from the screen, but also from our other viewing experiences, from sensitivities to the subtleties of life, and from the worlds we observe, live in, and dream about. Even though there may not necessarily be an unbroken continuity or mimetic relation between those sound and images and the other factors, they are a part of our meaning production and pleasures. It is the way we know things. We extrapolate from the world we know and the world we wonder about to domesticate the daily broadcast, to make it our own. But what of those sounds and images, that infinity of sadness and delight, the sprawling group of characters, situations, conversations, and an occasional event that are beloved by millions? We need to turn now to the textual features to which the audience is responding.

> But is there an elsewhere? . . . If it's not yet "here," it's already there—in that other place . . . where desire makes fiction exist.
>
> —Hélène Cixous

The Narrative Discourses of Soap Operas; or, How to Watch Soaps

Describing the soap opera text is a nightmare! What *is* "the text"? Is it the sounds and images emitted from the box during a daily episode? Or an afternoon's worth of stories? Sixty years of *The Guiding Light*?[1] Should we include the commercials; the promotional spots for the show; spots for other soap operas? How about publicity in other media? Dedicated websites? The backstory? What is it that viewers interpret and enjoy? Does "the text" have an existence beyond the actual screen time? Does it exist only in the mind of the contemplating viewer? As Charlotte Brunsdon has pointed out, what we recognize as a "text" is, consciously or not, a political as well as a critical matter.[2] And yet, we must ground our understanding of soaps in the specific instances to which the audience is reacting.[3] What is it that people are responding to and interpreting, and what provokes them to make meaning out of their "stories"? What *do* we mean when we say that we watch soaps?

How, then, to begin? Soaps clearly overflow the boundaries of a time slot. Since we rarely encounter a text as an isolated unit, perhaps we should start with more than simply the sounds and images of a daily broadcast. Each episode we watch is layered with our previous experiences with that particular soap, with our previous experiences with the genre, with the anecdotes and speculations we share with other fans, and with our knowledge of similar kinds of events and similar stories in real life. The "text" is influenced by publicity, promotions, and marketing efforts. It is invaded by various commercial and public service messages, and sometimes shared with other activities such as glancing at magazines, performing household chores, doing handicrafts, or eating lunch. It is not a self-contained entity:

it only exists within a context, thus its existence, like that of the viewer, is always specific to a particular historical moment.

Each time we watch, we bring in a variety of experiences, ideas, and information, a complex field of discourses, and these discourses infuse our understanding and appreciation, layering our viewing with various degrees of transparency, quietly transforming what we see and hear into our interpretations. The relations that these encrustations have with the daily episode's sounds and images are complicated and may sometimes be in conflict. Although the relations differ for different viewers and at different times, it is certain that this intertextual dialogue is an important part of the soap opera experience. As Tony Bennett and Janet Woollacott (writing about the James Bond novels) put it, "a text . . . is never 'there' except in forms in which it is also and always other than 'just itself,' always-already humming with reading possibilities which derive from outside its covers."[4]

Institutional Matrix: Genre, Seriality, and Repetition

The soap operas themselves, because of their extreme conventionality, seem to fold over themselves, creating a text always already seen.[5] Stories or story types are repeated on different serials and, over time, within the same serial, exhibited over and over again, generally using the same or very similar means of representation. That is why the woman tuning in the television-band radio on the bus, using her memory and imagination, was able "watch" her soaps. She was recalling what was about to be.

Because of this conventionality, soaps are closer to myth or fairy tales than to the modern novel. Like myths or fairy tales, soaps simplify situations. Characters are more typical than unique. And the outcome is predictable. We watch not for the *coup de théâtre* or the ingenious invention of unexpected events, but to see the expected happen. There may be some surprises but they are generally within well-organized, well-known, and, therefore, benevolent parameters. New embellishments are not lacking—indeed they have often already been announced in the fan magazines. They move us, not because they are novel, but because they bring us to the point where we realize we will be once again coparticipants in pity, sorrow, compassion, pain, condemnation, joy, or happiness. Soaps hold few shocks for the steady viewer. We never arrive at the point where we never have dreamed of going.[6] This redundancy, this repetition and regularity, can be comfortably reassuring, a sort of spiritual ballast. The days to come are very much like the days gone by; we look back at what will always be. Much as we loved to hear beloved fairy tales told and retold, we long for the consolation of the familiar. Even with the vast changes in the home media landscape in the past twenty years,[7] network soaps are always there, the same time, the same place. Generation after generation, day to day, soaps go on.

But as Jerome Bruner reminds us, we go flat with monotony.[8] Don't we steel ourselves against boredom? Watching soaps is playing with the comfort of the compellingly familiar, the rituals, *and* the allure of the possible, the odd deviation—the revelation that brings us to life. The comforts of predictability come alive with the excitement of the new opportunity. Although recurrent stock situations animate the stories, there are infinite variations on a situation and each instance has the possibility of psychological and social repercussions. The noteworthy moments may be those when we realize that, despite surface "novelty," the situation is the same, the gesture is repeated, and that this is the character whose stock behavior we already love. And this time, just as in the last, things will not go smoothly. This is what Umberto Eco calls a "hunger for redundance": something that we not only already know, but want to experience again.[9]

Each time we watch a new soap or a new episode, we understand it "through sedimented layers of previous interpretations, or—if the text is brand-new—through the sedimented [viewing] habits and categories developed by those inherited interpretive traditions."[10] Eco reminds us that what we usually call a message is really a *text,* "that is, a network of different messages depending on different codes and working at different levels of signification."[11] Roland Barthes notes that text and textile are etymologically related.[12] It might be best to think of a soap opera as a weaving, a fabric woven of not only narrative codes, but also of both intra- and inter-narrative threads. It is difficult to consider an individual character, incident, or even episode, without seeing it as a moment within an intertextual network or as a part of a dialogue already in progress.

One way to approach this intertextual network is to examine soap operas as a genre.[13] When I speak of soap operas as a genre, as a type of television show, a set of images and certain kinds of stories swiftly come to mind. The idea of soap operas manifesting a genre helps us imagine an individual show as similar to other programs, as well as different from other types of programs.[14] Being familiar with the genre helps us to formulate expectations (certain norms, possibilities, and limitations) and our expectations help us to conceptualize the genre. The intertextual elements of genre texts are one way to place them within a context.[15]

Genre, however, is more than a principle of classification or a critical category. It is also essential to production and dissemination, and an important way that we understand new texts. Most of TV programming consists of genres, and intertextuality plays a part in defining and constraining a genre. Some of the major conventions of daytime soap operas, their characteristic use of space and time, the characters, dialogues, story motifs, and rhetorical strategies will be discussed in detail below. These generic similarities function almost as a contract between producers and viewers.[16] Viewers know what to expect and they are generally given a consistency that they can count on. These resemblances also provide a cushion for introducing new shows, easing marketing by assuring new audiences of something with which they are familiar.[17]

Committed viewers often watch a chain of soaps, indeed are encouraged to do so, as the networks generally air their soap operas in blocks. A new program begins the same way that the previous soap ended, in the middle of a scene; the opening titles usually do not appear until several sequences and several storylines have been introduced. Pre-title sequences look and sound very much like the previous soap and like the post-title sequences.[18] Many of the ABC's promotional materials advertise their flow of soaps, generally including *All My Children, One Life to Live, Port Charles,* and *General Hospital* in the same ad or commercial. The recognizable continuity between shows lends itself to easy listening, encouraging the "viewer" to keep the set on (and thus be counted as a "viewer") even while moving on to other activities. These similarities and marketing strategies work to assure a predictable audience; however, the similarities also work to provide something predictable *for* the audience.[19]

Each serial's daily episode is in many ways a remake of previous episodes. *The Young and the Restless* on Monday is very much like *The Young and the Restless* on Tuesday. This is obviously an important factor in maintaining an audience, but it also has important production implications. Janice Radway has described paperback romance publishing as inspired by the vision of the book as an "endlessly replicable commodity."[20] This aspect of commercial production—a regularly issued, standardized, and renewable product—coupled with the notion of a reliable and identifiable audience for the product (along with the necessity to differentiate the product for commercial competition) is a good way to begin to understand soap opera production.

When I began writing about soaps there were thirteen (there are currently nine) daytime network serials being broadcast in most U.S. markets.

They are on the air five days a week (Thanksgiving, Christmas, and New Year's Day excepted for some of them), fifty-two weeks a year. Several of them have been on the air continually for over thirty years. *Soap Opera Digest,* writing in 1982, reported the average yearly budget of a soap opera to be about $30 million, the profits to the network reaching up to $150 million.[21] Peter Boyer in the *Los Angeles Times* claimed that in 1983 *General Hospital* cleared $1 million a week on an average weekly advertising income of $2.7 million.[22] Soap operas are indeed profitable! Various sources claim that daytime television accounts for at least 25 percent of the network's advertising revenues.[23]

Soap operas are cheap to produce (an hour or half-hour episode is generally rehearsed and shot in one day), costing one-fifth to one-tenth the price of prime-time shows with almost the same number of minutes.[24] Though commercial time is less costly during the daytime than in the evening, there is more time devoted to commercials and the proportion of commercial income to production costs or lease costs is higher. Hour-long soaps are popular with local stations (in the mid–1980s, *The Guiding Light* and *General Hospital* were reported to have 99 percent affiliate penetration);[25] and, very importantly, their targeted audience, mainly women between the ages of eighteen and forty-nine, appeals to a large number of advertisers.

There are three conditions that I see as important to my understanding of the institutional matrix of soap operas. The first is the "predictability" I earlier discussed: both the predictability *of* the audience, and the predictability *for* the audience. Basic to their profitability (and their continuation) is the idea that soap operas are a product designed for (and consistently appealing to) a predictable audience, an audience that can be identified and that is trusted to watch regularly. As the industry puts it—in highly moralistic terms—they depend on viewer "loyalty."[26]

Secondly, this predictability allows for an extremely rationalized production process. Soap opera production is less risky than prime-time production because the appeal is more certain and the production is less uncertain. Most performers' salaries are contracted on three-months, six-months, or yearly bases; there are relatively few extras or guest stars; sets are reusable; even stories are recyclable.[27] There is little remote shooting so that both rehearsal time and studio shooting time are limited and budgetable. Soaps are shot on videotape almost as if they were live (with few retakes), so post-production editing is minimal.

Thirdly, however much the rationalization of the production process and the standardization of the product sustain audience predictability, competition for sponsors, and therefore for audiences, necessitates some variation. Anyone who watches several soaps can tell you that despite genre similarities, they are not all the same. And particular soaps appeal to particular viewers and viewing groups. Shows differ in their humor, their intrigue, their pacing, the demographics of their characters, their attitudes toward controversial issues, their use of music, guest stars, exotic locations, and so on. Some allow the characters to be comically caught up in their own webs of hypocrisy. Others are much more staid. This range would make an interesting study in its own right;[28] but for now it is important to realize that differentiation is a necessary part of the standardization of American commercial television.

Whether a soap opera is considered as a constantly accumulating set of texts or as a huge unfolding text, viewers who have been watching over time generally find much intertextual resonance in the daily episodes. Even an unembellished scene where a young child runs through the room and calls out, "Hi, Uncle Lance!" (*The Young and the Restless,* winter 1982) can take on additional meaning when the viewer has known for several years that Lance Prentiss is really the child's father, not his uncle, and perhaps even more significance if the viewer remembers the romantic night of the child's conception. Longtime viewers bring much information and many associations to their viewing. New experiences are infiltrated by previous experiences and new information may even force viewers to reinterpret, retroactively, previous events. This is especially true in the frequent and kaleidoscopic rearrangement of families.

Soap operas often try to inform new, lapsed, or distracted viewers of past events by a soliloquy or dialogue that either reminisces or explains things to a character within the story unfamiliar with the past events or feelings. They also visually recreate scenes in the form of flashbacks (using footage specially created for the flashback or replaying old footage). These framed tales are generally marked by dissolves and/or gauzy mattes indicating that the footage is some sort of interior meditation. The repetition of sequences or the repetition of information are opportunities for viewers to remember along with the character, signs of communality, shared memories. These flashbacks and the special-event flashbacks, such as *The Guiding Light*'s newspaper montage, which collapsed the fifty-year anniversary of the show with the fifty-year anniversary of the fictional Springfield newspaper, enable viewers to review videotaped highlights of the show's/town's history (June–July 1987). Joanne's "memory book" of still photographs filled the screen and turned into video clips on *Search for Tomorrow* (fall 1986). Both commemorations incorporated sequences from previous programs into the shows' anniversary celebrations and served to remind us that our past is partially a television past, too. Flashbacks satisfy not only the commercial demands of informing new viewers, but also a nostalgic longing to experience the past once again. In this sense, soaps might be seen as symbolic of perpetuity.

If we think of these flashbacks as syntagmatic redundancies, they always exist in time, but they are also always undoing time, confounding any idea of linearity and subverting the very notion of beginning or end. Some flashbacks reiterate information for new or distracted viewers. But other flashbacks conjure up a past that precedes the debut of the show, and others evoke a past that occurred after the beginning of the show but hadn't yet had any screen time. Flash forwards are less frequent. However, if fantasy scenes (especially depictions of contemplated acts) are viewed as prolepses (Is this how it will happen? Will she really do it?), they are not uncommon on some of the shows. Such special events as *One Life to Live*'s trip to Limbo with dead characters returning to advise Viki on her "pending" demise (March 1987) or Erica Kane's "own story" fantasy (February 5 and 8, 1988) where "all the men she's ever loved" are brought back to comment on her past life, suggest a future that literalizes the idea that the character's actions and feelings are part of a narrative already in progress.

In flashbacks a character is doing, saying, experiencing again; however, the mass production of soap operas entails a certain repetition of character types and of stories so that other characters are also doing, saying, experiencing again. This reuse of the same story elements in "new" experiences or events (a repetition of the signifier) and the use of different characters in familiar functional roles (a repetition of the signified) are part of the familiarity we come to expect, part of the comforts of genre and seriality. Each telling resonates with past and future tellings, reverberating not only through history, but through ourselves.

The signified can never be exactly the same, however, as the differing context always conveys some difference and, perhaps even more importantly, the very act of repetition entails an accumulation of significance.[29] Is this too part of the pleasure of seriality, not only the repetitions and the variation, the regularity and the permutations, but also this accumulation, the collection?[30] The individual parts become less important than the way they are used in the logic and rhythms of the ongoing "whole." In this sense, soaps are very ordered, but from a point in the present, without omniscience. Because of this, for the viewer there is little uncertainty about the future in soap operas. In a period of profound social and cultural changes, these repetitions may serve as an assurance of the days ahead. Or perhaps they are symbolic of the certainty of the future.

In this certainty, we are watching to see the familiar happen. The conventions of soap opera storytelling are so strong that we can hardly say that we are watching to see *what* will happen. Rather, we watch anticipating what we *know* will happen once again and to see how it will happen this time, a bundling together of memories and expectation. Like little Alice's White Queen, we remember best the things that happened the week after next.[31]

Between the time we realize what story this is (and thus what will happen) and the time when it does happen, a lively anticipation imbues the events. All that happens occurs as though conventional events were surely going to follow. As one fan told Denise Bielby and Lee Harrington, "I have to say that very, *very* little of anything happens that I don't know about beforehand. Really, the pleasure is watching *how* they'll do what they do, not wondering what's next."[32] Alisa Holen's betting pool was premised on her coworkers' familiarity with the conventional outcomes and the possible permutations of the current stories.

But variations on the conventions can bring a smile. "It's hard to surprise a daytime audience today," explains Douglas Marland, head writer of *As the World Turns*. "They know all the formulas and are usually six feet ahead of you, but if the surprise is well thought out and justified, they love it."[33] There's no question that Tad Martin will receive his comeuppance (*All My Children*), but how will it come about this time? When things are *really* going to be different—when Stevie Wonder will be making a special appearance on *All My Children* or when *Search for Tomorrow* is taping on location in Ireland—the difference is generally proclaimed with much fanfare.[34] Network spots will forecast the occasion. In the case of the *Search for Tomorrow* trip, a full-page advertisement in *TV Guide* announced that the program would be bringing Ireland "into your living room . . . cottages, castles, beaches and misty mountains." Celebrating the show's difference—which in itself has an appeal—the ad at the same time, by proclaiming difference, intertextually referenced the conventional studio-bound domestic interiors from which it was deviating.

We are used to a certain familiarity and repetition in fiction. "Tell it again!" is a common refrain at children's storytime. As Eco has written about formulaic detective fiction, we continuously recover what we already know and what we want to know again.[35] The memory of infinite pasts and infinite futures makes time a void to be filled in. Though things to come are not yet, we have an expectation of them in mind, and that expectation acts as a structuring presence. For me, much of the satisfaction comes from the excitement produced by waiting. That is, the pleasure is not in knowing, but in the process of knowing, in experiencing the new telling of what is recognized as the same old story. If the relative eventlessness and duration of soap operas seem at odds with conventional narrative progression, it is only because we think of progression as an advance, rather than as expectation and elaboration.

However, soap fans will sometimes recognize and fret about recycled stories. The May 19, 1987, issue of *Soap Opera Digest,* for example, printed a letter from a *The Young and the Restless* viewer saying, "I was disappointed [with Ashley's nervous breakdown]. The exact same story was used (as any longtime fan will remember) for Leslie Brooks years ago."[36] Besides expressing discontent, the letter also celebrates the viewer's memory and his or her involvement in what the show is, has been, and could be. It's also an indication of what Roland Barthes calls the "flickering of meaning" that occurs with refrains.[37] The journeys back (the repetitions, the flashbacks, our recollections), the returns to and returns of, allow us, as Peter Brooks puts it, to bind one textual moment to another in terms of similarities or differences rather than mere contiguity.[38]

Some of the repeated stories resound with excess, an overabundance of effect, as when, for instance, a daughter experiences the repertory of ordeals that her mother had gone through. Like redundancy in significance in such aspects of production design as costuming, hair design, performance style, and makeup and, occasionally, lighting or set decoration,[39] there is a certain efficiency here: an intensification by repetition. Barthes points out that when different discourses represent the "same" signified, there is a surplus of communication, allowing one signifier to stand in for others who may be absent, or allowing some of the meaning to extend to other characters who share the "same" signifiers.[40] Such redundancy has the potential to initiate understanding that would otherwise require a more direct exposition.

There is also a certain amount of repetition within a single broadcast as the same information is passed from character to character so that a viewer who is watching and listening attentively hears the same material several times. Robert C. Allen points out that these "intraepisodic redundancies," far from being simply a retardation device or a tedious repetition of information, activate the viewer's knowledge of previous material about the various characters, opening up "major sources of signifying potential" that would not be available to a new viewer.[41] The reaction of each character to that information then becomes consequential: each reaction has the potential to unleash a rain of new events to complicate the situation. Each reaction contains a saturation of other stories that could, or maybe will, or perhaps already has. . . . To a new viewer, at that moment, it may seem like anything can happen. But the experienced fan knows that this will be a repeated occurrence of similarity. We encounter the "unexpected" once again, a performance of anticipation and timelessness. And in a short while we can claim a certain mastery. As we await the next interval, installment, week, we already know what will happen, a knowledge that evokes a sense of power, even in moments when viewers are unhappy with the turn the story is taking. Theodor Adorno and Max Horkheimer, writing about popular music, observed that once the trained ear hears the first notes, it "can guess what is coming and feel flattered when it does come."[42]

There must be some pleasure in the viewing ritual itself, its regularity, reliability, and familiarity. The tremendous amount of repetition in watching soaps might itself be a form of resisting change. My mother had asked me several times (during the first few years after I had begun my research) to recommend another soap because hers had changed and she didn't like it anymore. But sixteen years later, she was still watching the original show. Viewing seems to generate a compulsion to repeat. Several interviewees also talked about quitting a soap that they "didn't like" anymore and asked me with great concern why they hadn't been able to stop, for despite doubts and complaints, they tune in. Broadcast after broadcast, soap opera after soap opera, they watch on. I found myself wondering if what is often described as servitude, "addiction" to soaps, might also appear as evidence of free will. It reminded me of something that bell hooks wrote: "women who are exploited and oppressed daily [be it overt and brutal or silent and obliterative] cannot afford to relinquish the belief that they exercise some measure of control, however relative, over their lives."[43] Is the inability to quit so disturbing because it contradicts our fantasy of independence, contradicts our feelings of power and control over our own life?

On the other hand, another viewer boasted about not quitting *General Hospital* when she felt others were. When I spoke to her, she had been working a daytime shift and, like many fans, videotaped "her" soap so that she could watch it after she returned from work. This also allowed her to review particular episodes that interested her and to share them with friends. For a while, *Soap Opera Digest* ran a classified section that carried requests from fans and collectors to purchase, rent, or trade cassettes of specific episodes, events, or stories. The September 23, 1986, issue, for example, carried ads from viewers who requested tapes of events that they had missed or wanted to see again, such as "Bo and Hope's wedding" or "Tod Chandler's death." Some seem to be looking for tapes that predate their viewership or their own taping; Susan M., for one, asked for tapes of "*General Hospital* prior to mid-1985, especially those episodes featuring Jack Wagner." P. W. Cain from Pacifica, California, claimed to be a "David Renaldi loyalist" who missed him and was willing to pay "top dollar" for tapes to buy or rent. (In those pre–World Wide Web days, perhaps writers were also looking for someone with whom to correspond about their favorites and their fandom.) Kayla Lowrimore from Krebs, Oklahoma, wanted tapes of the "Rome and Greece nights of Frisco and Felicia's honeymoon." If it seems that soaps go on forever, but are destined to disappear, these private archives are personal viewing histories, allowing us to replay our memories. Without them, soaps are ephemeral.[44]

Soap operas also allow us to replay memories of current events, journalistic tales, as they often borrow stories from recent news. These "real world" stories mostly deal with "human interest" crimes or other public concerns.[45] *Capitol,* for example, had a story in March 1987 about a doctor who was accused of an unauthorized implant of a mechanical heart, soon after a similar Texas case was in the newspapers. The soap opera story, however, explored the doctor's personal motivation and the personal consequences of his act, not regulations or institutional policy. In 1985, *All My Children* had a story remarkably like New York City's Mayflower Madam, even riffing Sydney Barrows's name for their character, Mickey Barlowe. The soap opera Madam's "little black book" was updated to a computer disk. *The Young and the Restless* had a highly moralistic summer story (when school-age children often watch) involving teenage pregnancy and, like *The Guiding Light* and *Loving,* developed a storyline that acknowledged adult illiteracy (1987).

Several soaps have had stories situated in homeless shelters. The stories, no matter how sympathetic to the plight of homeless people, did not, however, investigate or expose, or even hint at, the social roots of the problem. They used the problem as a setting for more conventional stories. For example, the homeless woman whom Brooke English befriended (as a journalist making a television documentary about the shelter) turned out to be her long-lost mother; and Jack Abbott, sentenced to work time in a shelter, fell in love with the shelter's director (*All My Children,* spring 1986, and *The Young and the Restless,* fall 1986, respectively).

On soap operas ideological and social issues are generally experienced in emotional terms. *One Life to Live*'s 1992 summer story about homophobia concerned Billy Douglas, a non-sexually active gay teen, his lack of acceptance by his father, and his expulsion from the family. The other part of the story involved the Rev. Andrew Carpenter, who is accused of being gay, and his (rigid, homophobic) father Sloan's inability to accept the death of his other son, a gay man, from AIDS-related complications ten years earlier. The summer's penultimate tearful moment centered around Sloan Carpenter's reconciling himself to his guilt and grief. On the lawn of the church, with the AIDS quilt spread at their feet, Andrew embraced his father, "You are still the bravest man I know. I love you, Dad" (August 31, 1992).[46]

Defenders of soaps often point, a bit paternalistically, in my view, to these "social issue" stories as a positive attribute and a social service, conferring the high-toned aura of the worthwhile on a genre often deemed to be without social merit. These edifying "public service" stories exonerate the networks from charges of frivolousness and cloak the producers in the prestigious garb of social relevance. *The Guiding Light* began doing issue stories in the early 1960s because the head writer "was angry that soaps got no respect."[47]

These public service stories generally receive a good amount of press coverage. For example, the "Late Breaking News" section of *Soap Opera Digest,* which claims to report "all the juicy tidbits you must know" but seems to come directly from the networks' publicity departments, announced a forthcoming *All My Children* story involving Erica Kane's pregnancy: "Episodes will attempt to educate viewers on the dangers of toxemia, to mother as well as child."[48] Often naming the soap opera's professional advisors, the article implied viewers would be acquiring vigorously realistic details.

There has been an enormous amount of publicity and discussion of the several HIV/AIDS stories on soap operas. *All My Children*'s March 1988 AIDS story, for example, was covered in the New York City area by such diverse publications as *TV Guide,* the *Village Voice, Soap Opera Digest,* and the *New York Times. One Life to Live*'s discussion of AIDS and homophobia was highly publicized and covered not only in fan magazines, but also in the gay press. *As the World Turns*'s fall 1989 introduction of a gay character was accompanied by press coverage that almost "told" the viewers how to respond to the character. Several months later, *TV Guide* ran a picture and a blurb about the performer, Brian Starcher, knowing that "all eyes are upon him" as "daytime's first featured actor to play a gay male."[49]

Some of these public service stories seem to flaunt their value. They are so pedagogical that they exist in a relation of tension with the other stories—a dialectical tension that allows these stories to be perceived as "timely message" or "expert knowledge" and others (by contrast) as "fable" or "myth," dramatic portrayals of the contending forces of the world, which, although they are neither ideologically innocent nor uninformed by history, seem commonsensical and timeless.[50] *The Young and the Restless*'s story about Faren's tubal pregnancy included statistical information in her doctor's explanation of her condition to her husband that seemed clearly meant, like Erica's toxemia, to inform the viewer (April 29, 1987). Their summer 1988 story about a disabled woman's love life was so unashamedly didactic that it became an injunction to "be understanding." The romance was the indirect means by which the social imperative was communicated.

Both *Days of Our Lives* and *The Young and the Restless* in the winter of 1988 had stories involving alcoholism that reiterated many of the guiding principles of Alcoholics Anonymous. Similarly, after their young daughter was killed by a man driving under the influence of alcohol, Brooke English and Tom Cudahy visited a meeting of "Mothers Against Drunk Driving" which included information about the group, their legislative aims, their therapy (including a discussion about the stages of mourning), and their "red ribbon campaign" (*All My Children,* December 16, 1988). Such stories sometimes include hotline telephone numbers running across the screen or spots before or after the day's episode telling viewers how to contact the groups. It is the density—and plausibility—of contingent details that convinces us of the message's truth; yet the same density of details endangers the story's transcendental force: the out-and-out divine is reduced to a humble receptacle for the "real."[51]

Many of the current events stories have that same tension. Even though these stories may seem to be fictional (invented, timeless stories, which cannot and need not be verified), as "real" stories they are timely and embody a moral already well publicized by news reports (the "downfall" of the Mayflower Madam, for example, was known by the time the similar *All My Children* story aired).

No matter how emphatic and no matter how close they are to our daily life, however, soap's social issue stories and news stories cannot produce unambiguous or singular meanings. Even though we know these stories are not really "real," that they are fictional constructions, our knowledge from daily life inflects what they mean to us, and—conversely—in these public service stories, the increased knowledge gained from viewing is meant to inflect our daily life. But the relation between the different discourses can be conflictual, negating as well as affirming or reinforcing. TV stories and real-world stories inform each other in very complex ways. Of course, any indirect communication runs the risk of not being interpreted in the manner intended.[52] The didacticism of these stories is a way to try to obviate this danger, an attempt to fix the meaning of the story.

Because of the physical continuity between the show and our living room, or bedroom, or kitchen, this illusion of continuity between the fictive and the real is probably sustained even more by television than by theatrical films or newsreels.[53] Much of the publicity and promotion also functions to stimulate the illusion that the fictional places (e.g., Genoa City, Pine Valley, Springfield) and the characters coexist with us, or that there is a homology between our daily life and theirs. In February 1986, for example, *Search for Tomorrow* mailed a special edition of the soap's *Henderson Herald* reporting on Henderson's flood situation to the homes of *Soap Opera Digest* subscribers.

Promotions also often encourage associations between the daily life of the performer and the life of the fictional character. The October 18, 1988, issue of *Soap Opera Digest,* for instance, had a cover story about Jeanne Cooper and Jess Walton's "Real-Life Triumphs over Drugs and Alcohol." The article about the substance abuse of the performer (Cooper) who plays *The Young and the Restless*'s alcoholic Katherine Chancellor and of the performer (Walton) who had played a drug addict on *Capitol,* extended their personal experience to their acted roles.

A few years earlier, Jeanne Cooper's face-lift became a story as her character Katherine Chancellor underwent the same procedure on the soap opera. There was a strange collapse of the actual and the acted as the character Kay, explaining her reasons for the face-lift to another character, demonstrated the tricks of the television trade and revealed on camera the off-camera makeup secrets that had made her look younger. Then, with suitable publicity, Cooper's operation was taped and shown as Kay's on the show.

TV Guide awarded "Cheers" to *Days of Our Lives* for writing the actress Suzanne Rogers's neuromuscular disorder into her storyline so that she could cope with it on air.[54] When the wife of Doug Davidson (who plays Paul Williams on *The Young and the Restless*) played opposite him in a temporary role as his girlfriend, fan magazines forecasted hot love scenes.[55] The off-screen romance of Margaret Reed and Michael Swan, who were playing the spatting lovers Shannon and Duncan on *As the World Turns,* was highlighted with their appearance on CBS's *Morning Show* (July 2,

1987). Is it a wonder that fans speculate whether the actress who plays Dixie is really pregnant or compare Jeremy's televised sex appeal with the actor's looks in real life when he is seen shopping in a housewares store?

When Craig Montgomery was missing on *As the World Turns* (summer 1987) and his sister, wife, mother, and most of the other characters on the show were debating whether he would be found alive, any reader of *Soap Opera Digest* (and I'm sure many other publications) knew that the performer was leaving the show and was not being replaced right away, so that he had "an indefinite period of time to decide if he wanted to return to the serial."[56] We, along with the characters, were given a chance to reminisce and mourn the departure of both the character and the performer. His fictional mother, Lila, while waiting to hear if he has been found, reviewed (for us) his history, his anger, his misguided moments, and his recently found happiness "with the woman he loves" and his newborn son (July 2, 1987). Unlike Lila, *we* knew that he would not be found in the near future. Talk about such situations is an important part of fans' discussions and Internet postings. From the publicity about the performer leaving the show, we had information that infused our hermeneutic experience and predictions.

This critical dialogue about the shows and the performers is incorporated into our understanding of the daily broadcast so that some textual idea of real life and some textual idea of the fictional world act simultaneously. And we tend to judge stories by our experience: not only by our experience of real life, but also our experience with other known stories; that is, how faithful the story is to the conventions, logic, and values of a particular kind of storytelling. In August 2000, the *All My Children* website conducted a poll on what readers thought Dixie should do about the knowledge she had that Dimitri was still alive. I decided quickly that the option that was surely the most ethically responsible—to reveal it to the affected parties—was not practicable. It would have been the end of the story! This interplay of fiction and reality will come up again in the final chapter of the book.

Recent television theory has been exploring various notions of the text to acknowledge that the experience of watching American network television includes a flow of commercials, promotional spots, previews, newsbreaks, station identifications, and assorted other broadcast sounds and images as well as what is conventionally thought of as a show's narrative sequences.[57] The backstage information that we bring to the primary viewing event is also a part of that experience (and may be considered part of an expanded soap opera text). The conversations we have with friends and family members while watching, the subsequent discussions, debates, and speculations about stories and characters, the recaps and updates in fan magazines, in syndicated newspaper columns, on Internet sites, and/or the novelizations are, for many, a part of the discourse into which the broadcast is woven.

This weaving may include information from the telephone 900-number answered by a taped voice of an ABC soap opera character, or a 900-number trivia game, or the *All My Children* web page's weekly poll. Or other fans' opinions from *Soap Opera Weekly*'s "Viewers' Voice" or "Mail Call," or from an Internet chat room. Or information from ABC radio's one-minute daily "Soap Quiz," featuring questions about *General Hospital, All My Children,* and *One Life to Live.*[58] Or perhaps it includes hints from a videotape of "Hot Makeup Tips for that Cool Look" with the teen stars of *The Young and the Restless,*[59] or info from a video about the making of *All My Children.* The experience may include a coffee mug, an ashtray, a screensaver, a board game, trading cards, or a tee shirt with the show's logo and/or posters of and compact discs by favored performers. Soap operas are a part of our lives even when the set is turned off. The meanings that we make of the shows are entangled with a range of surrounding and supplementary material and are created within an interactive framework (a framework that is both formal and spontaneous). Like the stories themselves, the experience of watching soap operas seldom has a clearly or cohesively delineated space or time.

Much of this ancillary material is supplied or supported by the programs' marketing efforts, from fan club luncheons and shopping center appearances to a cruise with the stars of *Days of Our Lives.* Or perhaps a fan would like to meet two of the show's law enforcement characters at a three-day murder-mystery outing at a California spa.[60] Soap opera performers often make appearances on game shows and magazine shows, sometimes on talk shows and in commercials. When performers appear to discuss their personal or professional lives, the promotional function of these appearances is obvious. They sometimes appear in their fictive personae, however, or are cast in such a way that they seem to be in character. While still promotional, these appearances suggest that the characters have an existence beyond their thirty- or sixty-minute soap opera performances, expanding their fictional worlds, and at the same time, creating a more hermetic television world: television about television.[61] In 1985, for example, Danny and Tracy (then young lovers on *The Young and the Restless*) appeared as a couple on a game show; during the week of May 8 through 12 in 1989 cast members of *The Young and the Restless* opposed some members of *As the World Turns* on CBS's *Family Feud;* and *General Hospital* cast members appeared with their own domestic hints on ABC's *Home.*

Noncontract players often appear on the daytime courtroom dramas and performers sometimes appear in theatrically released films and made-for-TV films (which are generally promoted during soaps). Romance videos, written by paperback romance writers and starring some of the romantic men of soaps, sell for modest prices ($14.95 in 1987) at bookstores, drugstores, department stores, and supermarkets.[62] And soap opera performers have appeared on music videos: Andrea Evans, for example, who plays the sexpot Tina Roberts on *One Life to Live,* appeared in a similar role in the 1987 music video *No Such Thing.*

Soap Opera Digest had a two-page article on how USA cable network's *Heart Light City,* an hour-long music video show, "planned to fulfill the fantasies of soap opera followers." The article described the videos as having "themes [that] are tender, where people dress beautifully and speak lovingly." The program aired during the morning hours before soaps begin, and the magazine proclaimed the videos "a great way" to get into a "romantic frame of mind."[63] And daytime advertisements for prime-time specials often exploit the concerns of soaps. The 1986 prime-time miniseries "Christopher Columbus," for example, was advertised during the afternoon soap operas with the voice-over: "He discovered greed, love, power, tragedy, death, treason, and mutiny, then he discovered America." Distinctions between program types and what we generally think of as the narrative segments of soaps and other elements in television's flow are simultaneously subverted and venerated, as television creates its own world.

Soap performers appear on other daytime genres, and other daytime genres appear on soaps. On April 20, 1989, for instance, on *The Guiding Light,* Harley and Alan Michael, two characters, were guests on the show's fictional talk show *A.M. Springfield* and, according to the June 7, 1986, *TV Guide,* ABC's Bob Eubanks and *The Newlywed Game* made an appearance on *Days of Our Lives* and two of the characters became contestants. There are also some formal and thematic similarities between soaps and the flow of other current daytime genres. Game shows, talk shows, and courtroom dramas, for example, all share a similar question/answer format with soap operas, a predominance of one person in the frame, images of people's reactions, and so on. Many of the crimes, disputes, improprieties, and immoralities that are adjudicated on the trial shows are similar to subjects unresolved and continuing on soap operas.[64] Talk shows, which advertise heavily during soaps, often explore topics that relate to those represented on soap operas. *The Oprah Winfrey Show*'s promo for her discussion of "Sex and the Single Parent," for instance, aired just before *Loving,* when Stacey's sex life was being contested in court so that her former husband could try to gain custody of their son (December 12, 1988).

In the early days of *All My Children,* characters occasionally appeared on both that show and *One Life to Live.* Paul Martin, a recurring character on *All My Children,* for example, traveled to Llanview as Viki Buchanan's defense attorney, and Dr. Marcus Polk, a psychiatrist, was a character on both shows. The same device was used in the beginning of *Port Charles.* More recently, Jeremy commuted from Pine Valley to Corinth for several months before moving, as the producers attempted to attract viewers from the popular *All My Children* to the less-followed *Loving.*[65]

Performers also sometimes change soaps: the gangster who died under mysterious circumstances in a New York City jail on *Ryan's Hope* showed up two weeks later in Henderson on *Search for Tomorrow* as a cop (October 14, 1986). And Mary Stuart, who played the wise Joanne Tate on the same show for thirty-five years, appeared in the spring of 1988, after *Search for Tomorrow* had gone off the air, on *One Life to Live* as the wise Judge Webber. Lynne Joyrich tells of a period on *One Life to Live* when the actress Christine Jones substituted for Erika Slezak as the character Viki Buchanan. After Slezak returned to the role, Jones was hired to play a new character, Pamela Buchanan, Viki's father-in-law's bride. Imagine "the strange experience of watching the woman who used to *be* Victoria Buchanan [being] introduced to Victoria Buchanan"![66] *TV Guide* in the winter of 1988 reported that two performers who played the popular couple Drs. Rick and Lesley Webber on *General Hospital* in the late 1970s and early 1980s were appearing in new roles on *Another World* and forecast that they would certainly become a "dynamic duo" again.[67] The same issue announced "a reunion of sorts" on *One Life to Live* where three players who had performed on *The Edge of Night* were now working together again. How does this affect the way that we view new characters and new situations?

Colleen Casey, while playing the wholesome Faren, on *The Young and the Restless,* starred in a Cream of Wheat commercial, portraying the woman in the commercial in such a corresponding way that it almost seemed like Faren was endorsing the product. *One Life to Live*'s Slezak, or her character, the sweet family-oriented Viki, advertised prunes. And the actor who plays Benny Sago on *All My Children* appeared in a pizza commercial, still in his vaguely ethnic, working-class guise. The allusion to a performer's fictive persona and the strong performer/character association is used to advantage in a commercial in which a soap opera actor (Peter Bergman, of *All My Children,* for example), in his white-jacket costume as one of the serial's doctors, recommends the use of Vick's cough syrup by confessing, "I'm not really a doctor, but I play one on TV. And when you have a cold at home, you often play doctor, too."[68]

Soap opera producers may intend to create a unified and coherent text, but in practice this is not, and cannot be, achieved. Since any attempt to communicate a message is a stimulus for exchange, the potential for variable interpretation is inherent. The daily broadcasts are not simply an expression of ideology, nor simply a reflection of the mode of production, nor simply the reproduction of a larger socioeconomic reality. I think of them as fictional workings (a production and transformation) of all these and note how they interact with many other textual elements: the sounds and images broadcast are broken into by previous sounds and images, future sounds and images, other experiences, and other discourses, allowing viewers to bring their own understanding to bear upon the soap opera event, superimposing their own conceptual frameworks, creating their own interpretations and suppositions.

Though we want to be careful not to fetishize the text, we must also be careful not to abolish its materiality. The specific sounds and images broadcast do exert a certain determinacy over the conditions of interpretation. They provoke—but also shape and resist—our imagining. While considering watching soap operas as a cultural practice, we must not dissolve the soap operas into their various interpretations. Soap operas are not unknowable or nonexistent, but are multiknowable, multiexistent, multivalent, and are embedded with other texts and other discourses.[69] The shows' makers certainly have some meanings in mind when they produce the shows, and they arrange the elements available to them in a highly conventionalized fashion—one that they assume will be readily understood by their audiences. If the story is inferred by the viewer from numerous sources, among them must be the codes and conventions of the genre. These conventions themselves are not meanings, but are the conjunctures, the convergences that make meaning possible, the structures that help to produce the soaps' legibility.

In an attempt to explore some of these conventions, in the next sections I will turn to the major elements in this dynamic: the characteristic use of time and space, the main story motifs, the characters, the dialogue and its performance, and the common narrative tropes. This is an artificial separation, to be sure, but crucial to my effort to throw an "analytical net"[70] over the narrative discourses. I am not trying to describe the essence of the genre, but to look at some of the more prominent elements that animate viewers' interpretations. We will consider these elements as instances of storytelling (in their significant forms). Our desire for, and need for, such stories and interpretations will concern us more fully in the following chapter.

This study is certainly not an exhaustive one; it is selective and strategic. The descriptions offered here aim to suggest new ways of approaching the subject, a different footing for the debates on the pleasures of fantasy and reality. Of course, while watching soap operas, one might never think of the elements dealt with here. But I felt I had to, because they seemed to me to be important. *Any* description is "a particular activation of the text."[71] This might be seen as stating the obvious; however, it is important to recognize how my intellectual engagement and viewing experience are interlocking aspects of my descriptions.

Because of the quantity of soap operas, it has not been possible to follow all of them all of the time. The examples that I offer are not necessarily the best examples and may not even be representative examples. Rather, they were chosen because they illustrate my thoughts. Most of the examples come from my viewing experience between 1980 and 1990 and reflect both my personal preferences and a certain amount of chance (that I might be watching or thinking about a particular soap opera while I was mulling over specific issues).[72] Soap opera conventions are so strong, however, that my professional intuition convinces me there are few idiosyncrasies that would render my examples inappropriate.

Spatial and Temporal Unfolding

In order to investigate closer the use of space and time in soap operas, I chose one episode of one soap at random and analyzed it closely. The statistics and most of the examples are drawn from this episode (*The Young and the Restless,* CBS, Friday, November 27, 1981), though many of my opinions and conclusions are drawn from years of watching this and other soaps.

Each episode of *The Young and the Restless* has three main storylines, each revolving around the family, or relationships (friendships or love affairs) that closely resemble family, or are based upon it. In the episode under examination, Dorothy finds out that her boarder, Bobbi, is really her lost daughter; Nikki decides (after discussion with Jonas and Cash) to move in with Victor; and Patty Williams discovers (after confessing her love for him to her mother) that her boyfriend, Jack Abbott, is philandering. Except for the people in the scenes in Jonas's bar, every one of the twelve people pictured on the screen and the two people mentioned are related to at least one of the others by blood or close family-type associations (see Appendix I).

The family on *The Young and the Restless,* however, is not narratively constraining. It is "sufficiently commodious"[73] to accommodate a vast array of characters and ingenious plot situations, and convoluted enough to allow endless variations and interactions. In this episode, for example, Dorothy's husband informs her that he thinks that Bobbi, their lodger, is really their daughter, the lost twin of April. April is married to, but doesn't live with, Paul Williams, father of her "illegitimate" daughter, Heather. (Paul didn't marry April until after Heather was born.) Paul is the brother of Patty Williams. In an episode five weeks later (January 4, 1982), Paul, presumed to be searching for his sister Patty (who has run off to follow her boyfriend, Jack Abbott), is shown "the morning after" in a motel bed with Bobbi. Should there be an issue from that union—and soap opera characters are unusually fertile—that child would be both a cousin and a half-sibling to April's daughter Heather.

As in *Movie-Radio Guide*'s 1942 "novelette," "Lonely Women," the family is still the primary institution through which one participates in life, and the ideology of the family is the primary source of one's beliefs. Though some of the characters are shown as powerful and often in control of business interests, the family is their primary allegiance. Jack Abbott's company, Jabot, is a family-owned-and-managed cosmetics firm, and its business interests are constantly subordinated to family concerns. Paul Williams, in an extreme of filial piety, becomes a kingpin in the Mafia in order to clear his father of police department accusations. Nikki Reed, in subsequent episodes, chooses to give up her career as a celebrated stripper to be a mother.

In the Manichaean terms of the soap opera (its polarized moral forces), goodness and evil are grappled with, clarified and named usually within, but always in support of, the family. Or, as Gwyneth Alden, on *Loving* (January 18, 1988), explains to her daughter, "Family is the only thing that matters."

The family, writes Eli Zaretsky, is the "crucible in which our emotional life first takes shape and throughout life it is the major institution in which we expect to be recognized and cared for, for ourselves."[74] It is also, as

Nancy Chodorow explains, the place where we can experience "connection to, rather than separateness from others."[75] She argues that because of the conscious and unconscious effects of early childhood care and socialization, the feminine personality tends to identify itself in relation and connection to others; the family is a primary site for these attachments.[76] The narrative and spatial structures of soap operas reflect this socially constructed reality and enable it to be meaningfully experienced by individual viewers. Tania Modleski's study of soaps concluded that it is precisely this preoccupation with the personal and relational that makes soaps such a productive fantasy for homebound women.[77]

The soap opera viewer is close to and able to ponder and savor someone else's emotional life and private feelings, watch intimately a character reacting to, even thinking about, his or her individual destiny: the quintessential realm of the personal. At the same time, the personal is presented within an organic weaving of several plot lines, emphasizing the interdependence of characters and their interpersonal problems: the realm of the relational.

A close examination of the spatiality, temporality, and continuity of an episode shows how the personal and the relational are inscribed in, and conveyed through, the narrative structure. The most distinguishing structural mechanism of the soap opera is its serial form, an open-ended story "to be continued." It is implied in the very nature and structure of soap operas that they will last forever. There are many plots occurring concurrently, and climaxes or solutions to problems are usually such that they generate the potential for new tensions and new suffering. There is never a resolution, as such, but a constant search for tomorrow.[78]

In this search there are numerous interruptions and delays from within and without the narrative world. The episode of *The Young and the Restless* under scrutiny, for example, opens with a 3-minute, 17-second sequence of Dorothy talking to her lodger, Bobbi, about Dorothy's daughter April's search for her twin sister. The television audience has known for more than a month that Bobbi is April's twin sister, and it is evident from the acting style, editing, and camera work in this sequence alone that Bobbi knows she is April's twin. However, Dorothy doesn't find out until 27 minutes, 50 seconds later; there is first another scene in which Dorothy's husband, Wayne, becomes aware of it (the awareness is conveyed by a 40-second voice-over soliloquy); then follow seven seemingly unrelated sequences and three blocks of commercials.

Then in a 25-second sequence Wayne arrives home to tell Dorothy "who this girl really is." But the denouement is interrupted (and the narrative time extended) by a scene of Patty at Jack's office and another block of commercials before the scene continues and Wayne finally tells Dorothy. Then Dorothy convinces Wayne that it is untrue, that he has just been influenced by April's "fool notions." But when Dorothy goes to get Bobbi so that Wayne can see for himself that she is not April's twin, she finds out that Bobbi has moved out. Three sequences and one block of commercials pass before Wayne and Dorothy agree that Bobbi probably is April's twin sister, though it is never confirmed in this episode because of Bobbi's departure.

Thus, the delay is not only in the division and arrangement of sequences, but within the story itself. "Make them laugh, make them cry," Agnes Nixon has often remarked, "and make them wait."[79]

Since the viewers already know the truth, we must assume that much of the pleasure is in seeing how Dorothy will discover the truth, her reaction to the news and/or the consequences of the revelation. But to get from the state of expectation to its fulfillment is difficult and lengthy. If, as Roland Barthes says, expectation is disorder,[80] then the creation of disorder and the restoration of order is an ongoing and endless process in soap operas. Moreover, during the time that viewers are waiting to see Dorothy "find out," they are becoming involved with other stories and other characters' lives, constantly shifting perspectives and sympathies.[81]

The interruptions, the interweaving of stories, the constantly shifting point of view, the ongoing process of ordering call to mind (and probably reinforce) the traditional role of the homemaker/child rearer. And that traditional role is how many of the women whom I interviewed described their lives. Modleski quotes a moving testimony from Tillie Olsen's *Silences:* "Motherhood means being instantly interruptible, responsive, responsible. . . . It is distraction, not meditation, that becomes habitual; interruption, not continuity; spasmodic, not constant toil."[82]

The flow of *The Young and the Restless,* whose audience is mostly homemakers/caregivers (judging from the hour of the telecast and the commercials aired[83]) is, as Modleski, Lopate, and others have noted about soaps in general, very interrupted. In this one episode of the show, the day's three main plot lines are divided into twenty sequences. In addition, there are thirty-four sequences (commercials, titles, and network identification) from outside the story world.[84] Eight of the twenty narrative segments are "teasers," scenes that introduce a subject and then break off, generally after a question has been posed and before the response; in other words, in the middle of a conversation. The eight sequences that continue the teasers are often separated by more than just a block of commercials. In addition, one of the continuances is divided into two sequences. Only three of the twenty segments can be thought of as a scene in itself, a self-contained unit of narration.

Interestingly, in contrast to this, most of the commercial "interruptions" *are* self-contained units of narration: minidramas with hyperbolized closure where, in thirty seconds or one minute, the advertised product dispels problems or transfers tensions.[85] Although some recent daytime commercials may play with the idea of seriality (the MCI series of fifteen-second spots telling the story of the school nurse trying to reach a sick little girl's mother, each "to be continued," Duracell's "I wish this could last all night," Quaker Oats's "life is a compromise; fortunately, it's also a cereal," or the Taster's Choice commercial with its interrupted romance), the logic of consumerism and the dynamics of commodity culture do not include thwarted expectation.

The flow within each of the soap opera's segments is also quite disrupted, with the average shot duration being only a little more than five seconds.[86] Though each of the storylines seems to progress in some understandable temporal order, and there is a vague temporal parallel implied among stories, the exact temporal relation of one story's segment to another story's segment is seldom clear. Nor do contiguous segments have any evident causal or spatial relation. In this episode (and typically), there is no way of knowing which story's segment will come next.[87]

This discontinuous flow, thwarted expectation, and temporal disjunction create an attenuated and artificial suspense, a constantly delayed closure. The shot structure supports this suspense by ending almost every sequence (fifteen of the twenty in this episode) with a zoom into a close-up (or extreme close-up) of a character's face. Just as each story in the daily episode is to be continued, so is each segment within the episode. The zoom in to the extended close-up of the character's face at the end of the sequence is a close look at the expression to enable the viewer to gauge a character's mental or emotional activity, forecasting new possibilities. A climax may have been reached, but it is always undermined by the promise of new climaxes, the potential for and prospect of more problems . . . and pleasures. Peter Brooks writes that nineteenth-century melodrama often ended scenes or acts with characters in tableaux, compositions arranged and frozen for a moment, "a visual summary of the emotional situation," making "its signs clear, unambiguous and impressive."[88] In soaps, the passage of time is not as important as the intensity of the moment. We are watching a display of passion, an emotional spectacle that makes the moment intelligible.

The zoom at the end of a sequence also functions as a dramatization of the *importance* of the story. William Labov and Joshua Waletsky's study of oral narratives has found that they generally contain a moment when the teller pauses, calling attention to and self-consciously reflecting on the point of the story and its value.[89] Like the zoom and extended reaction shots in soaps, these moments implicitly or explicitly call the listener to attention, asking him or her to judge the story significant.

The prolonged large-scale reaction shots at the end of the segments, often of two characters in succession, also suspend ordinary time. In *The Young and the Restless,* meaningful intensity comes from dwelling upon an everyday moment. In most drama, ordinary time is foreshortened to achieve a meaningful intensity. In the daytime serials, time moves much more slowly. Ordinary time is portrayed as such on the television screen and is often extended to achieve poignancy. At breakfast in the March 3, 1986, episode of the show, Shawn tells Lauren that tomorrow will be a big day. The episode broadcast on March 25 was still that next day for Lauren and Shawn. Romance is often drawn out. Valentine's Day for Ashley Abbott lasted four days one year (February 14 to 17, 2000). On *Days of Our Lives,* Marlene and Roman's first wedding lasted three broadcast days.[90]

On soap operas, each everyday moment is always incomplete, poised between beginning and end. Viewers comment that time is like life; that is, it is not storylike with an "in the beginning" and a vision of the end. Time has always existed and will not stop.[91] As Frank Kermode has written, we are born *in medias res* and die *in mediis rebus,*[92] we are always in our spot of time "in the middle." Kermode says that one of the great charms of books is that they have to end.[93] Soaps are without that charm. They rush into the middle—an "infinitely extended middle," in John Fiske's words.[94]

Soaps, however, do not exist in an "eternal . . . present," as Dennis Porter has written.[95] The first line of the first page of every script refers to events, people, and things that have already happened outside the script (in the sense of *in medias res,* in the sense of outside the TV set, and in the sense of repeating once again the conventions of the genre). And characters are always haunted by their past, seeking their origins and plotting for the future; they search for yesterday as well as tomorrow. An important part of the narrative experience of soaps is this quest for what is past and passing and what is to come—ceaseless transition—from and to the middle. As Johnny Bauer, like many before him, announces to Roxie Shane, "I tried to think about our future but my past kept getting in the way" (*The Guiding Light,* December 5, 1986).

Even with new soaps, everything has already begun. The beginning of *Sunset Beach*'s first episode (January 6, 1997) establishes the main locale (with a helicopter shot of the ocean, a pier, the beach, a lifeguard shelter, and houses in the background), then, during the pre-title sequences we are quickly introduced to characters and their backstories. The dialogue of the lifeguards who discover a teen and her dog sleeping on the beach reveals that the homeless youngster has been found like this several times before; later, close shots of Meg's pensive face the morning of her wedding suggest she may already have had some doubts about her pending marriage (even before she sees her fiancé embracing a sexy blond woman in the chapel's anteroom); and, still later, as Ben walks away from his laptop, a zoom in on an impressionistic painting of a beautiful woman on a swing by the beach and, then, a voice-over of a woman promising undying love imply that he has experienced a devastating loss.[96] A new but comfortably familiar world is opening up.

There are some conventional pauses (the zoom into the extreme close-up at the end of a sequence, the pregnant moment at the end of the day's last sequence, a crawl of credits, a voice announcing the next show, or, occasionally in the 1950s and 1960s, an announcer posing a pertinent question: "Will Joanne Tate be able to keep little Patty? Tune in . . ."). But the story goes on, our day goes on, and there are many meanderings. As one soap opera story is intertwined with another, so are our other stories, the day's chores and dreams. We can never see a structured whole from our interminable moment in the middle. Brooks, describing nineteenth-century serialized novels, suggests that time in the representing was felt to be a necessary analogue of time represented.[97] Soap opera viewers also speak about the lifelikeness of the slow pace. They often joke about "children who grow up in a hurry" (reaching sexual maturity quickly), days that take weeks to happen; nevertheless, despite obvious discrepancies in representation time and represented time, they also find comfort in characters who pass time as they do and while they do. Perhaps this similarity implies probable further resemblances. What do characters do when they are offscreen? What we do when we are not watching?

The time of the story is both analogous to and separate from the time of the storytelling.[98] Unlike novels, whose verb forms temporally situate us *in relation* to the tale, soap operas by their very present nature (a story forged before our eyes) situate us *with* them; we are in the same time. We seem to experience a reality that coincides temporarily with our own reality. The characters celebrate the same seasons and many of the same holidays as we do. There is also a certain immediacy that is fundamental to seriality. The "recentness" of soaps almost has the character of journalism (the daily dissemination of information) or journal-keeping. The represented event hardly seems to predate the telling.

The past is generally treated as a mental state, remembering. It is signaled by optical devices and audio effects similar to those used for dreams and other interior fantasies. The iterative is seldom used; soaps are the here and now. Though they are no longer transmitted live, there is still a sense of timeliness and immediacy associated with the daily broadcast. The broadcast happens once, on schedule, never to be repeated.[99] When an episode is pre-empted, it is generally lost forever.[100]

Yet time in the daytime soap operas seems almost abstract. Dialogue sequences are represented in ordinary time within each segment, but, with the exception of the occasional mention of holidays and seasons, they are generally presented apart from any particular or material time. In the episode of *The Young and the Restless* under examination, all the scenes were videotaped in the studio; there are no exterior shots, no prominent windows or change in lighting to represent the time of day.[101] *Sunset Beach,* after the first week, seldom returned to the exterior beach scenes. There is an almost claustral confinement to most of the daily episodes. Soaps are less a filigree lace of leaves in springtime, than a hothouse jungle.

In contrast to this, almost half of the commercials in this episode contain some outdoor shots. Many of the interiors in the commercials have prominent windows or are backlit so they seem like a breath of fresh air. (The toilet bowl cleaner commercial with commodes marching in a field of wild flowers is the most stunning example.) Most shows have title sequences with shots of the characters out of doors. (*Ryan's Hope,* for instance, which seldom had much remote shooting, used a title sequence in the late 1980s full of exteriors; *General Hospital,* in the mid–1990s, used mainly formal portraits of characters, head shots, but interspersed them with eleven actions shots, all but two of them, exteriors.)[102]

The spaces portrayed in the stories themselves, however, are usually domestic or domestic-like, unrestricted by time. Jonas's bar is his "living room." He is the host and his friends can visit him there to discuss their personal problems almost anytime. Jack Abbott's office has a sofa and he uses it for activities usually associated with the home (or bedroom) and nonbusiness hours. In addition, 70 percent of the shots (excluding commercials) in this episode are close-ups or extreme close-ups of characters, isolating them from the spatial environment, de-situating them.

These close-ups are not only synechdochic (a part of the whole person), they are, importantly, also metonymic (the locus of thoughts and feelings). In soap operas, the face is the center of dramatic action. It is almost as if the box-room set, the center of action of nineteenth-century domestic melodrama, has been reduced to and concentrated in the face.

A character's main action is confined to mental and emotional activity—conniving, scheming, trusting, loving, fearing, loathing. Though physical action is spoken about, it is seldom pictured. The performers serve mainly as registers and relays of thoughts and emotions. When physical action is depicted, it is usually limited to "acting out," behaving in a way that expresses feelings or thoughts. Soap operas elevate thoughts and feelings to tragic status; but they are, at the same time, socially extended and quotidian. Each of the characters' everyday thoughts are favored in a close-up and shared with the television audience.

Dialogue is very important to soaps as we will see later in the chapter, though not all information is conveyed by words alone. In the first shot of this episode, it is through the close camera work and the acting style—the facial expressions and delivery—that we know that something special is being conveyed. The woman speaking *is* the twin sister of the daughter of the woman reacting in the same frame (see the frontispiece). A zoom into a close-up of a thought often communicates information not evident in the dialogue and not available to any character in the story. There is a constant and systematic play between what the viewer knows (Bobbi is April's twin sister) and what the characters know. Dorothy may be deceived, but the spectator is not. The viewers are in a position of superior knowing, of understanding more than the characters know or understand. This puts the viewer in a greater position to be responsive (and, according to Franco Moretti, it is the erasure of this discrepancy—when the character finally realizes what we knew all along—that is so moving).[103]

The many close-ups are opportunities for familiarity. The character's face is almost equal in size to the spectator's, mimicking face-to-face contact, a closeness generally associated with personal relations, a certain intimacy.[104] The character is portrayed in a way that almost conveys confidentiality, a mutual trust and sharing of the private. The daytime viewer may be isolated, but he or she is not alone.

Soap opera characters, however, are often represented as solitary in the frame. Though the plots always involve other people, and the problems are interpersonal, and characters are constantly being assured by other characters that they are "not alone," 77 percent of the total shots (excluding commercials) of this episode of *The Young and the Restless* are of a single person in the frame.[105] Bertolt Brecht, writing on theater, has noted that the smallest social unit is not the single person but two.[106] Soap operas depict not the social unit, but the personal; and it is the personal that viewers get close to. The most common (and at the same time, the ultimate) wickedness on soap operas is betrayal, which, as Brooks has pointed out, is a very personal version of evil.[107] It also involves interpersonal relations. The same, of course, is true of love.

Though the viewers appear to be offered access to the hidden motives and inner workings of a glamorous industry (such as Jabot Cosmetics) or the chance to penetrate behind the surface of an exotic occupation (such as Cash's "escort service"), a major institution (such as the numerous hospitals on soap operas), or a close-knit small town (Genoa City in *The Young and the Restless*); they are really offered access to the world of the personal. It is this microscoping of reality that is experienced by viewers.

Peter L. Berger and Hansfried Kellner have written that "the socially constructed world must be continually mediated to and actualized by the individual, so that it can become and remain indeed *his* [or *her*] world as well. The individual is given by . . . society certain decisive cornerstones for everyday experience and conduct; the individual is supplied with specific sets of typifications and criteria of relevance predefined . . . by society and made available for the ordering of everyday life."[108] This cumulative ordering, this open-ended project, this continual narrowing and stabilizing of reality[109] takes place in soap operas in the realms of the personal and the relational and within the audience's traditional patterns of right and wrong. The judgments are delayed, but they are inevitable and usually foreseen. The good or sympathetic must triumph and the wicked or destructive must fall. There is continual suffering, but within a structure of benevolent principle that reaffirms a commonly accepted moral universe; it is never overwhelming. The soap operas are morally predictable and morally reverent. Certain causes must bring about an effect. Suffering without cause is very seldom depicted. Our joy is not simply in seeing the wrongdoers suffer but in knowing why they suffer, knowing the conditions of suffering. Soaps have, as Laura Stempel Mumford puts it, a moral and ideological agenda that lends a sense of inevitability to the status quo.[110] As a character in a subsequent episode of *The Young and the Restless* says, "I've always believed that good has got to win out over evil. I know the odds are against us—we just have to hope; we just have to believe" (January 5, 1983). In remarkably similar language, on *As the World Turns,* Grant explains to Lisa that "the battle between good and evil has been going on since the world began. It takes a lot of faith to know that good will finally win out" (December 9, 1988).

"Suffering of the consequences," in Agnes Nixon's opinion, is the key to the soap opera's popularity and longevity.[111] Viewers certainly seem to take some enjoyment from their vicarious participation in the characters' adventures in pursuit of sex, wealth, and power; however, they no doubt also find satisfaction in discovering that only a return to conventional values of family life, personal integrity, and a romantic sexual relationship with a loving partner will restore the moral order and its essential "rightness." After spending the night with Paul, Bobbi says, "I knew you wouldn't respect me in the morning." Two months later, when Paul refuses to leave April for Bobbi, he eulogizes soapland's perfect homemaker/caretaker: "Let me tell you something: April does not have a jealous bone in her body. She's been put through a lot of hard breaks in her life and she hasn't become bitter, she hasn't become resentful, she hasn't become full of hate. She just takes it and goes on. Always willing to give more, to care more, to love more" (March 5, 1982). John G. Cawelti calls melodrama, in general, a "fantasy of a world that operates according to our heart's desires."[112]

Common Story Motifs

"Either all around or in its wake the explicit requires the implicit," Pierre Macherey has written.[113] In order to say anything there are some things that are not said, that cannot or must not be said, that are disavowed. But the unspoken term is still implied, even though the act of banishing it or its very absence is unacknowledged. Those things that are disowned or disavowed are, in essence, allowed to exist unquestioned, exercising power less visibly, more effectively. Therefore, we need to explore both the work and its silences, both the explicit and the implicit story motifs, for one cannot exist without the other. I am reminded of the search by the narrator in *The Quest for Christa T,* "The paths we really took are overlaid with paths we did not take."[114]

As we have seen, the concept of "family" is central to the various soap opera stories. A common motif involves the discovery that a character's parents, siblings, or children are not who or what he or she had thought, and hence the hunt for the true relatives. Families are perpetually under question and in the process of reconstituting themselves. It is not unusual for parents to hide paternity from their children and/or mates or for children to be given away, sent away, or kidnapped.[115] Family life is more emblematic of splitting, separation, and struggle than of a narcissistic merging or an imaginary unity of parents and children. Hysterical pregnancies, miscarriages, and deceptions about conception simultaneously act out and reveal conflicts about family relations.

Parents, spouses, lovers, sisters, brothers, and children thought to be dead will return and attempt to reclaim family relations. Characters also frequently fall victim to amnesia or develop a second personality, which isolates them from their families, allowing them to express and sometimes experience wishes otherwise forbidden in regard to the family.

In the fall of 1986, *The Guiding Light* had, at one time, stories about Vanessa Lewis searching for the daughter she gave away at birth; Dinah looking for her mother whose photo she had worn in a locket since childhood; Maeve Stoddard pretending that her child had been stillborn and the infant that she was caring for (who happened to be the same age that her son would have been) was "really" the orphaned cousin of the doctor at the hospital; and Alan Spaulding, who had returned from the dead (he was thought to have been killed in South America two years previously), conniving to have the coroner tag an unidentified corpse with the name of his son's missing fiancée. A full history of many of the show's characters would likely include other such misconceptions of family relations and the obvious confusions that these tangled bloodlines engender, including flirtations with incest.

Incest may be a sticky subject in the everyday world, but there seems to be a fascination with it on soap operas where it is a common story motif. In real life, our cultural codes of reproduction include some partners that are sexually barred, some desires that can only be experienced with dread, uneasiness, and opprobrium. In modern culture, the incest taboo defines "the forbidden," and as such sets the limits for desire and sacrifice. Of course, any social prohibition rests on the possibility of violations or attempted violations; however, the excessive potential for incest on soap operas seems to betray an ambiguity about more than merely family inviolability and family integrity. Perhaps the solicitations (and refusals) on soaps express important confusions in the real world about even more fundamental psychic relations and the larger social (dis)order. These acts of near-incest are certainly more than transparent manifestations of sexual jealousy.

Can such desires and fears be experienced without shame and disgrace? Perhaps they can be when the forbidden expresses itself by means of mistaken identity or misrecognition; that is, characters *unknowingly* move toward unspeakable acts. "Knowing" must be considered a major factor. On soaps, it is generally confused minds or confused blood ties, not violations of trust or the abuse of authority (i.e., social bounds) that permit the move toward incest. For example, on *The Young and the Restless,* when Cricket's long-lost mother returns to see her daughter once again and is hospitalized with AIDS, Cricket falls in love with her mother's doctor only to find out, when they are about to become engaged and she meets his father, that his father is really her biological father, and her prospective fiancé thus, her half-brother (winter 1988–89). The representation of incest on soaps is seldom a question of power (or exploitation, or coercion) as much as it is expanded and indistinct family ties (where, for example, "mother" may be second stepmother, "brothers" and "sisters" may not be blood relatives at all, or a stablehand may be an uncle). And, importantly, the ultimate revelation re-establishes the "natural" (i.e., repressed) family constellation. As it is represented, incest is more a threat to romance—that is, another hopeless situation—than a question of inbreeding.

But is incest just another convolution, a plot device to thwart romantic couples? It may be more in the service of narrative demands than an exploration of social concerns, but can it be considered apart from anxieties about larger social matters? Why incest and not another coincidence which might just as easily drive the plot? Despite the frequent suggestions of incest on soaps, in the real world, incest is still the unspeakable. The avoidance of a subject frequently imbues it with power. After being cleaned up, codified, and conventionalized in soap opera narratives, can the possibility of an incestuous relationship still produce revulsion?

Near-incest was not uncommon in nineteenth-century stage melodrama. A poster for the American play *Blue Jeans* that shows a young couple, an older couple, and another young woman in a genteel country setting, has as its caption the line: "You can't marry the gal—'cause she's your sister." The fact that the play was advertised by this "punch line" suggests that incest was not as much the operating hermeneutic as it was a conventional story type and an expected narrative rupture.

The ingénue in Gothic novels is often an orphan or of mysterious parentage.[116] This is important to the conventional subplot in which the ingénue's socially acceptable suitor, the young courtier, turns out to be her brother. This "often involves a series of false recognition scenes between now-they-are, now-they-are-not siblings."[117] Their ignorance, and innocence in thought (and usually in deed, having not yet consummated their passions), redeems their virtue. In soap opera's jumbled families, opportunities for incest are almost neverending. *As the World Turns,* during the summer of 1986, had a double incest story in which Lily Walsh, a young innocent who believes that she is the daughter of Lucinda Walsh, is dating the family's stablehand, Holden Snyder. Holden is thought to be the younger brother of Iva Snyder, who is known to viewers as Lily's real mother through a rape by her cousin Josh Snyder. But in August, Iva finds out *she* has been adopted by the Snyders, so that, in the words of *Soap Opera Digest,* "If she and Josh aren't cousins, Lily isn't an incest baby," and Lily is thus free to cavort with Holden, who is not her uncle by blood after all.[118] Mary Ellen Brown quotes a conversation from a *Days of Our Lives* discussion group, "Marie fell in love with this fellow who turned out to be her brother [laughter] with plastic surgery, and the one brother shot another brother . . . And Julie was married to Doug, who was married to her mother . . . [laughter] Doug's daughter was really Julie's sister [laughter]."[119]

Most of the threats of incest on soaps are among siblings or other "equals," and seem to be mostly about love, not sexual obsession, and are generally averted or shown not to be incestuous and thus represented as pardonable mistakes. There are many permutations, but most of the stories seem to employ one of two main schemes: either the stories involve relationships that are imagined as—then shown not to be—incestuous and result in romance such as the one between Lily and Holden; or they involve innocent lovers with unconsummated affairs that end in pathos, such as the story on *All My Children* in which Erica Kane is engaged to her long-lost half-brother, Mark Dalton. The revelation of the relationship generally involves the unveiling of a concealed past indiscretion on the part of one of the parents and always ends the romance. Incest averted (though implied or contemplated), where power relations are not involved, seems to be a forgivable mistake.[120]

Sometimes the story involves intrafamilial tensions that are acted out by surrogates. These contemplated or consummated affairs are among people close enough to be relatives and, as such, might be tinged with anxiety. For example, on *The Young and the Restless,* Jack Abbott has been flirting with his new stepmother, Jill Foster Abbott. This involves such obviously erotic play as "mistakenly" entering her shower as she is bathing. Finally, after Jill has a fight with Jack's father, she and Jack are marooned in an isolated cabin during a snowstorm and make love in front of a glowing fire (December 1983). The next two and a half years (broadcast time) involved many repercussions, complications, and punishments, including blackmail, pregnancy, miscarriage, and finally the expulsion of both members from the family.

Some cases of displaced familial relations are more benign yet are close enough to imply a moral transgression. For example, on *Ryan's Hope* (1985), Jillian is struck with amnesia and falls in love with Dakota Smith, who turns out to be her husband's half-brother. Promotional spots for *The Bold and the Beautiful* in the beginning of May 1987, when the show was only a little over a month old, featured a close-up of a handsome young man, introduced in a man's voice-over as "Thorne Forrester, obsessed with forbidden desire." A clip from a forthcoming episode showed a heated conversation between Thorne and his sister, "She's your brother's fiancée!" "I happen to be in love with her!" On *The Guiding Light,* Reva Shane has been married to (a deep breath here) H. B. Lewis and to his son Billy. She has had a passionate affair with Billy's half-brother, Kyle Samson, and then, in May 1987, was pregnant by Billy's full-brother Josh Lewis. Ashley Abbott (*The Young and the Restless,* 1983) was engaged to her mother's ex-lover.

Parental love and romantic love are often in conflict as mothers and daughters or fathers and sons are rivals for the affection of the same third party. Natalie Hunter had been Jeremy Hunter's lover before she married his father, Alex. After Alex's death, her plans to marry Palmer Cortlandt are upset when she thinks she is pregnant with the child of Cortlandt's son Ross (*All My Children,* April 1987). Cassie Callison falls for her mother Dorian's live-in lover, Jon Russell. In a moment of turmoil she wonders, "Who will you chose, my mother or me?" (*One Life to Live,* April 14, 1987). In these stories of displaced incest, biological relations are replaced by relations of competition, making familial struggles for possession concrete.

While considering the incest motif and its relation to the misrecognition of family relations, one might be helped by examining Sigmund Freud's discussion of "family romances."[121] In a 1908 essay of that name, Freud writes about the process in which a small child struggles with independence from the authority of his or her parents by getting to know other adults and so coming to doubt "the incomparable and unique quality" (p. 41) that the child has attributed to his or her own parents and even coming to imagine that other parents might be preferable. Freud ascribes the "intense impulses of sexual rivalry" (p. 42) that come from a child's feelings of being slighted and the regrets for having to share his or her parents' love as some of the factors that contribute to this. Family romance, then, is a specific kind of imaginative activity where children fantasize that they (or their siblings) might be stepchildren or adopted or even the product of secret infidelities in order to fulfill their wishes for an ideal family of "less complicated" sexual relations. A form of revenge and retaliation that might be considered intrinsic to separation, family romance is also an intense expression of affection, for indeed, it frees the child for imagined sexual adventures with the ones to whom he or she feels closest. By exalting one or both parents, the child is also expressing a wish to return to that blissful period, "the happy, vanished days when his father seemed to him the noblest and strongest of men and his mother the dearest and loveliest of women" (p. 45), and, we might add, when the child thought himself to be the sole object of his parents' desire. As part of a process of transformation from helplessness and dependency to independence and autonomy, the child begins to see an object of identity as an object of love. It is a fantasy of overvaluation and compensates for feelings of loss.

The many near-incest stories on soap operas suggest that family romance is still ethically and morally ambiguous. Of course, all the stories of romantic love contain some degree of obstacles and trespass and it might be argued that all romantic love is a nostalgia for a fantasized image of a parent. Perhaps romantic love is so valued on soaps precisely because it is seen as an intensification of an idealized parent-child bond?

But the social utility of the incest taboo (where the lack of the taboo is thought to cause family friction) might seem to be under question on soaps since it is obvious that the taboo itself cannot assure family stability. If the incest prohibition is a part of the child's realization that he or she cannot be the parent's lover, protection from both overwhelming desire and re-engulfment,[122] do the threats to the prohibition confront the limits of familial responsibility? For Michel Foucault, the family has taken on the role of anchoring sexuality and providing it with a permanent support. The family has become "an obligatory locus of affects, feelings, love," and since sexuality has "its privileged point of development in the family, [it] is 'incestuous' from the start."[123] Does romanticized incest navigate around this unspeakable? While recent studies of family violence have found that actual seduction and incest may be more prevalent than Freud's theories of fantasy suggest, I wonder if soaps have a fascination with incest as such, or with mapping out the boundaries that constitute acceptable social behavior, testing the "intolerable limits of common sense."[124] Could it be that incest is the extreme, the threshold to be undermined? The leap into limitlessness that opens up the question of the problematic ambiguity of all limits?[125]

Although it is implied in the other stories, actually consummated incest is very seldom dealt with, and when it is, is generally retroactively introduced to "explain" later deviant behavior (thus becoming a highly moralistic social-issue or public-service story about abuse). In *Loving*'s story about the Garth Slater family, for example, father-daughter incest was disclosed as the origin of the schizophrenic daughter's second personality (1983–1984).

Doubles of all sorts (twins, amnesia victims, split personalities) are also a familiar motif on soap operas and often permit characters to indulge in forbidden fantasies. The Slater girl's second self allows her to express her hostility to her father. On *As the World Turns,* in the fall of 1981, a normally "good" character, David Stewart, could engage in an extramarital affair without guilt during a bout of amnesia. On *One Life to Live,* after witnessing her husband Clint arguing with her first husband's long-lost twin brother (December 1986), Viki Buchanan experienced a traumatic loss of memory of the previous eight years, which meant that she had no memory of Zimbabwe ("That's what we call Rhodesia, now") or her current husband. The amnesia also allowed her to mistake her ex-brother-in-law for her beloved late husband, and there were hints of a reunion.

On *All My Children,* the brilliant millionaire-schemer, Adam Chandler, has a sweet, friendly mentally retarded twin brother. Doubles of the same gender appeared frequently in nineteenth-century novels written for women in which they often acted out the subversive elements felt by people confined by more traditional roles and traits.[126] In soap operas, the double might also embody a character's unacknowledged traits. Not long before her amnesia, Viki Buchanan was the victim of a split personality (reoccurring after a fifteen-year dormancy), and the kindly, responsible newspaper editor has had to do battle with her free-spirited and frequently naughty alter ego, Niki Smith.[127]

Another familiar motif and fairly common peripeteia (the sudden reversal of circumstances) is the return of a character thought to be dead or terminally missing. Serious illness and bedside vigils are commonplace on soaps and patients sometimes recover miraculously. Those who verge on death or are rumored to be dead are often revived. In the meantime, the hospital is important as a station for interaction and also as a site where, under the stress of separation, truths pour out. In a hospital scene on *One Life to Live,* for example, Cordero Roberts's vital signs have stopped and he seems to be dead after having been slashed with a machete during his honeymoon. His bride, Tina, confesses all her wrongdoings, including not telling Cord who his real father was and tricking his grandfather into giving him a legacy in exchange for her silence. However, it is just the monitor malfunctioning (August 18, 1986).

The physiological origins of illness are seldom discussed (can it happen to me?) but the moral origins are often implied (he or she deserved it). Jack Abbott, a philanderer, is shot by his deranged wife and is paralyzed "from the waist down" (*The Young and the Restless,* 1982). Few recurring characters die of old age or even offscreen.[128] They usually die violent or exotic deaths, making death a catastrophic accident, which is an *individual's* problem (rather than the inevitable ontological ending).[129] But a character's death usually affects many other characters. Though the details of the death are usually known to the viewer, they are often a mystery to those other characters. Therefore, investigations, accusations, and retributions often follow someone's death. Even when the circumstances are less mysterious, there are usually realignments of affections and, or, of power. Dead characters seldom rest in peace and they sometimes come back to exact their own revenge.

On *Ryan's Hope* (December 11, 1986), Siobhan Ryan Dubujak finds out that her chauffeur is really her ex-husband, Joe Novak, who she thought had been killed in a 1984 bombing. His face had been extensively reconstructed after the blast and he had returned to reclaim Siobhan from the man who had tried to kill him.[130] On *Loving,* Clay Alden, thought dead in a boating accident that happened before the show's debut, has returned alive (also with a new face) to rid his family of his wayward wife (January 1987). On *All My Children,* a newly remarried Nina Cortlandt Warner Connelly finds herself an unintentional bigamist when Cliff Warner, her first husband thought to have been killed in a train accident, is discovered alive in a hacienda in South America (January 1988). Cordero Roberts is surprised at the church, during the recessional after his marriage ceremony, by his "late" wife carrying an infant she claims is his son (*One Life to Live,* June 1987).

On soap operas, even death has a future that is ripe with possibilities. James Stenbeck, a very villainous character *(As the World Turns),* thought to have died two years previously when he fell from an airplane while trying to destroy all its passengers, returned to Oakdale in a monk's robe just in time to rescue his ex-wife from an attack by the crazed Scotsman, Hensley Taggart (December 1986).[131] One of the February 1987 promotional spots for the program showed Stenbeck in a close shot, looking at the camera and announcing that he's going to build a new life with "a fortune from Lucinda, my son from Barbara, and Emily at my side." These are instances of "family romance" that stress the fantasy's capacity to unsettle. In the returns from death, the disavowed takes on a material presence, the obverse of the amnesia victim's new identity, two sides of the same coin.

Many stories also involve detection, policing, and the law.[132] There is a certain irony (or contradiction) between the frequent appearance on soap operas of the police and policing, and the general moral and legal truancy, misconduct, and lawlessness that are a vital part of most of the stories. It is almost as if the police stand guard over an order fated to be transgressed. In episodic dramatic series, the police (or the private eye) generally intrude upon the lives of people not seen before and not to be seen again. Their presence, and the need for their presence, is represented as aberrant moments in a social world not normally needing police ordering. At the end of the episode the police (and usually the criminals) are withdrawn or deported elsewhere. Of course, that they are needed again the following week by someone else somewhat mitigates the idea of an orderly world; however, police activity in most cases is represented as exceptional and effective in a social world posited as well behaved.[133]

On the other hand, the everyday world of private life in soap operas is far from well behaved. Although private life is not an area where police law is ordinarily the supervisory principle, in soaps police intrusion seems to be a quotidian event. If this shimmering world is one of anarchy and chaos, it is not because of the lack of police presence. In order to see how the police and lawlessness function in soaps, we will have to acknowledge how soaps (as a set of representational strategies) function to police both the cops and the transgressors. Soap operas are organized in a way that circumscribes criminal activity and limits the pertinence of police activity. Even on shows such as *Ryan's Hope,* where several members of the Ryan family are law officers and the police supposedly hold center stage, the main interests transfer the policing to the periphery.

For example, on the episode broadcast July 22, 1986, Detective Siobhan Ryan Dubujak returns to the precinct to pick up her badge and weapon the day before she is to return to work after her leave of absence. There she overhears that Father McGuinn from Saint Ann's Church has been reported missing. In the previous episode Siobhan had told her husband Max that she had confessed to Father McGuinn that she had searched through Max's papers and that she was beginning to suspect him of gun smuggling. In later episodes, Siobhan works on Father McGuinn's case, but it is obvious that gun smuggling or the missing person are not as important as marital (dis)trust and betrayal. Father McGuinn is not a recurring character. The crimes and the investigation are a key to Siobhan and Max's marital problems. Later, when she finally begins an investigation of her husband, it is instigated by the return of Siobhan's ex-husband, who accuses Max of having attempted to murder him. Her investigation indicates not a triumph of police procedure but a shift in Siobhan's affections (winter 1986–7).

On *As the World Turns,* Frannie Hughes sees a woman who looks remarkably like herself. At first curious, she begins investigating, but soon, after several mishaps and a couple of deaths, she finds herself in the middle of a murder attempt. She rescues the woman, Sabrina Fullerton, from an assassin, only to find out that she is her half-sister, the "illegitimate" daughter that Kim Hughes thought had died at birth twenty-two years earlier (January–February 1987). The attempted assassin was the hospital administrator who had switched a stillborn baby for the healthy, newly born Sabrina. On *The Young and the Restless* in the summer of 1985, an African American law student and district attorney's assistant, Tyrone Jackson, infiltrates a crime syndicate in an attempt to stop the threat on his brother's life. Tyrone's disguise includes being made over to appear white ("a total") and most of the story time concerns the deceptions involved in his interracial romance with the mob boss's virgin daughter. Both police work and criminality are marginalized; that's not what soaps are really about.

Organized crime is the "official" criminality on soap operas. Even though they are repeated offenders, mobsters are less threatening to the home than less-organized crime. In soap operas, as a matter of convention, organized crime is more likely to be penetrated by regular "ordinary" characters than the other way around. The criminality that invades the home is seldom either organized or random. It is generally the result of a romantic involvement or part of living dangerously; that is, it is represented as if it were of the victim's own causing. Brooke English (*All My Children,* spring 1986) is being threatened by the murderer of her ex-lover Gilles. The murderer turns out to be the estranged husband of Gilles's ex-girlfriend (Brooke's competitor for Gilles's affections) and he is trying to stop Brooke from writing an exposé about the affair. The police officer who helps Brooke with her investigation ends up dating her, and it is Brooke's ex-husband who rescues her during the final showdown. On *Loving,* Dane Hammond's white-collar crime involves his wife's family's corporation and results not in police action but in divorce. His ultimate downfall, after long plotting (1984 through 1986), is caused by his affair with his sister-in-law, not his attempt to take over the corporation. On *The Young and the Restless,* Victor Newman's wedding day is threatened by the deranged Eve

Howard who plots to murder him so that her "illegitimate" child will inherit his "benefactor's" (possibly his father's?) fortune.

Soap characters seldom get robbed or mugged. They are more likely to get kidnapped or murdered, crimes that have the potential to disrupt and/or consolidate family life or family-type relations. Erica Kane on *All My Children* has been abducted (and almost sexually abused) by three different men in one year (summer 1985 through summer 1986), and each time rescued by her boyfriend, Jeremy Hunter. On another occasion, she is threatened at gunpoint on a tottering elevator structure by a jealous, pregnant woman who thinks *she* has a claim on Jeremy; Jeremy rescues both Erica and her assailant (July 1986).

While white-collar crime and business conniving have long been represented, the shady methods of multimillion-dollar family-held corporations have become popular narrative fodder since the early 1980s (no doubt influenced by the prime-time serials such as *Falcon Crest* and *Dallas*). While their illegal activities are not treated sympathetically, big-business villains (and sometimes their politico cohorts) are usually depicted as mainly menacing each other. Their dubious dealings, corruption, and compromises of basic moral values are posed as personal conflicts derived from personal motives, not as a structural part of the corporate (or economic) system or as a threat to a larger order.

Monopoly capitalism itself is not questioned or even very ambiguously represented. The fault lies in the individual players. On *The Young and the Restless,* Jack Abbott steals a perfume formula from the Jabot Cosmetics safe and has it duplicated and marketed by Mergeron U.S.A., his mother's conglomerate. Jack had been president of Jabot, but his father kicked him out when he found out that his married son had been sleeping with one of Jabot's models. Furious when his sister (the company chemist) took over the presidency, Jack takes her formula and passes it on to his mother's company hoping to secure a job there. On *All My Children,* the feud between Adam Chandler and Palmer Cortlandt (of Chandler Enterprises and Cortlandt Electronics, respectively) has involved theft of corporate secrets, bribery, graft, condemned property, and attempted murder (in 1986 alone). These maneuvers are not represented as a natural part of doing business, but as maniacal revenge originating in the two men's hatred for each other because of an affair Palmer had with Adam's older sister in Pigeon Hollow, West Virginia, forty years earlier. When corporate crime is punished, it is generally not by the official law, but by family law.

Interestingly, transgressions that don't involve the police, such as disobedience, inattention, or selfishness, are often embedded with excessive guilt and atonement, and decidedly disproportionate punishments. These extreme measures, however, are generally not directly related to the "crime" (such as revenge or retribution by other characters) but are threats normally thought to be outside of human control, primitive or elemental threats, such as fatal disease or accident.

The down-and-out or petty criminals are seldom portrayed, but when they are depicted, they are generally represented with sympathy for their social situation and they serve as a contrast to middle-class standards and mores. This contrast is somewhat self-serving, as it helps to reinforce an appreciation for the middle-class standards themselves, for the class habits and securities that make the benevolence and sympathy possible. In the *The Young and the Restless*'s mob story, for example, Cindy, a prostitute, is shown (in flashback) to have been sexually abused by her father. Jazz Jackson has become a syndicate underling so he can send his orphaned younger brother, Tyrone, through law school and Kong, Jackson's colleague, thinks he has little choice in employment because he is illiterate (1984).

Regular characters often go undercover to investigate the underworld or infiltrate organized crime. Few of the stories contain much investigation or detection; they are more a series of an individual's heroic adventures. The infiltrators generally operate out of their homes and either lie to their families about their activities or lie to them about their affections so that they can leave their family (hoping not to endanger them). This causes unending complications and tensions, and the families are almost always imperiled.

Jesse Hubbard, on *All My Children,* after clearing himself of a petty crime, is convinced to help the police by going undercover to look for the real gangsters. He makes up lies about what he is doing every night and his wife begins to suspect that he is seeing another woman. His efforts to protect his family are miscalculated, and his wife, son, and mother-in-law are held hostage by the people he has been trying to expose (fall 1985).

Police officer Rick Hyde, on *Ryan's Hope,* lies to his wife, Ryan, and separates from her so he can penetrate the mob as a hit man. After a period of being single again, and even an attempt at dating, Ryan by chance finds out about the deception and is affectionately reunited with Rick, just in time to be part of the final shoot-out (summer 1986).

There is a certain element of adolescent fantasy about these adventures, an obstinate personal confrontation with the bad guys. Similar to the various amnesia stories, good people descend to the erotic, powerful, exciting, and dangerous; enter the world of the unavowable temporarily; then return home.

The police and the amateur systems of investigation and regulation almost always support each other. The amateurs could hardly be considered vigilantes, as there seldom seems to be a conflict of purpose or interests between them and the legal and police apparatus. When the private investigator Paul Williams (son of a Genoa City police detective) goes to San Francisco to rescue his wife, Lauren, from her crazed companion, Shawn Garrett, he immediately seeks out Detective Young, previously a member of the Genoa City police force (*The Young and the Restless,* winter 1986). Though it is generally the private citizens who act most heroically, they usually have either the implicit approval of official law agencies or explicit help from its representatives. Often they are actually acting on behalf of the police or the district attorney. The law (either official or moral) generally punishes the guilty party for the amateur. Very often the evil person's associates do him in. If the transgressors are captured, they are generally quickly dismissed and seldom tried on air.

On the other hand, regular characters are frequently in courts of law. When they are brought up on criminal charges, they are likely to be wrongly accused and sometimes wrongly convicted. It might seem that the justice system is being seriously questioned; however, it is ultimately redeemed when the innocent are eventually exonerated and truth wins out (though usually by quirks of fate rather than through the designated social institutions). Tried for the murder of Zona Beecham, Lorna Forbes's plea of self-defense is denied (*Loving,* spring–summer 1986). She is convicted and jailed but is absolved when her lawyer, Zack, falls in love with her and uncovers Zona's diary, which details her plan to kill Lorna. On *Days of Our Lives,* Kimberly Brady is convicted of murdering her boyfriend's ex-wife and is saved from life imprisonment only when Barbara Stewart makes a deathbed confession after an auto accident (March 1987). The following month on the same show, "Patch" Johnson confesses to murdering his father after the man raped his sister. He is being sentenced to ten years in prison, when his sister rushes into the courtroom, suddenly remembering that it was she who killed their father in self-defense.

Even in a case where the actual culprit is not known, the audience often does know that the person being accused did not commit the crime. In addition to the convention of a truth that is veiled and later uncovered and the convention of a "good" character wrongly accused, the narrative arrangement often gives the viewer privileged information not available to characters. For example, on *One Life to Live* (August 4, 1986), the first pre-title sequence shows Cassie (who has been infiltrating "Brother" Mitch Laurence's "mission"), drugged and being knocked unconscious by "Brother" Mitch in a room at the Waterside Inn as he continues to threaten her with rape. We then cut to Tina professing love to Cord; then to several Llanview residents waiting for "Brother" Mitch to appear and proclaiming their various reasons for hating him; then, after the title and commercials, to the hotel room with Mitch already dead on the couch, Cassie just coming to on the floor, and Cassie's mother, Dorian, entering the door. Although the still-drugged Cassie thinks that she has killed Mitch and is eventually brought to trial, the arrangement of information allows the viewer to know Cassie had been unconscious and couldn't possibly be the murderer.[134]

The soap opera investigation stories generally work on a double system of information: one available to the viewer and characters within the story who are doing the investigating or who are victimized, and another that is available to the viewer and sometimes to the criminal. Though a character is seldom privy to both systems, it is important that the viewer is. Most conventional detective/crime stories open with what appears to be a random crime and move toward showing the act to be full of meaning. In soaps, because of the viewer's privileged position, the illegal act generally resounds with meaning from its inception. The apprehension of the criminal is not so much a recuperation of order as it is a confirmation of the viewer's power. Soap opera detection does not loop back on itself, as in conventional investigation stories. The investigator doesn't gather all the suspects around and explain the happenings for the innocent parties and the viewer, providing closure or some sense of erasure of the story. Rather, in soaps, sooner or later, the mise-en-scène, camera work, editing, and/or dialogue isolate the true criminal. The guilty party becomes televisually individuated so that eventually there are few aspects of "mystery" for the viewer. It is the moral horror of the event or pity for the victim (emotional qualities) that are moving rather than the unique puzzling aspects of the crime. The solution to the investigation becomes of secondary importance and seldom ends the story. Even though new information may force us to reshape our previous interpretations, the story is clearly not teleological. The solution of a crime or the end of a legal disputation is not the end of a narrative line, but, at most, a temporary moment of stasis.[135]

The institutional law, rather than clarifying, often creates more ambiguity by introducing false leads and false accusations, and it is generally the amateur detective/lover who extracts sense from the confusion, rescues the importance of meaning, and reveals what the viewer at home already knows. Soap operas celebrate individual heroic action and implacable justice, but without the viewer's affective experience of ignorance there is little celebration of, or even exercise of, ratiocination. And the achieved order is usually undermined by its temporariness. Lorna Forbes's absolution begets conniving and betrayal from her lawyer/lover's daughter and sister-in-law as they try to break up Lorna's and Zack's relationship (*Loving,* fall 1986).

Whereas Sherlock Holmes (in *The Adventure of the Copper Beeches*) claimed that his motivation was impersonal, "a thing beyond myself,"[136] soap opera detecting generally involves a personal motivation that is usually defined within the family or family-like relations. In classical detecting stories, the unusual element—the strange bell-pull or the eccentric closet—is of interest. The crime is generally what disturbs the unexceptional life. In soaps, it is the usual, the ordinary, that is both threatened and tested. Love, the family, and personal relationships that might seem superfluous to classical detecting stories are exactly the subject of soap opera detecting. In the fall of 1986, *One Life to Live* had a story of a crack ring and a related murder. Dan Wolek has been indicted for the murder, but the real criminal is the son of his defense attorney, Judith Sanders. The viewers know it all the while, so it is her failure and possible redemption as a mother that are really under surveillance. Detective Carl Williams on *The Young and the Restless* spends months trying to find out who shot Jack Abbott, while the audience knows that it was his own daughter, Patty. (1982).

In conventional police or detective stories, the police or detectives seldom get involved with the specific grounds for the illegal actions, or even their consequences. They are only interested in the agents. The actions themselves are generally defined as violations; that is, they are defined by a frame that doesn't question the rest of society. In soaps, because the police or detectives are generally personally involved, the reasons for the crime and its consequences seem to have a special importance. The illegal actions are still framed as violations, but usually as personal violations. No matter how often crimes occur, or how many times a crime occurs, they are represented as deviations from the social norm. And it is generally the social sphere (rather than the institutional) that provides the most effective means of policing.

Guilt is always individual and voluntary, rather than collective, social, or universal, and the guilty parties (and this often includes the victim) are generally seen as suffering long before the law metes out punishment.

Since the criminals always bare themselves to the world (televisually, at least), generally admit their blame, and are usually punished by extra-institutional sources, the police and the institutional law become almost irrelevant symbols of power. Investigation and policing do not provide cathartic action. Such tales are primarily an expiation of the personal and the familial; like the threats of incest, the appearance of doubles, and the instances of amnesia, they serve to both rupture and repair family bonds. These stories speak to a homemaker's pleasure; they both valorize her concerns and, in their framework of moral certainty, reaffirm her comfort in the enclosed world of the family.

Characters

Soap plots are, in Agnes Nixon's opinion, motivated by character.[137] This section is an attempt to analyze the functional roles of the different kinds of soap opera characters and the different ways that they are characterized.[138] Like mythic or fairy tale figures, soap characters are clearly drawn. Viewers generally recognize characters' roles quickly as they are familiar types: familiar in the sense that we have seen them on soap operas before and in that they have traits that are not too dissimilar to people we know or know about from real-life stories (news reports, a friend's account, or community gossip). Of course, many of these stories are fashioned to fit soap opera conventions, sometimes even in installments, and often only loosely based on reality.

Soap operas have no superheroes (equipped with powers superior to, or unimaginable in, common folks), few fairies or sorceresses,[139] or truly repugnant freaks. Since the characters seem fairly ordinary, they seem almost accessible, or "normal" as one viewer put it.[140] Yet these people are not *just* like we are or might be; they are exceptional. They are exceptional not only because they are on display (via mise-en-scène), but also because they have only significant qualities and are surrounded by consequential circumstances. Banalities are missing. On soap operas, characters seldom watch TV unless they are about to see their long-lost husband on the screen and never take out the garbage unless they are about to be kidnapped doing so. Their lives are extremely concentrated, so they can be simultaneously ordinary and outrageous.

Since there is little uncertainty in soap operas, there is little room for mediocrity. Absolute good and evil demand absolute heroes and villains.

In a world so full of tensions, where good must always win, in order for the fights to still seem like fair play, the predetermined winners must be the most deserving, the most virtuous, the best.[141] Although the victory may be thwarted or far off, it is expected and must seem merited and reasonable. When a virtuous character is occasionally knocked off for plot or, more likely, for contract reasons, fan magazines invariably publish letters questioning the justification for the move and the justice of it, and Internet bulletin boards and chat rooms are full of protests.

Soap opera characters, like those in myths or fairy tales or melodramas, are generally represented as very good or very bad, models of virtues and vices, without too much ambiguity. Not that characters' histories are not complex, or that they do not change, or that we cannot sympathize with someone who is "bad." But at any one moment, they seem to embody clear attributes and refer to absolute moral imperatives. Almost everything positive and commendable is concentrated in one pole (making others seem more contemptible). Most everything negative and disdained is concentrated in the other pole (making others seem more innocent).[142] They function very much like a pair of mirrors, polarized yet endlessly reflecting each other.[143]

Those characters who are good are generally wise and reliable, often protective and helping, and usually the guardians of rites and tradition. Good people are the product of the search for justice and order. These characters are generally patient, receptive, and relatively passive. For a good character to seize power and still be good, he or she usually neutralizes the negative effects of a previous abuse of power. For example, on *Loving,* when Ann finally acts to assert her voting control over Alden Enterprises, she does so to redress her husband Dane's grievous misuse of his position in the company (winter 1985).

On the other hand, those who are bent on doing evil (who are ruthless, immoral, full of guile, jealousy, and/or treachery) are, in most instances, represented as the product of their drives, their individual passions.[144] Their motives are generally abstract and internal (e.g., "greed") rather than specific lived conditions ("the pressure of financial difficulties"). The abstraction and internalization of lived conditions make it easier for characters to "cure" themselves. For example, on *The Young and the Restless* (spring–summer 1983), Cindy's prostitution is portrayed as "sin"; she is treated at a convent and ultimately redeemed when she sacrifices her life for her "good" boyfriend. (As in the nineteenth-century tradition, her redemption comes from a double process of purification: true love and self-sacrifice.)

Bad characters' actions are sometimes "explained" by their past histories and it is not uncommon for wayward characters to have their past histories introduced just as they are about to reform. As the prostitute Cindy is beginning to see the light (that is, fall in love), the serial introduces a backstory telling through dialogue and flashback that she had been forced to have sexual relations with her father as an adolescent.

Villains in their aggressiveness often offend middle-class norms. Villains, especially the poorer social climbers such as the young Meg Snyder on *As the World Turns* and Ava Rescott on *Loving*, and those climbers who have already achieved their wealth, such as Gwyneth Alden on the same show and Jill Foster Abbott on *The Young and the Restless*, find their personal needs more important than social norms. For most of the women I spoke with these characters were both acknowledged as bad and found intriguing precisely because of these violations. Under the practical demands of many people's daily existence, the contradictions between our personal needs and social norms are often restrained or repressed. In soap operas these contradictions bloom; villains uninhibitedly act them out as individual dramas. Ava (*Loving*, summer 1985), afraid her marriage to Jack Forbes is on the rocks after her miscarriage, feigns continued pregnancy, purchases her impoverished sister's infant child, and passes the boy off as her own in order to trick her husband into remaining with her. (Many villains have an entrepreneurial outlook toward procreation.) In soap operas, women needn't acquiesce to cultural imperatives to limit sexual activity; however, those who don't are not generally rewarded. Sexuality used for social mobility seldom upsets the power of hierarchy for very long.

Power (the ability to dominate others) and privilege (the exploitation of others) are socially extended across gender, age, and even class.[145] For a villain, the struggle for pleasure is transformed into a struggle for dominance. This dominance is generally represented as compensatory and spurious, however; and it is also coded as risky and uncertain, no matter how long it may have been going on. The power-hungry millionaire Palmer Cortlandt on *All My Children* has been a villain ever since the character was introduced in 1979. To list all of his evil doings would be too lengthy, but in the character's first decade on air, they generally clustered around his obsessive need to dominate his daughter, Nina, and eke out revenge on his archenemy, Adam Chandler. He has lied to Nina about her mother's death, plotted and paid to try to break up his daughter's marriage, and schemed to keep her in a state of semi-amnesia (Nina had lost her memory about everything that happened to her after she turned sixteen) so she would forget his pernicious acts and retain her girlish affection for him. But his domineering always seems to be threatened (and mediated) by his daughter's sincere love and the counterintrigues of Chandler.

Many of the characters behave in a somewhat romantic way, impulsively, like adolescents whose excessive sense of obligation is more a function of the importance of their superegos than of their real situation. Stubbornly insisting on being faithful to themselves, these characters take values seriously, living them "to the limit," often putting themselves and others at risk.[146] Erica Kane (on *All My Children*), for example, is represented as imaginative, adventurous, and brilliant, though she is scarcely rational enough to cope with adulthood. When her fiancé is falsely imprisoned on the suspicion of murder, she stages a wedding in the prison chapel, a "news" helicopter overhead to cover the event, and attempts to fly away with the unsuspecting groom (November 1986).

Yet she is admired—or at least found intriguing—by almost all the women with whom I've spoken. Erica, enchanting Erica, we watch her with obstinacy, passion, and despair. The very women whose daily practice would seem to call her attitudes and actions into question responded with enthusiasm when I mentioned her name. Images of independence and power are sometimes so attractive that we willingly ignore the palpable evidence of impotence in our own reality. Or perhaps, as with the "good" characters, there is a certain tension between recognition and negation. Similarly, Jack Abbott, on *The Young and the Restless,* when played by Terry Lester, is depicted as thoroughly enjoying forbidden pleasures. His obedience to his family's welfare seems to be in conflict with his pluck and enterprise. Can it be that his resistance to civilizing efforts and his defiance of family authority constitute part of his charm? One of the women I spoke with certainly felt so.

The soap opera world is a world that seems to be geared toward power relations but one in which rational models and moral ends win out. (Erica's fiancé refuses to break out of jail because it is morally wrong and he has faith in the system.) It is a world where characters revel in independence and power, where selfish aspirations are exalted, but seldom realized.

But it is only after being defeated that the individual aspirations are declared mad. Viewers familiar with the narrative world and the narrative conventions will certainly anticipate some ramifications. Perhaps it is because of this expectation that the revelries are so much fun to watch. Foucault locates madness "at the point of contact between the oneiric and the erroneous," transversing "the surface on which they meet, the surface which both joins and separates them," between infatuation and delirium.[147] It is not that Erica Kane is beyond morality, but that she moves in a transitory space between a proscribed morality, which we hardly dare to identify, and an exalted one, which for the greater common good, we don't dare to practice.[148] Erica Kane is not only a fictional character; she is also a coordinate in a mighty moral debate.

Economic success is seldom realized through positive action, individual accomplishment, or achievement; high aspirations in both romance and careers are generally related as dreams and if they come about, it is generally either through personal initiative in the form of conniving or exquisite luck (characters marry "well," or their real father turns out to be a millionaire, and so on). When fortunes have the potential to rise and fall rapidly, social or economic mobility suggests instability as well as hope. Career and marriage strivings spurred by plotting and manipulation are generally unrewarded (or not long lasting); real advances come about only through love or benevolent powers. For example, Dolly, the warm-hearted madam who cared for Keith when he had amnesia, becomes an executive in his fragrance company and marries him (*Loving,* fall 1985). Harry Sowolsky (on the same show), an ex-convict, proves his worthiness by exposing his boss Dane Hammond's treachery, wins seven million dollars in the lottery, moves into his boss's old duplex apartment, and begins dating Hammond's ex-wife (summer 1986). On *The Young and the Restless* (winter 1982), April's long-lost twin sister, as good fortune would have it, turns out to be very wealthy and moves her entire working-class family to New York City (and off the show). On soaps, hard work and self-denial are not the usual paths to success; yet, working-class poverty is generally the experience of only one generation. Class conflict, like gender conflict, is usually subsumed under individual conflicts (and depoliticized), and social contradictions are "resolved" by their denial.

In the sexual representations on soap operas, women are not reduced to the mere fact of their gender. Rather they have personalities, dreams, needs, and desires. Erotic relationships and expressions of desire exist freely but self-consciously. Class, age, education, morality, retribution, or corporate deals can be important aspects of sexual encounters.[149] Sexuality can be deployed for advantageous alliances, and women can approach men without jeopardizing their fulfillment and pleasure, though generally only the most brazen or devouring do so.[150] Such aggressiveness may even be enough to mark the woman "bad" or signal unhappy repercussions to come, defeating any temporary satisfaction. Gwenyth Alden on *Loving* seduces her sister-in-law Ann's husband, Dane, and later Ann's fiancé, Harry, each time causing chaos in the family and the family corporation. As in Victorian literature, an amazing number of women get pregnant after one illicit night (Maeve Stoddard on *The Guiding Light,* for example). Sexual relations, like other social relations on soaps, are enlarged, simplified, and then presented as most significant.

Female characters can be represented as licentious or promiscuous, but with the men whom they love, they are generally moral and virtuous. Though neither pole excludes the sexual and pleasurable, soaps continue to reproduce traditional male definitions of female behavior and the power relations integral to them. (*The Young and the Restless,* for instance, had a light-hearted story in 1985 in which the kindly whore, Boobsie, falls in love with a retired British officer, gives up her profession, and marries him.) Some characters (generally "good" characters) do act as though sex were justified only by love (in heterosexual, potentially permanent relationships) and this feeling is sometimes shared by couples. However, when reciprocal pacts of tenderness do appear, conventions tell us that they're very precarious. Even the most blissful of relationships can break up (though generally because at least one of them seeks a new relationship), and these breakups are usually tumultuous.

Ellen Seiter and her collaborators found, as I did, that fans were openly delighted by these types of stories. They cite a discussion in which one woman tells how angry her husband gets when she is enthusiastic about an extramarital affair: "Oh Bruce gets so angry with me when I'm watching the show and they're married and I'm all for the affair. [Laughter] It's like, it's like [Voice changes to imitate Bruce]: 'I don't like this. I don't know about you.'" The two interviewees agreed that there were "lots of times when you want the person to dump the husband" and get it on with the new partner.[151]

While subjugation and humiliation are never eroticized, domination in marriage or romantic liaisons sometimes is. The protection that traditionally accompanies domination seems to be an even more powerful erotic force. After Victor Newman rescues Ashley Abbott from an attempted rape and nurses her back from her amnesia, she falls in love with him (*The Young and the Restless,* spring–summer 1985). Erica Kane is threatened by one of her ex-husbands, her current lover's father, her current lover's father's widow, and Latin American terrorists, each time being saved by Jeremy Hunter, who during the course of the events progresses in their relationship from the celibate friend of Erica's late husband to her fiancé (*All My Children,* summer 1985–summer 1986).

Young women characters sometimes have sexual fantasy sequences romanticizing and eroticizing their subordination to their boyfriends or husbands. These are generally set in the past with exotic costumes and the young woman and her lover play the primary roles. The women are generally powerless and physically vulnerable in a menacing situation and are rescued by their lovers. But only their husband's or boyfriend's social and physical power over women is portrayed as sexy. Other men's violence or power is threatening. Ryan Hyde, for example, a young journalism student on *Ryan's Hope,* envisions a story on an eighteenth-century sailing vessel that is attacked by pirates. The fantasy is shown on screen in a dreamlike manner, in soft focus with the edges of the frame blurred, and uses the language of paperback romance fiction, including a first-person voice-over by Ryan describing her husband/rescuer as "pulling me up against his hard body" (September 14, 1986). In another fantasy sequence, she exalts her husband/rescuer's "wonderfully strong but tender hands" (October 7, 1986). Less explicit maybe, but no less fantastic, Detective Siobhan Ryan Dubujak (on the same show) is taken by her wealthy husband to his family's chateau in Switzerland, where in a designer gown she waltzes with him and tells him that she would be happy with him in a fishing shack (October 16, 1986).

Social barriers and social conventions are often undermined by the power of sex. The usual obstacles are temporarily overcome by the passion, and the unavailable or the unattainable is provisionally conquered. Generally one indulgence topples all resistance, but happiness is certainly not assured. Cross-class encounters are probably the most common (the intertwining stories frequently unite disparate classes), but there are others. On *The Young and the Restless,* for example, Traci Abbott, an innocent young woman, has her first sexual encounter with her college professor. She becomes pregnant, sees her teacher with another student, and attempts suicide (fall 1984). On *Loving,* gentle Father Jim Vochek, a Catholic priest, had had a youthful love for Shana Alden. He had rejected marriage and decided on ordination, but following an automobile accident, he loses his memory of his ten years in the priesthood and the two are able to pursue their love. They marry in the fall of 1986, but after almost a year and a half of marriage (broadcast time), Shana, now pregnant, is still worried that Jim will regain his memory and his "dedication to God," and destroy their future (January 15, 1988).

Like Jim Vochek (or Doctor Cliff Warner on *All My Children*), many of the men on soap operas are so feminized that they seem to be a critique of traditional macho masculinity. Jeremy Hunter, for example, is caring, creative, vulnerable, nurturing, patient, and tender.[152] But these almost maternal characteristics are balanced with physical and public power and, although unconventional, Jeremy is perfectly heterosexual. He is also represented as an object of desire and is astoundingly popular with the women I spoke to. Frequently shown with his shirt off or in a stance that emphasizes his physique, Jeremy, one might argue, is further feminized as spectacle. This spectacle, however, is not the point of view of anyone within the narrative. There is seldom a shot of someone looking at him. He is, rather, exhibited for the home audience or, more precisely, for the female viewer, although one can imagine that he might be admired or desired by men as well. (Such "hunks" are also regularly on display in fan magazines.) In the early days of his relationship with Erica, Jeremy's "femininity," like his celibacy (he had sworn vows to a Tibetan monk after his fiancée was killed), served as both a contrast to and a containment of Erica's hyperbolized and flamboyant sexuality.

Soap opera's successful marriages are represented as allowing both partners romance and a passionate and equal sexuality.[153] This is a treatment of sexuality that is in dialogue with viewers who are progressively reflective about sexual pleasure, and with feminist debates on the subject on television talk shows and in other popular media. However, it should not be seen as necessarily having a radical autonomy or even as disruptive of conventional social relations. In fact, the conservative social setting of this sexuality may provide precisely the privileged space where these fantasies may be "safely" indulged.[154] The very romantic Travis Montgomery proposes to Erica Kane by telling her that he needs someone he can trust, someone he can talk to, someone to take care of (*All My Children,* May 18, 1987). John Ryan courts Lizzie by telling her that he will always be there for her and that he wants to take care of her (*Ryan's Hope,* April 1987). On soaps, there is seldom a conflict between the demands of bourgeois marriage or cultural notions of femininity and the desire for sexual excitement and pleasure. Is this an odd little exercise in wishful thinking, a projection of both our limitations and our longings? This "scenario of extreme heterosexism," as Alison Light's discussion of romance fiction puts it, should probably be seen as as much a measure of our "deep dissatisfaction with heterosexual options" as of any desire to identify with the safe versions of femininity that the texts construct.[155] It is as much a discourse on insecurity and discontent as it is a reactionary impulse. "Marriage is not a point of narrative and ideological closure," John Fiske points out, "because soap operas interrogate it as they celebrate it."[156]

Dialogue and Its Performance

One of the major ways that we get to know characters is through their delivery of dialogue, their conversations. Talk is, as Robert Cathcart and others have pointed out, the action of soap opera.[157] *Days of Our Lives,* more action-oriented than most soaps, is, in Mary Ellen Brown's estimation, 90 percent talk.[158] In the next few pages, we will look at the dialogue and its performance as boldly spoken verbal acts that express and inform and provoke responses. On soaps, as in nineteenth-century melodrama, nothing is left unsaid.[159] The censorships, accommodations, and tonings-down of daily life are broken through by soaps' desire to express all.[160] And much of the excitement in soap operas derives from these exchanges of dialogue.

Soap dialogues are a series of complex interactions full of, among other things, reasons for the characters' speaking and listening to each other. The dynamics of the transaction are not always equal, but they are generally economical. Information that should be garnered by the viewer is expressed through the words and through the speaking character's intonation, diction, and bodily gestures. It is also expressed through the reaction of the character listening in the story, the music, and the camera work.[161] The camera can convey information not evident in the words. Sometimes the listening character's reaction provides or emphasizes information not available to the speaking character. Such televisual means as the framing angle, the scale, or camera or lens movement, can help to produce meaning that can clarify, contradict, or reinforce the information expressed in the words, intonation, and gestures. The use of silences within the story and both ambient and background music (that is, music coming from the story world or accompaniment from outside the story space) may also affect the meaning. In soap operas, what is said may be somewhat obscure, but what is meant is generally very clear to the home viewer (who is, after all, the intended recipient of the dialogue). In this sense, the text is both ambiguous and precise.

These dialogues also function as occasions from which characters and viewers can infer or speculate on the conditions that caused the utterance or on the consequences from the fact that it was said. This is important because on soap operas, causes and consequences can be more important than an act itself.

Misunderstandings (and concealment) are rampant in the stories, but they are generally dispelled when the protagonists become willing to explain themselves and pay heed to one another: to speak and to listen.

Often disagreements and quarrels can easily be avoided, if only someone speaks and someone listens. Unbeknown to her husband Paul, Lauren Fenmore Williams submits a nude photo of him to a magazine contest (*The Young and the Restless,* November–December 1986). When the pinup wins and is published, Paul is furious, especially since he had just been appointed to the mayor's committee on pornography. The problem is not that she took the photo or that she submitted it to the magazine, but that she does not communicate with her husband. Several times along the way Lauren could have escaped her troubles if she had told him what she had done. But she keeps silent. It is not the fear of punishment that keeps her silent. She is foolish, stubborn, pigheaded—and childish. Silence is often represented as though it were an infantile disorder that is overcome when one grows up to conversation.

Many problems germinate from the interruption of communication, or the inability to use or decode it properly. Misunderstanding is not only the effect of not communicating but is often the cause of it, making the "conflict" itself seem superfluous. The final recognitions are touching because they demonstrate that if communication and understanding had come earlier, the conflict could have been easily avoided. After trying to withdraw the prizewinning nude photo of her husband and failing, then attempting to buy up all the issues from all the newsstands in Genoa City, Lauren finally overcomes her silent pride and admits that she is acting childishly and selfishly. She talks to her mother about how her neglectful childhood has made her strive for attention. She speaks to her husband about her need to be noticed (December 12, 1986). Conversation is both social mediation and cure.[162]

Conversation is a serious matter on soaps. Conversations seldom take place while the speaker is doing something else (washing dishes, watching television, knitting, shelling beans).[163] They are shown in close-up, both literally and figuratively. Although it seems to us that characters on soap operas are engaged in conversations, their dialogue is in fact very much more "literary" than the socially used language we experience everyday. Soaps have no "umms" and "ahhs," few asides, seldom any abandoned thoughts. The characters' sentences are logical, organized, and generally grammatical. If they pause, repeat themselves, overlap someone else's words, or become unintelligible, we think that the performers have flubbed their lines. Yet these are common occurrences in improvised conversation. The disparity between our talk and their talk is a disparity not of class or education, or even linguistic ability, but of representation and imagination.[164]

The importance of talk in televised soap operas certainly reflects the genre's heritage from radio. The other predominant daytime TV genres—talk shows, court shows, and, in the 1970s and 1980s, game shows—are also marked by a dialogic format of talk. Soap opera talk, however, is a different case because it is fictive. Fictive dialogue should function to represent an "historical" utterance, that which the character composes and says, and which is therefore, unless quoting, always "original." That is, fictional dialogue should function as if it were a "unique" occurrence.[165]

But on soaps it is often doubly fictive as characters overtly fantasize, pretend, and lie. For example, on the half-hour episode of *Ryan's Hope* chosen at random for examination (ABC, Monday, August 6, 1986, see Appendix II) there are at least two instances in which characters make patently false statements, intending to deceive the listening character. Frank Ryan has been shot and is in the hospital "fighting for his life." His family, his ex-wife, Jillian, her current boyfriend, Dakota, and Frank's current girlfriend, Diana, are at the hospital waiting for some news. In this day's episode, Frank regains consciousness for a moment when Diana is with him and he called out Jillian's name. Later Diana tells Jillian that Frank opened his eyes for a minute, but when Jillian asks if he said anything, we cut to a close shot of Diana as she turns her head away from Jillian, with strained facial gestures, and nervously says, "No"; and the background music swells as the screen fades to black.

In this case, the fiction within the fiction is marked with stylistic and intonational features, which clearly signal its fictiveness. This is meant to be clear even if we happened to have missed the contradictory evidence in the previous scene. Later Dakota tells Diana how happy he is that she has been "standing by" Frank and that Frank has told him how much she means to him. The narrative situation (Dakota's been trying to get Jillian to leave the hospital and go home with him and, in the previous sequence, Dakota had complained to Melinda that it looked as if Jillian was still in love with Frank) and the several close reaction shots of Diana's puzzled face seem to imply an alternative intention to Dakota's words. Diana, herself, verbalizes her doubt that Frank has told Dakota anything about their relationship. The context incites an interpretation by warping its literal meanings.

After the scene in which Frank calls out Jillian's name and after the one where Diana lies to Jillian about it, there is a scene of Dakota and Jillian arguing in the hallway about Jillian's refusal to leave the hospital to go home. "While I was out here dealing with your insecurities," Jillian whines, "Frank came to for a moment." Dakota replies bitterly (although neither he nor Jillian could possibly be aware that Frank had said anything), "You know something, I think you should go back in there, because I certainly wouldn't want you to miss it if he called out your name." He turns and walks off camera, and the oboe takes over as the camera zooms in closer for Jillian's significant reaction.

In this episode there are also at least two instances of speakers choosing words carefully, so as not to lie, but nonetheless to mislead the listener in the story. We see and hear Max Dubujak (who unbeknown to his wife is the leader of a crime syndicate) interrogating his underlings about who ordered the hit on Frank Ryan and, in a threatening tone, telling them that he *will* find out who did it. Right after that, we see and hear Max reassuringly telling his wife, Detective Siobhan Ryan Dubujak, that he knows her usual good police work will uncover her brother Frank's assassin. Ryan Hyde, who has been hiding out with her estranged husband, the hit man, arrives at the hospital to visit her Uncle Frank. When her family asks her where she has been, Ryan tells them that she has been "just working things out." Until the time that the character who is being misled finds out about the deception, dialogue and performance is rife with intense and multifold meanings as new characters become involved in the deception and, importantly, as new viewers are informed about it. As Al Rabin, supervising executive producer of *Days of Our Lives* told Martha Nochimson, the characters may lie to each other, but they never lie to the viewer.[166]

But there are frequently multiple meanings to words. Such semantic ambiguity often implies that there is a significance that transcends the usual literal meaning. A fortune cookie that reads "a new person will come into your life soon" (*The Young and the Restless,* January 23, 1987) may seem to refer to the happy newlywed and newly pregnant woman's child-to-be or to that same amnesiac woman's other husband (who the viewers know is about to discover her whereabouts). The character generally understands the meaning unilaterally, though both the import and duplicity of the words and the character's ignorance of the duality are usually obvious to the viewer at home.[167] Sometimes the hint of additional significance is indicated by phonological means (such as tone of voice, volume, stress, tempo, etc.). These aspects of performance have semantic value, often expressing shifts or innuendo not available in the words alone and sometimes difficult to express in verbal language. These nuances are seldom subtle.

Though sincerity cannot be taken for granted, characters seldom take due or paranoid caution; they rush in without qualification. Mistaken interpretation seldom undermines their confidence in verbal exchange.

Since lies and evasions are pervasive and often continue for some time, the performance style—vocal idiosyncrasies, intonational features, facial gestures—may need to convey the information that a character is lying or avoiding. Performance style in soap operas cannot really be separated from the use of the close camera and the moving lens. The lengthy duration of the zooms in on the face seems to necessitate some facial movement ("waving eyebrows"[168]), not only to inform the viewer, but for visual interest as well. But the facial expressions are seldom abandoned as soon as they can be understood; they are displayed, held for a while (like a pause in musical performance), amplified with a duration and intensity that seem to demand response. Like a mask representing suffering, defeat, justice, humiliation, rage, or triumph, the facial expressions make plastic what is often unsayable.

Roland Barthes, in an article on wrestling, discusses a type of performance in which reserve is out of place.[169] He says that reserve wouldn't serve the ostentatious nature of the spectacle because the whole reason for the fight is not to get a winner, but to display suffering (p. 19). It seems to me that this is very close to the overstated acting style that we see on soap operas, but unlike wrestling, where physique and gesture are often endowed with meaning, soap opera performance is mainly concentrated in the face. Performers empty out all their interiority (in a sort of pantomime) so that everything is excessively clear through exterior facial signs. Like wrestling there are no allusions; everything is presented directly and exhaustively (p. 25) so that the performance is "endowed with an absolute clarity" (p. 16) or a "moral beauty" (p. 22). Barthes argues that wrestling is not really a sadistic spectacle; it is an intelligible one (p. 20). He writes that the audience that goes to wrestling matches—and I think we can substitute "watches soap operas"—doesn't want passion, but the image of passion (p. 18). On soaps, motives and feelings may be concealed from other characters, but they are exhibited with conviction to and for the viewers.

Characters often spout proverbs, aphorisms, or other "timeless wisdom" or "universal truths." Patrick Ryan, for example, tells his new wife Melinda (who has just found out that her dizzy spells are caused by an environmentally produced cancer), "We'll just have to play the cards we're dealt" and, later, "I promise you, I'll be with you every step of the way" (*Ryan's Hope,* March 25, 1987). Each time these sayings are used a particular context is conferred upon them; however, they appear to be instantly applicable to other contexts (perhaps even *all* contexts), adaptable with inexhaustibly broad analogic value. The adage's truth also seems to be reaffirmed by its recurrence. It's implied that if it were not true it would have been forgotten by now, even through it might be a sorry wisdom.

Though characters do not address or discuss the viewer, the recitation of shared knowledge ("it happens with those December–May affairs") and other collective generalizing ("those are feelings we know so well") seem to include us. But when these truisms are used in dialogue, the speaker, by quoting the eternal, also seems to be disclaiming responsibility for it. It's a dodge: wisdom without commitment. Universals dull the pain of particular circumstances, obscure the complexity of social relations and our ability to make history (Pat's "We'll just have to play the cards we're dealt," for instance).

One of the most popular of these sayings is the reassuring, "Things always work out the way they're supposed to," said, for example, by Joanna Manley to John Abbott after he finds out that his son has had an affair with his stepmother (*The Young and the Restless,* December 11, 1985). Or, "You just got to believe. You can't lose faith," as the housekeeper Vivian says to her mistress as she is about to forfeit her family's mansion because her errant husband has exhausted her fortune (*Generations,* March 30, 1989). Or, as Sonny, on *General Hospital,* tells his father, Mike, "Sooner or later, everybody pays" (July 25, 1996). The Panglossian doctrines that Herzog observed in 1942 may still be declaimed, but the immortality and anonymity of such timeless wisdom can also undermine its power and invite skepticism. The same is true with such threadbare phrases as "trust me." There is a double entendre implied in every use. The character may say it sincerely, but it has been said so often that its truth is dubious.

The more specific and precise the dialogue, the more restricted and particular the meaning and the context to which it is appropriate. Restriction and specificity serve to establish distinctiveness or uniqueness (of character or situation or feeling). But soap opera characters and situations are not striving for the unique, just the mildly differentiated. The overblown rhetoric, ingenious dialogue, powerfully romantic dialogue, and feisty argumentative dialogue constitute "memorable" exchanges. They are bits that bear repeating and invite use apart from the context in which they occurred, an instruction manual for the inexperienced and an opportunity to rejoice in a chat room, as the *All My Children* fan's celebration of Anton's line, "I have better things to do with my life than kiss up to archaic Euro-trash!" on the America Online bulletin board indicates. (Outstanding fashion concepts and sophisticated manners may also serve a similar purpose. On the August 25, 1986, episode of *General Hospital,* for example, in a moment of high romance, Duke Lavery pours champagne for Anna Devane, sampling it first before handing her the glass.)

Sometimes dialogue serves primarily to inform the viewer of a character's state of mind. For example, in the same episode of *Ryan's Hope* that we have been examining, there is the conversation between Dakota and Melinda in which Dakota expresses his feelings about Jillian. Melinda is sympathetic but the conversation (instigated when Melinda sees that Dakota is upset) is primarily a device for Dakota to express his frustrations and doubts. It could have been a voice-over soliloquy.

The soliloquy in the form of musing, talking to oneself, wondering out loud, is one of the few types of nondialogic speech on soaps. The monologue, a talk with an absent or imaginary partner or before another party or parties without their intervention, is seldom employed. But by far, the preferred mode is dialogue, usually in the form of questions and answers, assertions and rejoinders, statements and replies, promises and responses. Even emotive outbursts are generally responded to (although sometimes the only response is a reaction shot and swelling music). Many of the characters' questions function as "rhetorical" questions, since the viewer already knows that answer ("What calculating scheme is hatching in her sick little brain?" asks Katherine Chancellor about Jill Abbott on *The Young and the Restless,* May 8, 1987). Other times, the replies can be anticipated by viewers from having "witnessed" the events or previous dialogue, flattering and affirming the fans' sense of belonging.

Soap opera dialogue seldom directly commands actions or meets specific immediate needs. There are few "please close the door"s on soap operas. Practical affairs are seldom discussed and there is little small talk, unless it is intended to reveal concealed information. For example, "What did you do for lunch?" might be understood as "Will you lie to me about whom you lunched with?" Whole conversations are sometimes made up of the two-part exchanges of questions and answers. Soap opera dialogue is a series of provocations and responses, interrogations and interruptions, concealments and discoveries, which prolong, hold off, or forestall the conclusion for a future moment, all the while, by frustrating, inscribing a desire for that prospect.[170]

Background instrumental music sometimes reinforces the performances, heightening the emotions and guiding our attention and interpretation. (The name "soap opera" is itself fundamentally linked to the use of music.) Background music is used to introduce characters, to mark their moods, to set an emotional tone, and to highlight climactic moments.

This use of music in soap operas seems quite similar to Peter Brooks's description of nineteenth-century theatrical melodrama, where music often expresses another register of feeling, outside of language and gesture.[171] On soaps, the music sometimes continues (or crescendos and continues) even after the image fades. This style has a long history. In the October 2, 1963, episode of *The Guiding Light,* for example, as Bert and Papa Bauer find out that Mike Bauer's pregnant young bride, Julie, has been in an automobile accident, is unconscious, and is going into "involuntary labor," a series of close-ups of their troubled faces fades to gray as the organ music swells and continues over the empty image for several seconds.[172] Today, it is more common to hold an intense moment for a duration and a long—often five seconds—fade, with the music rising, then eventually fading along with the image. More than simply underlining the significance of the feelings, the music both isolates and expresses emotions not available in the visual discourse, emotions that might be in excess of what can be expressed by the visual discourse, or emotions which are too overwhelming to be represented by any character's performance. This is similar to what Mary Ann Doane hears in Hollywood love stories of the 1940s when she observes that music has the burden of evoking "that which is unrepresentable: the ineffable."[173]

No longer the simple organ music of the past, soap music is now more elaborate, using imaginative instrumentation. The music sometimes indicates humor (much the way a laugh track is used on situation comedies), adventure, or romance (special motifs for particular loving couples, music that triggers a whole scenario of passion and desire, are used frequently).[174] In the past fifteen years, singers have become common characters on such one-hour shows as *General Hospital, The Young and the Restless, Another World, The Guiding Light,* and *As the World Turns.* The stories include concert scenes, nightclub performances, and music videos. Songs often express (and augment) the emotions of the singers or the emotions of a person or couple within the story (usually indicated by extended reaction shots). The music performed almost becomes a soundtrack of their thoughts and feelings. The performers (Michael Damian, for instance, while playing the singer Danny Romalotti on *The Young and the Restless* in the late 1980s) sometimes cut CDs and cassettes that were marketed in soap opera fan magazines. In 1992, Quality Records put out an album of songs performed (and sometimes written) by soap actors, including Damian, Matthew Ashford (Jack on *Days of Our Lives*), and Jeff Trachta (Thorne on *The Bold and the Beautiful*).

On soap operas, muteness (from amnesia or severe trauma), although widespread, is represented as an extreme and harsh affliction. Ashley Abbott, on *The Young and the Restless,* troubled because she had refused to tell her family and her boyfriend Victor about her pregnancy and abortion, on the way to a mid-winter vacation goes mad and is found wandering mute in New York City (January 1987). The muteness is both a consequence of her silence and the key to her ethical conflict and Manichean struggle. Muteness is the extreme repression exactly because she is unable to talk about her moral and emotional state. (It is because melodrama is about expression, Brooks writes, that it seems like an apparent paradox that so often in climactic moments and extreme situations it resorts to nonverbal means of expressing its meaning.[175] These "texts of muteness" seem to have been as common on the nineteenth-century stage as they are in today's soaps.) While Ashley is unable to express herself, the spectator is informed of her conflicts through the performance style, expressionistic camera work, voice-over flashbacks, and audio fantasies. Also, the sequences of her voicelessness are often ironically intercut with scenes of her family (unaware of her dilemma) discussing how happy they are that she finally got away for a vacation and of Victor talking with his brother in an effort to come to terms with his feelings about Ashley's abortion. Ashley's inability to express herself also isolates her. Aloneness may be the usual state of the average viewer, but it is the scourge of soap opera characters.

Common Rhetorical Tropes

Soap operas employ many of the other plot devices of nineteenth-century melodrama: overheard conversations, missed meetings, disguised identities, last-minute rescues, and letters that go disastrously astray. The stories are full of astonishing acts, extreme passions, outstanding heroes and heroines, and dreadful villains—exuberant characters and tall tales, all of which seem to be simultaneously disbelieved and appreciated.[176] The maternal excesses of Lucinda Walsh (*As the World Turns*), the intense self-absorption of Erica Kane (*All My Children*),[177] the incongruities of the back-from-the-dead storylines, the face changes, the outlandish coincidences, and the sudden reversals are an important part of the allure. On soap operas, moderation itself might be a vice, as it makes a character or situation seem suspiciously insipid, boring, and therefore unbelievable. For example, one of the women I interviewed, Marilyn Morales, spoke about the easygoing nature of Melanie on *All My Children* as "dull" and "not too realistic." "Why's she acting like that? People in 1989 do not act like that!" Later she and Awilda Valles agreed that they didn't like Erica Kane as much since she had had her baby because she is now "more steady, more realistic," and they remembered with relish one of her more grandiose stunts, "Right, oh, that part was good!" Describing an ingenious incident on another show, Marilyn said, "I liked that part! Like, that's interesting. I said, 'Let me see this. What *is* this? I can't believe that this is going on!'" On soap operas the commonplace, the down-to-earth, is most radically unlikely.

Let's look at the ideas of "unlikeliness," and "credibility" to see how they might relate. Nancy K. Miller, in a fine essay on plots and plausibility in women's fiction, quotes Bussy-Rabutin's critique of *La Princesse de Clèves* in which he complained that Mme. de Clèves's confession "is extravagant, and can only happen in a true story"; he goes on to say that "when one is inventing a story for its own sake it is ridiculous to ascribe such extraordinary feelings to one's heroine."[178] The reasoning is that in life, unlike in fiction, anything can happen, so we really can't complain of unlikeliness. In fiction, however, we should be more responsible and not violate readers' expectations. Could this be related to the early English novelists' ritualistic denial of authorship (as in, for example, Samuel Richardson's original preface to *Pamela*) by claiming to be merely recording or editing someone else's true story (i.e., the facts)?[179] It is possible that the "veracity" of the story left them more leeway for uninhibited extravagance. That is, the disavowal may have had the double benefit of making the story seem more acceptable to readers and giving the authors a certain amount of rhetorical freedom. Samuel Richardson himself speaks of "that kind of historical faith, which fiction itself is generally read [with], even tho' we know it to be fiction."[180]

At the turn of the twentieth century, Dorothy Richardson's American autobiography discussed the reading habits of her fellow workers in a box factory, as women who "will not read stories laid in the past, however full of excitement they may be [but who] like romance of the present day, stories which have to do with scenes and circumstances not too far removed from the real and the actual." But Richardson also tells us about describing the plot of Louisa May Alcott's *Little Women* to her coworkers and the reaction of one who grumbled, "that's no story at all—that's just everyday happenings. I don't see what's the use putting things like that in books. . . . They sound just like real, live people."[181]

This tension between the ordinary and the out-of-the-ordinary, a knowable landscape populated by extraordinary characters and events, seems to operate today on soap operas. They are spectacles of the outrageous. But as we have seen, soaps also conform to real-life seasons and holidays, use recent news stories, and refer to contemporary social issues. Their publicity and promotional campaigns indulge in public anecdotes about performers, casting, and backstage antics. These current affairs, even while they suggest a certain ontological insecurity about the categories of fact and fiction, may also serve to fix and displace a more fundamental defense of the truth of their stories, possibly even permitting them a margin for excess. That is, the "veracity" of these stories may leave them more leeway for uninhibited extravagance.

Some of the most distinctive rhetorical figures used on soaps—coincidence, sudden reversals, concealment (and revelation), and hyperbole—might be seen as excessive and implausible. And this is one of the first things that people who decry soaps gripe about, either from a realist critique or from an aesthetic one. They find fault in the lack of credibility, the lack of plausibility, the arabesques. Soaps are unfaithful to one's idea of reality. That is, the extravagance, the unlikeliness, departs from the limits of common sense.[182]

Yet all of these tropes seem to be enjoyed. Viewers often refer to instances of excess and folly as "great." Extravagant feeling, extravagant behavior, and extravagant circumstances may strain credibility, but they also provide a source of energy and excitement.[183] The question is how these tropes function, both narratively and socially.

Soap operas are full of remarkable coincidences and sudden reversals, from the doorbell that rings just as the virginal couple is about to embrace to the paralytic who can walk again, just in the nick of time. On *Search for Tomorrow* (November 1986) the drunken driver who killed Suzie McCleary and crippled her husband, Cagney, turns out to be not only the mysterious and reclusive surgeon who has developed the special procedure that is the only hope for curing Cagney's paralysis, but also the only doctor available to perform the extremely difficult operation. On *Days of Our Lives,* the blind Kimberly regains her sight just in time to save her boyfriend from being killed by a falling beam.[184] Her sister Kayla, who has been struck deaf and mute after a mugging, is about to express her wedding vows in sign language when, as *Soap Opera Digest* put it, "miraculously, the power of love" cured her and she regained her voice just in time to say "I do."[185]

The same kinds of remarkable coincidences and sudden reversals occur in nineteenth-century stage melodrama. For example, Brooks describes Philippe Dumanoir and Adolphe Dennery's *Le Vieux Caporal,* in which an old soldier is struck mute, unable to disclose essential information. "At the moment of final crisis—as the heroine is about sign a wedding contract with the villain, and her adorer has cocked his pistol to end his days—the Caporal leaps to prevent the suicide, the pistol goes off next to his ear and the shock restores his power of speech in time for the saving recognitions to be effected."[186]

These uses of coincidence and reversal—the miracles—emphasize the role played by circumstances external to the characters—chance and fate—forces we cannot control. By giving chance and fate major roles, essentially good people can suffer. Because the forces are outside their control, any moral onus is removed from the protagonists, allowing them to be afflicted without personal blame or flaw. Their suffering, then, can achieve nearly tragic intensity and still sustain the viewer's sympathy. Although there is seldom a clear, overt, or conscious causal relationship implied between the characters and their fate, there is often a logical one. The effects of contingency and chance make it clear that events could have turned out differently. That they turned out as they did implies not that the events were bound to happen, but that there is some underlying moral order to the world. Such contrivances may underline the contingent nature of fictional causation and lay bare the tension between story and plot, but they are so conventionalized that they seldom ripple the surface of our anticipation.

However, sometimes the reversals, recognitions, or rescues are too late, reminding us that time is irreversible and causing a rupture in our notions of fairness. Franco Moretti writes about untimely deaths in literature, "This is what makes us cry. Tears are always the product of *powerlessness.* They presuppose two mutually opposed facts: that it is clear how the present state of things should be changed—and that this change is *impossible.*"[187] That is, it is something that, if we had our way, would not happen. On *Ryan's Hope* (November 22, 1988), a "good" and loving character, Joe Novak, a decent guy, dies from a bomb planted in the family music box. Even though there was quite a bit of prepublicity about Roscoe Born's return to the role on a "limited" contract, and even though the home audience had known about the bomb for several days, his death brought tears to this viewer's eyes.[188]

Sometimes the recognitions move us, not only because they are too late, but because they are the consequence of a series of causes seemingly beyond a character's control. On *The Young and the Restless,* after a courtship of over a year, Victor Newman and Ashley Abbott are finally about to marry when Victor learns that his soon-to-be ex-wife, Nikki, has developed a possibly fatal, unnamed disease. Victor tells no one about the illness and decides to remain by Nikki's side. At the same time, Ashley discovers that she is pregnant. Ecstatic, she goes to tell Victor, but before she can talk to him, she overhears a conversation that he is having with Nikki's doctor and she learns of Nikki's illness. She decides to break off with Victor (so he will be free to stay with his wife) and to have an abortion. When Victor learns of Ashley's pregnancy and her planned abortion, he rushes to the hospital but arrives seconds after she has had the operation. Upset, Ashley takes off for New York City and is soon found wandering aimlessly in Central Park. Unable to speak even her name, she is diagnosed as having had a nervous breakdown. Later, when Nikki learns that she is in remission and dashes off to tell her husband, she comes across Ashley (well again and back in Genoa City) and Victor, speaking intimately in a secluded grove. Desiring to free herself in order to indulge her growing affection for her psychiatrist, Ashley decides to come forward with the truth and explain to Victor why she has broken off with him. Nikki misrecognizes the meeting as a sign of Victor's continued affection for Ashley, and decides not to tell him of her remission. Right after Ashley marries her doctor, Victor discovers that Nikki has been deceiving him (1986–1987).

This, as well as most of the storylines already discussed, with their emphasis on the intertwining layers of secrecy and revelation, on obstacles and nonfulfillment, on tragedy and trespass, and on loss and frustration, illustrates the prevalence (and the narrative importance) of both coincidence and the concealment of important information. Acts of omission are often more important than acts of commission. The "truth" is constituted as a secret and thus an object of suspicion, a secret whose dramatic discovery is doubly pleasurable because of the attempt to conceal it.[189]

But it is not simply a matter of something being unknown or the character being unaware; rather, it is usually intentionally hidden and there is often an ironic asymmetry between the "appearance" and the "reality." And, of course, despite the confidence of the character, the viewer generally knows that things are not what they seem and is able to participate with privileged insight in the situation. The spectator (unlike the characters) recognizes her hero or villain beneath all the masks, double identities, and misfortunes.

Soaps are full of "falsehoods" which the knowing viewer can be relied upon to see through by a counterassertion, as when, for instance, George Rollins tells Paul Williams how much he values his honesty and friendship, and the viewer knows that Paul is having a secret affair with George's wife, Cassandra; or when George, suspicious that his wife is being unfaithful, goes to Paul's detective agency to hire Paul to check up on Cassandra (*The Young and the Restless,* summer 1988). The pleasure in interpreting is increased by seeing a situation or a meaning that "is not there" and which contradicts the meaning that "is" there. The awareness or recognition of the "true" nature or intention of others or seeing someone unaware of being in a position that is so different from what he or she thinks—knowing the secret—is part of the enjoyment of soaps precisely because the viewer can imagine delightful new developments. (For a while in the mid-1990s, one of the characters on *General Hospital* was marketing a fragrance named "Deception" and even the simplest dialogue was full of innuendo and double meanings.)

The revelation of secrets *does* often release more intrigue and more lying, denial, or deceit, and generally numerous confessions. As Brian Rose points out, however, the process of discovery is more in the service of narrative momentum than it is a stimulus of suspense.[190] On soap operas, revelation is constructive. Unlike the opening of Pandora's box, where the pursuit of knowledge releases destructive forces, forces that should have remained in darkness and in silence, on soaps it is darkness and silence themselves that are dangerous and a burden for as long as they remain unpenetrated. While Sloan Carpenter is struggling to accept his feelings about his gay son's death, Viki Buchanan counsels him, "Whatever it is you've been keeping inside, I can see how terribly it's hurting you. It won't stop until you let it go" (*One Life to Live,* August 31, 1992).

Laura Stempel Mumford argues that soaps' treatment of the concept of privacy actually redefines both the public and private spheres. Characters live much of their lives in spaces whose communal nature make privacy impossible. Personal life is open to public scrutiny. Jonas's bar, the Jabot offices, the General Hospital lounge, and the many multigenerational family mansions are all spaces where secrets are exchanged and indiscretions are enacted—and often overheard or observed. On soaps, characters are very seldom alone. The dominant mode of representation may be a close shot of an isolated person in the frame, but when the camera pulls back someone is watching, eavesdropping, or turning the doorknob to enter the room where the other has been snooping. Ashley Abbott's muteness was moving because it left her so atypically alone. According to Mumford, soaps collapse the private into the public, or, drawing on Christine Geraghty, colonize the public sphere and claim it for the personal.[191]

Even when a character declares a need for privacy, the audience shares knowledge of his or her secret. In *One Life to Live*'s 1992 homophobia story, the minister accused of being gay asks people to respect his privacy and steadfastly refuses to disclose his sexual preference, but the audience is aware, from previous broadcasts, of his heterosexual involvements and that the rumor had been started by a woman whose advances he had spurned.[192]

The Sloan Carpenter case and the homophobia storyline is an exception, however. More often there is obvious furtiveness and deception on the part of the concealer (more than merely needing privacy or needing to control access to one's personal domain). Soap opera characters seldom say that they want to be alone and they seldom withdraw from public life unless they are concealing something (Margo Hughes's flight from Oakdale, for example, conceals her pregnancy from her husband and from her police partner, the father of her child [*As the World Turns,* fall 1988].)[193] Characters never have privacy. In order to make sure that the viewers are aware, they confide their secrets, lies, and deceit to another character (or, occasionally, muse about it in soliloquy). (Margo, in this case, tells her mother, her father, and her brother of her pregnancy, her planned flight, and the child's paternity.) The viewers have already been taken into the concealer's confidence, have intruded upon the unspoken. Therefore, there is little sense of violation when secrets are probed. Still, *As the World Turns*'s secret codes and bank accounts, hidden diaries, and locked rooms all testify to a felt need for additional protection and to an obsessive, conflict-ridden longing for the private, to be let alone. (One of the many contradictions of a homemaker's life is that despite her isolation she nevertheless feels the need for time for herself and a sense of a private life.)

Aloneness and isolation are pictured in the single images on the screen, yet at the same time constantly subverted as the characters talk things out and as the stories tell of endless commingling, caring, and sacrifice for others. The narrative discourses of soap operas legitimate the preoccupation with the private, the personal. They are both a symptom and a ratification of the socially constructed role of women in the domestic sphere (the effect and the support of women at home in their "felicity" and confinement).[194] Watching soaps engages our own loneliness, endlessly titillating but never confronting it. For soaps entice us to care by weaving webs of relationships,

relationships on which we in turn rely. Yet however cunning they may be in their power to arouse our desires, they are not, in themselves, able to satisfy them—or to liberate us. The privacy of our home is invaded by these longings at the same time that we are being comforted through the fantasies we extract from the fictions.[195]

We seem to take a certain pleasure in the uncommon aspects of others' lives, that which transcends the ordinariness of our everyday life. (*The Star*'s report of an eight-year-old who delivered a ten-pound baby, for example, or the *National Enquirer*'s announcement of Hillary Clinton's lesbian affair, or the *San Francisco Chronicle*'s article about the oriental carpets and faux crystal sconces in the porta-potties at a Hollywood benefit.) Does part of the pleasure lie in the fact that other people's lives, at least, are knowable? According to Brooks, this clarity is a primordial concern of melodrama.[196] Lynne Joyrich notes that in melodrama, personal and psychological conflicts are externalized "so that they may become clear as fundamental forces."[197]

Even if we waver between enchantment and denial—or hesitate between a certain playfulness and a more maternal concern—perhaps we can also read the landscape of our lives in that other world. This may be, as Christine Gledhill suggests, how the unthinkable and the repressed achieve a material presence.[198] If so, then the excesses of the daily broadcast should be seen as a form of emphasis, markings of intensity, italicized versions of the real. Brooks writes that nineteenth-century melodrama constantly reached toward a sublimity of expression, maintaining a state of exaltation where hyperbole became the "natural" form of expression because anything less would convey only the apparent, banal drama, not the "true" moral drama.[199] On soaps, however, because they appear nearly every day and because the rules of the genre are so ingrained, the exceptional, the larger-than-life, the uncommon play against a more ordinary reality that builds, over time, the known and the familiar, which we come to take for granted.

A new soap, or an unfamiliar soap opera, at first seems almost tongue-in-cheek, so over the top that it might be a parody.[200] But once we become involved with the stories and the characters, we generally grow accustomed to them and the excess is no longer so laughable. There is a to-and-fro between an overheated excess—which catches the imagination and almost seems to wink at the viewer—and the knowledge that it will, eventually, settle down to a more ordinary probability. One pulls against and expands the limits of the other.

Of course, it is possible that even after becoming involved in the stories, some viewers will continue to feel the outrageousness provokes irony and distance. Mary Ellen Brown points out that the opportunity to discuss soaps can bring out a playfulness and even some self-parody. She quotes a discussion about *Days of Our Lives* that was full of raucous laughter, which began with one of the fans admitting, "If you try to explain it, it really does sound absolutely ridiculous."[201]

Whereas classical poetry uses verbal extravagance to praise love and flatter kings, excessive language when used on soap operas is much more quotidian. It is often coupled with an inflated diction and acting style, a more general, hyperbolized manner of expression. Phoebe Wallingford, for example, seeing her nephew, Dr. Chuck Tyler, with Donna Sago at a night club, tells her husband Langley, "If they get back together again, I'll just *perish* from the earth" (*All My Children,* February 5, 1990).

However, most of the hyperbole is in the form of exorbitant situations and unrestrained actions. Paul Williams, about to be falsely convicted for murdering George Rollins, fakes his own suicide, escapes from jail, and in several elaborate disguises pursues the person he thinks is the true murderer, his former lover, George's wife, Cassandra (*The Young and the Restless,* fall 1989). The intensity of the feelings and the relationships seems to justify the excess, the audacity, and make them acceptable. The unmitigated Manichaean terms of the story proffer "life" as a heightened drama, a moral combat. After a couple of months of pursuit, when Cassandra is finally brought into court to answer charges for murdering her husband, the prosecutor tells the bail-hearing judge that another person, Paul Williams, wrongly accused, has died for her crime. When Cassandra's defense attorney replies by telling the judge that there is only circumstantial evidence against her, Williams, still in disguise, angrily steps out of the gallery to address the court. When the judge asks who this man is, Williams, in grandiose gestures, tears off his hat and fake mustache, and speaks his name. Cassandra, fully acting out her emotions, faints, and we fade to black and a commercial (January 15, 1990).

Such hyperbole (in dialogue, delivery, or situation) invites the viewer to interpret metaphorically, parabolically, or ironically, implying some other, more general or more important, significance. There seems to be another articulation being implied, another level of meanings or volume of consequence or opportunity. The metaphoric or analogic implications of Duke Lavery's suaveness with champagne might be that it almost *exemplifies* something else, perhaps a more general proposition about chivalry or love.

This resonance is part inference, part hypothesis, part conjecture—an exercise in imagining. Given the practical demands of our everyday lives, our perceptions are usually fairly directed and selective. Personally, I can seldom give relaxed attention to all events and there is not always much room for creative cognitive adventure in my daily life. But isn't that part of the appeal of soap operas? A new viewer might understand them more literally or less imaginatively than one who is familiar with the backstory and has more resources for play.

The soap world appears to be full of chaos and conflict: people are not what they seem; situations are shrouded in double meanings; psychological forces are impelled into the open space of familial battles. But at the same time it is a world that is clearly polarized and unambiguous; that is, there is a moral order implied in the chaos and conflict, an almost excessive clarification and rationality. Perhaps this heightening and intensification of experience has an expressionistic purpose.

Soaps neither address the viewer the way the "classic realist text" does, nor do they attempt to engage the viewer with issues of surface, representation, or narration. But this is not to say that they are no more than meets the eye. The refusal of a realist economy, as Nancy K. Miller points out, may mask the inscription of another. This other may appear silent or unarticulated ("It may simply be inaudible to the dominant mode of reception"), but it is not absent.[202] To experienced viewers, soaps invite an understanding as metaphorical dramas pointing to hidden forces and truths.

Maybe soap operas also point to a need for more than the ritual pieties of family. The stories of confrontations of good and evil, the instances of grandiose moral exchanges, the workings of "chance," the heroic gestures, all postulate a significance that goes behind or beyond surface, representation, and narration. This melodramatic mode of excess isolates and dramatizes a morally legible universe, stages its existence, and affirms its relevance to daily life.[203] If tragedy's anguish is from "one noble conviction coming into conflict with another,"[204] melodrama "becomes both legible and consumable," writes Joyrich, "in the clash and play of . . . visible oppositions."[205] If tragedy allows us to grieve, soap operas, with their roots in nineteenth-century melodrama's constant state of exaltation, the fiery right versus fervent wrong, exhorts the world to live up to our impassioned expectations. They are, to recall Cixous, our "elsewhere" where desire makes fiction exist.

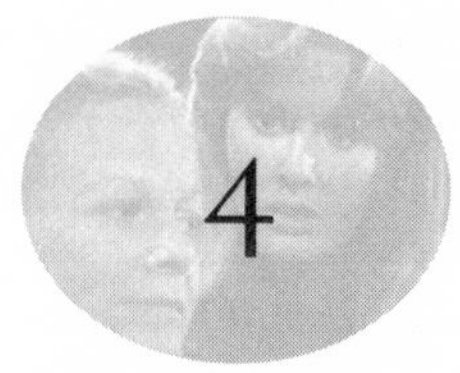

They who live to please—must find their enjoyments, their happiness in pleasure!
—Mary Wollstonecraft

The Power of Pleasure; or, How to Enjoy Soaps

Our pleasures and displeasures—like our desires—are frequently private and, because they are often rooted in and draw upon unexpressed or unrecognized feeling, they are sometimes difficult to acknowledge or talk about. Indeed, we sometimes live and feel in ways that we cannot put into words. Our feelings and what things mean to us, besides being difficult to know, may also be too important, too precious, to share. Understanding, reporting, and interpreting subjective experience is certainly a difficult task. There can be a substantial rift between feeling and telling. But if we avoid interrogating the personal, we will never learn the specific ways our conflicts and contradictions are lived—and we run the risk of denying the political in our daily lives. Accounts of personal experience can point to senses of pleasure—and discontent—that, though they surely have a material basis, might be difficult to articulate (or experience) in other than subjective terms.[1] Does part of the power of pleasure lie in the very invisibility of the experience? Possibly. The degree to which it resists language may be an exact measure of how closely we have come to understand something as important. Perhaps we can never talk *about* pleasure, only within it.

There may be some insights in the tension between how we live and feel, and what we think we are allowed or able to express. Most of us have been taught to suspect or distrust our deepest and nonrational knowledge and cravings; the threat of passion when it implies selfishness or self-indulgence and uncontrollability is a disturbing possibility. From there, it is only a small step to the fear of our desires, a fear that keeps us docile, loyal, obedient. And it is another tiny step to the false belief that only the suppression of pleasure within our lives and consciousnesses can give us strength.[2] Sigmund Freud says that adults cherish their daydreams as their most intimate possessions and would often rather confess their wrongdoings than their fantasies.[3] Writing about literature, he suggests that part of the enjoyment of reading comes from the release of our mental tensions and perhaps, he goes on, "much that brings about this result consists in the writer's putting us into a position in which we can enjoy our own daydreams without reproach or shame."[4] Such pleasures are neither reflections nor consequences of personal power, but forms of personal power in their own right.

This chapter is an attempt to develop a compassionate understanding of how television soap operas—how these psychic and cultural pleasures and displeasures—work in women's lives.[5] It is also an attempt to understand the powers that arise out of our deepest desires (conscious or unconscious). If, as Audre Lorde puts it, "we have been raised to fear the yes within ourselves,"[6] if our desire pulls us toward self-denial, then what are the possibilities that watching soap operas offer us?

I mentioned earlier that this study would have to be sensitive to differences within viewers: we need to acknowledge that household responsibilities are often met with both ambivalence and creativity, and that there may be both divergence and diversity in our thoughts about daily life. However, it may sometimes be difficult to recognize the deep conflicts around fantasy, pleasure, and desire, and around the articulation of subjectivity. They are not simple processes structured around fixed "selves" which we either are or are not, nor are they sites of autonomous identification. Much as there is a struggle between forces of domination and resistance, there is also a dialectical tension between how we live (and this includes extracting pleasure in and from our lives) and how we would like to live. So this book is not simply about what it means to engage with soaps; it is also about the contradictions that structure our lives.

Some of the women I spoke with describe watching soap operas as almost therapeutic, a source of comfort as well as a distraction, both calming and exciting. Candy Lampropoulos talked about how she used soap operas during times of emotional stress: "[Watching soaps] distracted me in a way that a book wouldn't [or] starting a movie that I was not invested in any characters . . . So it was an easy distraction to slip into." Later she continued, "There is something comforting about just hearing the sound. It's something that's helped me through hard times, my divorce, adjusting to living alone, being in bed for five months [when I was pregnant]. It's like an old friend, you know. It is something familiar that's there for me. It has been very positive for me." She further elaborated, "It's the level of concentration that you have to give. When you're tired, when maybe depressed about things, you don't want to have to give as much concentration."

Ann Weinstock said, "If something is really bad in my life, if I'm upset about something—I can turn them on and get involved very quickly and so for a half an hour or an hour—I can just forget about what is bothering me. You can just kind of forget that you have three feet of water in the basement and it's gonna cost $50,000 to have it fixed, or your child has just called and said that life is coming [apart] and it's terrible and 'that and that' is awful. Even though you know twenty minutes later everything will be fine, you're not there and there's nothing you can do about it, and I find [watching soaps] very helpful for that." Ellen Seiter, a feminist academic, spoke about soap operas as an emotional resource while her mother was terminally ill, and the "use value of soap operas as a distraction" from pain and suffering.[7]

Diana Ortiz mentioned that when she was working during the day (boxing mail) she used a TV-band radio to listen to soaps. She still watched them at home on tape before she went to bed. One time when her VCR was broken and she couldn't watch her soaps she said that she noticed that she became "very cranky." She described watching soaps as a "relaxing time when you forget about everything." And "on Sundays, when I have nothing to watch, it's like [she laughs], it's really like depressing."

Charlotte Siegel is at home during the day but watches *General Hospital* on tape before she goes to bed at night. "My mother never read the Bobbsey Twins to me as a child, this is my regression . . . it's really my bedtime stories." When I first began teaching at night, I stayed home to prepare during the day and enjoyed watching a soap to unwind before taking a nap.

Perhaps that is why we tune in: it is an indulgent invitation to repose. Whether amicably settled into domestic banality or exhilarated by utopian dreams, many women are snaring an afternoon—or an evening—for quiet consolation.

The regularity, constancy, and familiarity of soaps are surely part of the comfort. For most of my lifetime, all three networks have scheduled soaps solidly from late morning until the late afternoon. Because of the flow of soaps, you can tune in anytime in the afternoon and find a soap opera—or a commercial. But if you miss an episode, either from absenteeism, preemption, or (a recent complaint) VCR malfunctioning, it is seldom redeemable.[8] This sense of potential loss might actually stimulate viewership. Jennifer Hayward quotes a mid-nineteenth-century sermon (around the time of the serialization of *The Pickwick Papers*) about the "great and grievous" evil of installment fiction. "The works of amusement published only a few years since were comparably few in number; they were less exciting, and therefore less attractive; they were dearer, and therefore less accessible; and, not being published periodically, they did not occupy the mind for so long a time, nor keep alive so constant an expectation."[9] It is the seriality, stories easily available at regular intervals, and the expectation that comes with such a steady narrative progression, that seemed most injurious to the clergyman, the habit-making aspect of serial fictions. As Candy put it to me, "I guess the feelings that I have definitely grow. I mean, time is important. If you watch every day—you get so invested." Although her schedule has changed drastically, Alisa Holen says that if she runs into any of her old Penney's co-workers, she always asks them what's happening on *The Young and the Restless*.[10]

Unlike theatrical film, which we can hear about from our friends and then go to see, soaps must be witnessed (or taped) at the same time to be shared. The women I spoke with who tape their shows also seem to watch them in a timely fashion, making sure of being current. None lets the episodes accumulate for more than a few days, unless she is on vacation. There is even timeliness to discussions on the Internet. Much of the discussion (75 percent to 80 percent on most days) is on the episode aired that day; people seldom comment on events that are more than four or five days old. There must be a sense of commonality created as we all watch together, a sense of belonging based on the shared experiences of viewers, providing women of diverse social groups with a basis for imagining interests and values in common.

Soap opera commercials often try to forge an imagined solidarity among women. Correctol laxatives, for example, tells us that "women don't have time for irregularity, but they are constipated three times as often as men." In an Always sanitary napkins commercial, a woman identified as "Jane" in a superimposed title speaks to the camera, extending her space into ours in an extremely close and intimate shot, and asks, "Did you ever wonder. . . ?" In another commercial, a mother assures her daughter and us that "every woman on the planet has that not-so-fresh feeling one time or another" and suggests Massengill douche "for that pure, fresh, absolutely clean feeling." "We all do it," claims Secret deodorant. A summer 1987 commercial for Bounce passed along the "testimony" of several women and even of the child of one of them about what the smell of the fabric softener reminded them of, by implication eliciting our opinions, as well.

Other ads provoke an experience of community as they proffer good advice from "one of our own." "Judy Kennedy, mother and Citrus Hill Plus Calcium technician," for example, offers us an accepted truth, "At fifteen kids don't want to be mothered anymore," and she wisely counsels, "You have to pick your opportunities. Citrus Hill Plus Calcium is one of those opportunities." Cybill Shepherd, in a commercial for L'Oréal hair coloring, looks into the camera and asks us, "Do anything wonderful for yourself lately? You should! We *all* should . . . we're *worth* it!" She seems to be proposing not only that this fictive "we" needs improvement and deserves indulgence, but also that the product can make us the exalted objects that we all agree we ought to be. Whether for hair coloring, lunchbox food, or back pain medication, these commercials are based less on competition among women (as we often see in the soap stories), than on a comradeship that is premised on the assumption that we are not alone in our wish to observe the procedures that ensure desirability. They are occasions to see one's self as not one's alone, but in community with others, a sort of collective self. This is important because any group gains a distinct identity not only from a shared material reality, but also from a shared consciousness, that is, from their "image of their communion."[11] Cybill Shepherd, Judy Kennedy, and the other individuals are both confirming and confirmed by this illusion of community.

One of Alisa's coworkers, Heather, began watching *One Life to Live* during her maternity leave (the show coincided better with her son's naptime than did *The Young and the Restless*).[12] When she went back to work, she had no time to watch, but on-line frequently in her new job, she was able to follow the show on ABC's web site. After corresponding with the volunteer who writes the daily recaps, she joined a Listserv of *One Life to Live* fans from all around the country. Her interest in *One Life to Live* was enough to integrate Heather into the group. The participants have exchanged Christmas cards and scanned photos. When the husband of one was diagnosed with cancer, she asked the list to pray for him, or think positive thoughts, or whatever they thought might help. After it was established that he was in remission, she made a trip across the country to meet and thank the participants. Friendships can start with what people have in common, a collective activity, like watching together, touching base with something familiar and dear, reminding themselves of what they share. Such continuity can enhance intimacy and create camaraderie among posters who do not know each other personally. Tania Modleski points out, "it is important to recognize that . . . [t]he fantasy of community is not only a real desire (as opposed to the false one mass culture is always accused of trumping up), it is a salutary one."[13] But if this is a community, it is fundamentally fragmented and celebrates not interdependence, but the narcissism of similarity. Marshall Berman describes modern experiences that cut across boundaries, that can be said to unite all people, "But it is a paradoxical unity, a unity of disunity: it pours us all into a maelstrom of perpetual disintegration and renewal, of struggle and contradiction, of ambiguity and anguish. To be modern is to be part of a universe in which, as Marx said, 'all that is solid melts into air.'"[14]

Dorothy Hobson reports that many of the British working-class women whom she interviewed perceived television and radio as their only connection with the "outside world" (not that it necessarily was their only connection, but that it was seen as such).[15] Listening to the radio or listening to or watching television were not mentioned as leisure activities, but as "integral parts of everyday life" (pp. 85–86). Hobson argues that the phone-in programs, which are important in counteracting the women's isolation, also "reinforce the privatized isolation by reaffirming the [supposedly] consensual position—there are thousands of other women in the same state, a sort of 'collective isolation'" (pp. 94–95).

American Christian television evangelists also often calculate on people's loneliness and isolation. The preachers directly address the camera and the viewer, using the imperative voice, with such instructions as, "Kneel by your television set. Close your eyes. Pray with me" (assuring the viewers that not only Jesus, but also the preacher, his on-screen entourage, and others in their homes, are with them). They also have telephone banks, inviting viewers to call a toll-free number: "Tell us how you feel. There'll be someone to talk to you."[16]

In one sense, this is a social community (imagine all those people kneeling by their television sets at the same time or all the members of the Listserv thinking good thoughts for the cancerous husband). But it is a community of separateness, a community that both is built upon and builds isolation. Arthur Kroker argues that the television audience is Jean-Paul Sartre's serial culture *par excellence,* a culture where absence is a mode of connection between people, where exterior separation is the negative principle of unity.[17] I would argue that the soap opera audience is Kroker's television audience *par excellence,* electronically composed and rhetorically constituted, the viewers isolated not only from each other, but also from their families, a serial unity experienced as a negative totality. The eighty million people across the country who tuned in to the final episode of

Roots in 1977 were mainly watching in families. More viewers than not who are watching soap operas are sitting alone (isolated in different places and, thanks to the VCR, perhaps even at different times) experiencing a public spectacle that is capable of being very private, but also capable of being shared. We might think of this as a dialogue between belonging and lonesomeness.

Many fan activities are opportunities to demonstrate not only enthusiasm, but also loyalty. Diana Ortiz claims that, at one time, as a teenager, she belonged to about twenty-five fan clubs.[18] Peggy Orr said that she often browses at a thrift shop not far from ABC's Manhattan studio and once bought a blouse that had the wardrobe tag of "Nina" (on *All My Children*). Lee Meltz told Peggy and me about the time she was shopping for a shower curtain and ran into the performer who plays Jeremy on the same show. They picked the same style curtain and Lee switched the two as they were checking out. She invited me to go into her bathroom and see "Jeremy's curtain" and gleefully reminded me that "hers" was in his bathroom. Diana insisted that she "always kept up with *General Hospital,* even when it was borderline cancellation . . . I even liked Laura when everyone hated her, in the beginning." Although Lee said that until we had begun speaking she had never told anyone she watched a soap opera, she was also proud of her fidelity and bragged that she had been watching *All My Children* for as long as it had been on the air. Awilda Valles's soap opera watching is famous in her neighborhood. She invited a protégée to the interview, a high school student who sometimes watched with her.

In this sense, the interview situation itself might be seen as not only an instance of validation but also one of solidarity. People's eagerness to talk to me should be seen, not only in light of their generosity, but also as a potential for bonding. A woman I met at a party, a travel agent in Miami, invited me to call her collect anytime I wanted to talk about soap operas and reiterated the offer as she was departing. Another, after my tape recorder broke down, offered to return the next day with her own tape recorder. All the women have questioned my own viewing practice and many asked if I watch soap operas for myself, for enjoyment, or if I watch them for my work. "Is this for pleasure or because you have to?" Several times when I asked someone for what she thought was a commonsense answer, she would reply, "Well *you* watch them, don't you?"

Soaps seem to be seen by many women as gender-specific behavior. They often fuss about their mates' disapproval or insist that the men in their lives really *do* like them. For example, one woman told me that her husband resents very much that she watches *General Hospital,* "He's very funny. If he comes upstairs and if *General Hospital* is on, he'll say, 'Well, I guess I have to go downstairs until *this* is over!' I have a theory that—there is a modicum of interest and an addictive quality about these programs and the reason that he gets so vituperative about it is that he is afraid he's going to be too interested in it and get hooked on it himself."

One of the first things that Lee Meltz mentioned was that her brother became "addicted" after a week of delivering groceries to her during his lunch break while she was laid up with a broken foot. And Candy Lampropoulos, as I mentioned in the first chapter, immediately after being introduced to me told me that all the men in her life had watched soaps with her. The predominance of these remarks made me wonder if they were taking the opportunity to speak about gender issues "among women," or if it was a preoccupation. I began consciously to avoid directing their attention toward gender, but the references continued.

Almost all the women I interviewed mentioned beginning to watch with female friends or their daughters or their mothers. Peggy Orr told me, "My mom started me on *General Hospital* and *One Life To Live* when I was about nine." Lee said she had gotten so tired of her grandmother telling her that she had to be quiet when she was watching her soap that Lee began watching *All My Children* so she would have a soap "of her own."[19] For them, as for me, soaps mesh with memories of their childhood.

Charlotte Siegel was becoming annoyed with a close friend who was always talking about *General Hospital* until she began watching the show when her teenage daughter took it up; Charlotte and her friend have been talking together about the soap ever since. If she's home during the early afternoon, Ann Weinstock very efficiently watches *The Young and the Restless* for the ten or fifteen minutes while she's eating lunch, "and that's enough so that I can talk to my mother about that." Lee and Peggy had been acquainted for about ten years before they discovered that they both watched *All My Children;* soon afterward, they spoke with me in a double interview and six months later Lee mentioned that they now often meet to discuss the soap opera and it had become a bond between them. Mary Ellen Brown found several already constituted soap opera discussion groups when she began her study.

Candy, her husband, and a very close friend all watch *All My Children,* "So we share that, so we can kinda make fun, you know, and laugh and guess, whatever, together." Two of the women I spoke with mentioned that they often conversed together about how they felt the show should evolve.

"[We] would speak and divine how we would do it if we were doing it." Another woman told me that she and a friend "have this dialogue every couple of weeks about what's going on on *The Bold and the Beautiful* and what's going to happen and *inevitably* we are wrong!" and, "We think that we're better than the writers on *The Bold and the Beautiful* because we come up with things that are more interesting." She mentioned that she used to enjoy speculating with another friend; they imagine what might happen *if*. . . . "We used to do it with 'General,' one or the other of us, maybe it's an easier show to read, but one or the other of us would come up with something and say [laughing], 'Oh! My God, that's good, Alice,' or 'Oh, Wilma, you're so smart!'"

Forecasting is also an important part of the dialogues on Internet bulletin boards and chat rooms, as is conjecture about off-screen romances, performers who are about to be written out, and lines ad-libbed. Posters also often express pleasure and displeasure with what the writers are up to or the way a storyline seems to be going. On Yahoo!'s *All My Children* board, gigi_cam writes, "I adore AMC, but I wonder what the writers are thinking when they bring someone as lame as Esther back to the show. As many great villains, vixens, and troublemakers as they've had, you think they would do a little better than this." And jimiphil agrees: "With all the people to make a return/we get/ester/and not even the pitiful ester that we came to know and loath/but the evil bitch that shes become/god its time for some heads to roll in the writing department. . . ." But _elfin_ approaches the problem more structurally: "Given that they needed Stuart to disappear for a bit . . . but basically not be in danger as he recovers, this was actually a pretty logical choice. Esther is not here as a villain but more as a plot device. In soap logic, this seems to make more sense than anything" (May 11, 2000). Under the subject line, "The show's going down the tubes," fmelcarek, on the same board, aggressively expresses annoyance: "When are the writers going to beef up this show? . . . I have watched this show since the beginning of it's run and I have never seen it get so bad. It seems that they are running out of story lines. . . ." Once again, jimiphil agrees: "The show has been going downhill for months and now without janet i cant bear to watch it . . .you know its really bad when you turn to 'passions' and enjoy it." Cobris suggests tossing out "their writing staff and hir[ing] several of us." And "I'll be dipped if these boards aren't a hellvua lot more fun than the actual show" (May 18, 2000). "Okay, what do they think, we are stupid?" wrote morris 2280, on ABC's *All My Children* board (August 17, 2000).

The prevalent attitude toward the writers seems to be "If we can see this then why can't [they]?" as one fan put it.[20] "Please, tell me she won't have that ugly clown outfit on tomorrow," one *The Young and the Restless* board participant commented on Jill's pregnancy wardrobe.[21] Although based on critical interpretations of storylines, characters, and costumes, these more vitriolic attacks on the production staff are seldom mitigated by "IMO."

But for many women, watching soaps is not without conflict. One of the students in my "Women and the Media" class told me, "It's funny, too, because until I took your class, I never would tell anyone that I watched soap operas, never. It's something I had done all of my life—all of my adult life. When I was getting ready to write the soap opera paper, I thought, 'This is nothing to be ashamed of. This is fun.'" Another woman, of working-class background, spoke tenderly of her memories of her mother and her grandmother watching soap operas. Yet later she called watching soap operas her only "flaw." Like many other regular viewers, she associates soaps not with misfits or dreamers, but with the "typical" housewife, itself an occupation regarded with quite a bit of ambivalence. This woman works full time as a hairdresser, goes to school, and occasionally also cuts some additional clients' hair after hours in her apartment. "I work six days a week, fifteen hours a day; that's my average week, I work very hard. And I feel like, God, I'm out there and doing so much and I still watch soap operas? You know, it's like I still can't get out of that housewife mentality."

Another woman, who was educated as a lawyer and had a more privileged upbringing, mentioned that she remembered the family maid listening to soaps on the radio. "I found out after a while that my mother had been watching *As the World Turns* for twenty-five years and had never mentioned it." When asked if it was embarrassing, she laughed and said, "Yes, it was the kind of thing, you know, people like us didn't watch soap operas!" But after she began to watch *General Hospital* with her own teenage daughter, "And then I branched out, it was like this whole new world." She is one of the women who said that she enjoyed speculating about the show with friends; however, at the end of the interview, when I ask her if she would like me to use her name if I quoted her, she immediately requested that I use a pseudonym: "I'm still ashamed enough."[22]

Perhaps the pleasure and displeasure are entwined? Are these necessarily incompatible feelings? One begins to wonder if part of the experience, part of the entertainment, is in doing something that is disapproved of, or secret, or if it is possible that part of the appeal is precisely because their husbands or established critics find soaps so unappealing. Viewing seems to be, for some women, women whose lives are full of commitments, an area of autonomy, a place and time of free will and a certain freedom, a site of possibility.

Yet when I asked one very poised, articulate woman (who was also raised in a home where the household help listened to radio soap operas) if she ever spoke to others about soap operas, the space between us thickened, her tone lowered, and she responded slowly, "I'm sort of defensive about it because—[you have] much more education than I have—I only have two years of college. I think that if I had the degree of education and all and your credentials that I would be much freer talking about it in front of other people. I think that with me the package is: very little formal education and soap operas equal bimbo. With you, it would be: that's your little *mischegas* [craziness], that you like the soap operas." Social distinctions are maintained through exactly such expressions of embarrassment, disgust, and exclusion. No wonder we feel guilty about our pleasures.

Minu Lee and Chong Heup Cho studied middle-class, college-educated Korean women in the United States and found that their husbands compared their viewing choices to the tastes of a housemaid, someone at the bottom of their social order, making them feel shameful for damaging the family image and honor.[23] Soaps force social differences in our faces: not only class differences and the differences between men and women, but the range of differences among women as well.[24] My cousin was so embarrassed when I grabbed hold of the most recent issue of *Soap Opera Digest* at the supermarket checkout that she made me put it in a separate bag from her groceries. When I mentioned this curious act to Natalie Portman, a well-read, culturally savvy neighbor of mine, she immediately replied, "Naturally!" Telling me about a friend of hers whose "whole family" (later revealed to be only the women in the family) watched soaps, Natalie proclaimed that she could see why someone who was home all day with kids might watch, but not this highly educated, career-oriented woman! "Do we have to *watch* them?" one of my classmates asked when I announced I would be talking about soaps in a graduate seminar the following week.

Although women viewers seem to be denied the solace of "respectability" and "good taste," many of the women I interviewed seemed to feel they had an intuition for the divine where others find only coarseness. They also seemed confident that they deserved some pleasure. Yet, at the same time, many of them, especially the more middle-class, felt that watching soap operas was an activity of little worth.[25] Echoing the Frankfurt School's concern for the degradation of "free time," many seemed to distinguish between "real pleasures" and "mere diversion."[26] Candy, who worked as a social worker before she became a mother, for example, said, "There were times that, I mean I was very involved with the soaps after I had the baby, and so when I first started making friends and stuff, I would try to get together before one o'clock or after three. And I thought that that wasn't very good. I have relaxed about that." Hanni Lederer, a retired bookkeeper, mentioned that she loves classical music and had expected that when she stopped working she would play the piano more; an activity she clearly felt was worthwhile. Instead, she finds she watches two and one-half hours of soap operas each weekday—including one show that she doesn't really enjoy. And she feels that if she didn't watch that show, she "could do something more constructive" with her time.

When I asked Charlotte Siegel if she watched any soaps other than *General Hospital,* she giggled and told me how she was once convinced to watch *The Bold and the Beautiful* but wouldn't allow herself to get committed. "I'm very involved in volunteer work for our synagogue, that's my, you know, my work now. I don't really do anything that's income producing. So I just couldn't do, I mean, I'm not ashamed of watching *General Hospital* but I could not—something stops me from getting involved with the other ones."

My mind was stirring. Charlotte's moving testimony reminded me that how we spend our day can become an important source of self-esteem. What we do often translates to what we "are." In a world where women's work is often defined as contributing to some common good, where unselfish devotion is still the ideal of wifely behavior, and where personal growth and self-fulfillment are supposed to lead one into productive relationships with others, how one spends one's free time is often fraught with tension.[27] As we saw in Chapter 2, the relative autonomy of women in the home places an enormous burden on their self-interested choices. Caught between obligation and freedom, soap opera viewers enter a "permissible" nether world, but one where desire can be transversed with contradiction. While it does not seem very helpful to dismiss soaps as merely the commodification of unconscious desires, watching soap operas may be one of the discursive sites where social classifications and psychological processes intersect, where ideology and fantasy conjoin, and where longing and loss are produced and reproduced through one another. Many of my conversations with viewers did seem to reflect real conflict about the unstable and suspect nature of pleasure, and, when it came to soaps, there often seemed more a sense of regulation than fierce abandon.

The seriality and segmentation probably lend themselves to a scheduled, ritualized viewing experience. Even those women I spoke to who tape their shows seemed to have a regular, habitual time for viewing them. If we are torn between necessity and freedom, family service and individuality, responsibility and romance, or duty and desire, watching soaps offers us both terms together. We can be seduced by the familiar, can revel in the trifles, the frolics, and the reckless misdemeanors, and can take comfort in the fact that, barring a change in the viewing schedule, soaps are reliable, recurring, faithfully there. "You just get into it, " Candy explained, "because you know these people, they're familiar, they're a part of your life, you know."

Seriality itself perpetuates the entrenchment of habit. For almost all of the women I spoke with, watching soap operas is part of a pattern of weekday life, another activity in a task-oriented perception of time. Anne van der Does, for example, described her day to me by talking about what chores she performs at what part of the day. She had an analogic sense of time in which each moment is seen in relation to other possible moments. This is very different from time on soaps where each moment exists only for itself, soon to be replaced by another (in an almost digital effect), fantasy time, dream time, relief from the discipline, duties, and obedience of home life, and opposed to the profaned time of everyday life, which relentlessly subordinates all things to itself.

Some of the women who mentioned performing chores while watching, also spoke about how they felt soaps were particularly suited to distracted viewing. Candy, for example, told me, "When we rent films, Senovia has to be asleep, I have to be settled down. I know that I have to give more concentration. Whereas when I start the soaps I can still wash the dishes, feed the cat, do all these things, and then I can be right into it. . . ." Hanni said that she sits silently and immobile during the two shows she likes the most, but sometimes straightens up or puts on makeup during the show that she least prefers.

The woman whom I mentioned in the second chapter, whose children are in school and now views alone, sewing for her family while she is "watching" *Days of Our Lives,* continually denied that she enjoyed the show. It is possible she used the sewing to assuage her guilt over what she sees as self-indulgence? A very conscientious woman, she told me that when she quit work during the last six weeks of her first pregnancy, she didn't go out because she was so embarrassed not to be working. Denise

Bielby and Lee Harrington tell of a woman who stopped watching *General Hospital* during one job-hunting period because she didn't want people to know that she was at home without anything "productive" to do. Once she was employed again, she resumed watching.[28] Another woman told me that she felt that for a while she had "gone overboard." When I asked her what she meant by that, she said, "I was really watching too much of it" and "always knew what was going on" on all four ABC soaps. When I asked her if she sat down and watched the whole afternoon, she quickly responded, ". . . never sit down, having them on in the background when I'm paying bills, cooking, putting away."

Most theorists have seen the film spectator positioned either in terms of identifications or desires, generally along gender lines. While this might be relevant for the conventional Hollywood film, it doesn't seem to operate with soap operas, and maybe not for television in general. The furtive pleasures that Christian Metz writes about are based on the experiences of a darkened theater and are not really applicable to the domestic viewing circumstances where the television is usually part of many activities going on (or available) concurrently.[29] Even in houses with a separate television room, it is seldom a black box or velvet light trap. Such TV rooms have windows, magazines, family photos, and other objects of distraction. And even if we were to watch soap operas in a black box, the commercials, newsbreaks, network spots, and promos for official websites would certainly mediate any identification. Even if they were "interruption" free, soap operas' narrative structure, the short sequences interspersing many characters and stories, would make any sustained identification difficult. Perhaps viewing film in a theater is not the best model of soap opera spectatorship. It may be that television offers very different kinds of attractions. Though TV shares with film many means of representation, it shares much of its institutional structure and the type and flow of its programming with radio. Most importantly, television shares radio's domestic reception, a part of the flow of household activities and living habits. It is a matter of both placement and positioning.

I would argue against seeing an easy concept of identification or a neat separation of cognition and affect. How we relate to the soaps and to their publicity and promotion is complex; soap operas articulate subject positions that are often multiple and contradictory, and our identification operates in relation to difference and dreams as well as to resemblance. It is not simply that we "are" or "want to be," or that we can put ourselves in the place of, or occupy the perceptual space of, a particular character. For example, as I have already noted, we often know more than the characters do during many of the stories. Our feelings for a character are certainly other than simply feeling "at one" with that character; they involve both psychological and critical processes. But our feelings for a character or a situation surely have some elements of desire. We are all looking not only at but *for* something.

Part of the process of watching soap operas is the fantasy of getting to know characters, as Candy articulated so well. In fact, we may feel that we know a character in a soap opera better than we know some of our own friends or colleagues; after all, we are privy to their "innermost thoughts and motivations."[30] Or we may feel we know characters with whose type we might not be friends in the course of our daily activities. *As the World Turns*'s head writer Doug Marland, in an interview about a new gay character on the show (fall 1988), said, "For a lot of people in the audience, Hank may be the first gay person they'll come to know."[31]

But in fantasy, identification can be multifocal and promiscuous (even the particularity of gender or other practical realities may be ignored); and it can be the result of highly ambivalent feelings. One of the women I have interviewed, for example, discussed Jack Abbott on *The Young and the Restless* and said, "I like him as entertainment. I wouldn't want to meet him; I mean I wouldn't want to get involved with him. I probably *would* like to meet him because he's sharp and sarcastic and—I can be like that!"

There is not much fear or danger in this kind of ambiguity or in this kind of relationship to a character. One might ask if these feelings mitigate, or perhaps satisfy, the isolation and fragmentation of our day-to-day experience. But perhaps they increase our dissatisfactions with our own alienated lives? If soaps' splendid characters and eventful moments are fascinating, encrusted with portent, then do we become, by definition, increasingly dissatisfied with the finiteness of our own life? It may be that soaps thrive on precisely these sorts of dissatisfactions, a basic and systemic discomfort with daily life.

The idea that we locate ourselves *in* characters, or merge with characters—or that the strong bonds between viewer and characters replace or overcome the weak bonds of family and friends—does not account for our analytical capacities, the thinking and imagining that are certainly a part of the viewing experience. Being "invested" in characters and their adventures, be it Erica's shenanigans on *All My Children* or the mysteries and miseries of suburban family life on *The Sopranos,* does not preclude a critical self-consciousness about viewing.

Even emoting can be reflexive. For example, although we may weep at a particular feeling of sadness (generally connected with a situation or an event), there is also another type of tears, tears that are admittedly self-conscious and enjoyed, where pleasurable feelings and emotions are sought for their own sake (a sensuous delight in weeping).[32] Although tears of sensibility seem "justified" by the moving work, tears of sentimentality are thought by many to be an artificial and gratuitous indulgence.[33] Nonetheless, many of the women I spoke to mentioned "the pleasure of a good cry."

Though not everyone admits to weeping, those who do feel that it is a significant part of the experience. One woman told me, "You know, I really *live* [soaps]," and with a change of tone that seemed to indicate some embarrassment, she explained, "I cry." Awilda Valles bragged that she was crying so much when Jenny died on *All My Children,* even after the broadcast was over, that her grandmother came in to find out what was the matter. But she also wrote to the production company to tell them off for killing Jenny. She discussed other forms of emotion that she enjoyed, "I get excited, you see, I get *into it,* and when something bad happens, I throw myself on the floor and I go [laughing] 'You bit . . . ,' you know, I start yelling." Lee Meltz, who also watches *All My Children,* said that she cried for days when Jenny died, and later when I asked how she felt about us watching the show together, she admitted a bit of anxiety, "I *react,* you know. Like, 'Oh, my god, what happened? Why did this happen?'" Peggy Orr also admitted crying when Jenny died but then went on to justify her reaction by telling me what a "good" character Jenny was, good because she was such a nice person *and* because she was central in the narratives, affecting the lives of many other characters.

Marilyn Morales, herself a mother, admitted that she cried when one of the characters was sobbing over the fate of her child. "Don't you cry when Dixie's thinking about the baby and crying . . . that's emotional, right?" And later when we were talking about the child's father, Adam Chandler, an evil character: "He's terrible, but you imagine if it happened to you, how would you feel? I cried then." But I too found myself choked up at that scene, and I have no children.

Does crying need solitude or the company of those who do not make you feel ashamed?[34] Does it even need the suspension of disbelief? Candy Lampropoulos was telling me how much she cried when Brooke English's and Tom Cudahy's little girl died: "I was *very* upset." Then she laughed and said, "I was really upset because for years a creepy kid played her but then when they got a cute kid they killed her."

One of the more popular images of a soap opera viewer is someone who is unsure of the difference between reality and fiction (the "Nurse Betty" syndrome): women attacking the performer who plays a villain on the street or sending wedding presents to characters who marry on the show. What we think of as a knowing suspension of our disbelief, or our simultaneous interest in characters as people or story as event and characters or story as fictional devices, or our appreciation of the suspense of a tale whose ending we already know, involves a certain gap in our viewing experience, but one that is seldom disconcerting. For example, I overheard a conversation between my mother and my grandmother (who both watched *Days of Our Lives*). My grandmother had not seen the show in some time and my mother was bringing her up to date. What interested me about the exchange was that they were switching, without effort or confusion, from the narrative world of the characters and the plot to extranarrative information about the performer:

> Mother: They killed off Marlena, but she is on another show now.
> Grandmother: Who did it?
> Mother: The same guy who's been trying to for a while.

("They [the writers/producers] killed off Marlena [a character on *Days of Our Lives*], but she [the actress, Deidre Hall] is on another show now [the prime-time series, *Our House*]." "Who did it?" [refers to the character who killed Marlena]. "The same guy who's been trying it for a while." [refers again to character].)

When I asked Hanni if there were some characters she liked better than others, she paused and then referred to Jack Abbott on *The Young and the Restless* and said, ". . . he's a bastard. But then you give him credit for good acting [laughter], so you don't really dislike him!" If one reason soaps are so compelling is that they make us believe that we are actually getting to know about people and life, the characters are also, however, at the same time clearly constructs who meet the demands of narrative conventions.

The anonymous letters to the editor of *Soap Opera Digest,* like the postings on the bulletin boards and in chat rooms, regularly comment on writing, performance, and other aspects of craft. Couldn't these be the same people who give advice to characters or send wedding presents?[35] Are different viewing attitudes indicative of different viewers, or different postures, or the complexity of the viewing relationship?

A 1988 issue of *Soap Opera Digest* printed two letters to the editors commenting on the realism of the recent death of the character Jesse Hubbard on *All My Children.* Each letter both acknowledges the story as a construct performed and discusses the truth in the performance. The letter from P. B., in Washington, D.C., begins, "As a faithful viewer of *All My Children,* I was very sad to see Darnell Williams leave his role of Jesse Hubbard. I never cried so much for an actor on a soap opera. Every time I saw Angie [the character, his wife] after his death, I would cry. It all felt so real." The writer goes on to wish Williams good luck and thanks the writers for the Angie and Jesse story. K. H. in Detroit wrote, "Debbi Morgan [who plays Angie] deserves an Emmy. She is an excellent actress who constantly performs with such strong emotion and sensitivity that she can't help but touch everyone's heart. Her portrayal of grief at Jesse's death was so moving that I felt as though a member of my immediate family had taken the deadly bullet. I was able to feel deeply the hurt, pain and agony that she portrayed at that particular time. I cried when she cried, and I cried when she tried to be so strong. So, Debbi, I hope you get the prize you so richly deserve."[36]

Soaps are fictional and yet are about the world. We gently imagine, are immersed, but never completely leave familiar ground. Or as Wolfgang Iser writes of works of fiction, they are not about contingent reality, but about "models or concepts of reality."[37] Soap operas might be seen as both representing and interfering with—or challenging—our formulations of the world. They are, for many, both the product of our thoughts and a departure from the limitations of those thoughts. In fact, these plays of fantasy may come to signify a provocative arena of truth. Robert Musil observed in his novel, *The Man Without Qualities,* "If there is such a thing as a sense of reality, there must also be a sense of possibility." He went on to elaborate, "A possible experience or a possible truth does not equate to real experience or a real truth minus the value 'real'; but, at least in the opinion of its devotees, it has in it something out-and-out divine, a fiery, soaring quality, a constructive will, a conscious utopianism that does not shrink from reality but treats it, on the contrary, as a mission and an invention."[38] Our real is seldom very static.

A performance is true because it has a special relation to our feelings and our fantasies. It is familiar, and as its familiarity adds to its credibility, it seems genuine. Hanni spoke about her unhappiness with what she called the "unnaturalness" of *As the World Turns,* especially its convoluted families. "Nobody lives with their parents; everybody has been married to someone else. I don't think that real life is as mixed up as this show is." That is, she expects the show, or the writers, to know something of life. Yet she considers herself an experienced woman and doesn't easily cede authority if her beliefs don't coincide with those in the show.

The idea that a coherent and rationalizing authority creates an orderly world is not a given; it is negotiated. What is real is not universally acknowledged but is problematically at stake with each viewing and each viewer. As literary theorist Mieke Bal has noted, each interpretation is a proposal, a well-founded proposal that makes logical connections if it is to be accepted.[39] We speculate, form propositions, formulate views of our worlds. This is a way of historicizing the fictions, of naming and transforming them, domesticating them, making them our own. Discussing Cecily and Sean's broken romance on *All My Children,* Lee told me, "I think they really loved each other, I really think so," and then moments later, laughing, she forecast that Cecily's current "platonic" business-arrangement marriage with Nico would turn into love. "I can't wait! It's gonna be so great!"

Feminist soap opera scholar Charlotte Brunsdon wrote of her pleasure in seeing how her predictions come true.[40] Charlotte Siegel was telling me about the previous Friday's episode of *General Hospital* in which Frisco, not knowing his two buddies were aboard, blew up Domino's ship, "Let's see, if I were writing this, that's part of the fun, wondering if Anna Devane were comatose and on the brink of death and her daughter Robin will be without a mother; Bobbie is adopting Robert's new infant and maybe she'll be involved. . . . That's part of the fun!" When a group of four of us watched a Friday afternoon episode of *All My Children,* we speculated during the commercials about who had kidnapped Adam and Dixie's baby and if the child were still alive. When the show ended with a shot of the kidnapped baby in a hotel room, alone and well, we were all impressed when Awilda blurted out the name of a new suspect, one that we hadn't thought of before, but who seemed so dazzlingly logical, so elegantly rich in new possibilities. A circular relation is forged between soaps and their viewers; soaps offer a kind of salvation that depends on our obsession with them.[41]

This anticipation and the ability to run ahead of time, to see into the future, to play with the predictable, are forms of mastery, transforming the uncertainty of history into readable spaces. Both a stage for memory and a stimulus for making connections, the new meanings we invent make older ones visible and, likewise, the story forms we uncover elsewhere help us to sharpen our inventive tools. Such pleasures can be both a response and a threat to the alienation that is a part of everyday life. (What a lark to conjure Jenny back from the dead!) Of course, the rebelliousness of viewers must not appear too evident in the halls of the networks. Ironically, although the mass-market nature of soap operas makes viewer involvement a necessity, an ideal of passivity, conformity, and the comfort of being under the thumb of the sponsor is one of the major operating assumptions, "the reality" of the institution.

Hanni spoke to me several times about how she felt characters ought to behave (if they had the same scruples that she has), and then in the next sentence discussed the narrative necessities. For instance, commenting on Caroline Forrester on *The Bold and the Beautiful,* she remarked, "I don't know how I would feel if I were marrying the guy, but I think that I would say that he had a last fling. Why cancel the wedding. . . ?" and "Wait 'til she finds out . . . what a sleaze her father is!" When I asked her, "Do you think she will?" she replied, "Of course! Why would he be like that if she [weren't going to find out]?" And later, "You knew that Ridge wouldn't die [when he was shot] because then he would be out of the picture, right? Then there would only be half the story."

If the boundary between image and reality, the real and the acted, is constantly being challenged, is the line erased when guests (such as Hulk Hogan, Ron Darling, Roberta Flack, or Stevie Wonder) appear as themselves? Is it effaced when well-known film and television stars such as Liz Taylor, Carol Burnett, or Sammy Davis Jr. appear in temporary roles "as characters"? When Rosie O'Donnell was about to make a guest appearance on *All My Children,* July 30, 1996, fifteen-second spots (with clips) advertising the date of her forthcoming appearance played with this disjunction: "Is it Rosie O'Donnell or Naomi the maid?"

What happens when performers change soaps, or when characters are played by a new or substitute performer? Were we thrown into a tailspin when Daniel Pilon appeared as both Max Dubujak (on *Ryan's Hope*) and as Alan Spalding (on *The Guiding Light*) simultaneously (November 1988)? Or when a performer appears on commercials "in character"?[42] Is there a blurring of the distinctions between illusion and reality, sign and referent, rendering both artificial, as Jean Baudrillard might say? Is it, as Lawrence Grossberg claims, that television's "in-difference" to this distinction has changed its effectivity? That the distinction collapses and becomes irrelevant?[43]

It seems to me that it is not a matter of failing to distinguish between fact and fantasy or a narrowing of the distance between reality and fiction; they coexist. If there *is* a blurring of distinctions it is because neither fact nor interpretation is a given.

Watching soaps is experiencing a fantasy not our own but one which we believe to be true enough to draw moral conclusions about, to form opinions of, and to compare to our own life.[44] The more detailed our experience is with the subject or similar subjects, the more likely that pieces of what we know from the real world will infiltrate the glowing screen. This is an important part of the numerous "public service" stories and those that borrow from news headlines.

But the truth of soaps lies not simply in their referentiality, in their relation to our lives, daydreams, or nightmares, but also in their rhetorical power, in their relation to possibilities. They are at once relevant and imaginary. Yes, they are clearly make-believe, but they must somehow ring true to hold our interest. As Michael Riffaterre has demonstrated, adhering to the rules of the genre intensifies a story's authenticity. Truth, then, occurs when the narrative accomplishes the expectations it sets up.[45] Marilyn Morales commented on the "realism" of some exorbitant occurrence on *All My Children* and tried to justify the relevancy: "It *does* happen but it doesn't happen in—in everyday form of life, you know. It happens to someone else, not to me."

Many of the women with whom I spoke seem to take a playful stance, eschewing narrow-minded seriousness and dogma, seeing humor, gaiety, and mocking the outrageousness of what they watch. Ann Weinstock, for example, said that she thought that *The Bold and the Beautiful* was very funny. When I questioned what she meant (I found the show practically humorless), she replied: "I find things to laugh at not because they are meant to be funny, but because they're so bad, because they are so absurd and horrible." Others seem to take a critical position that tests the stories against their experiences and those of others. Awilda Valles, talking about the birth of Adam Chandler's son (*All My Children,* summer 1989): "That part was phony—he wanted a boy and he got a boy. Get out of here." But neither stance seems to prevent the viewer from becoming involved in the fictions. Awilda also told me that she cried when the newborn's life seemed to be in danger.

For soap fans, there doesn't seem to be a conflict between our quest for authentic, "human" stories that address essential concerns and our desire for triumphant stories that soar, in which determination, decency, and courage win out. Hanni reflected on a state of affairs on *The Young and the Restless,* "I was thinking today that if [Brad] would have told Tracy when Lisa first came into the picture, 'I have been married before.' You see, I'm a very honest person. He could spare Tracy and himself all this grief now if he would come out and explain it to her—I would have told it, and there wouldn't be a threat, but then," she laughed, "there wouldn't be a story!"[46] The warmth of her delight enveloped me like a hug.

Soap opera publicity and promotion encourage this comparison of the story and the real. In the November 15, 1988, issue of *Soap Opera Digest,* the news section by Seli Groves asked readers if the plot of a soap opera had ever helped them in their own lives and requested that readers send in their experiences.[47] A month earlier, the magazine published the results of a romance survey. Readers were asked to respond to eight questions. Six of the eight questions related the readers' own romances to those represented in soap operas, and one asked readers about some of the values they felt were important in "real-life" romances. Only one question referred solely to the representation of romance on screen. With this emphasis on the factual worthiness of the fictions, it is not surprising the magazine found that "[a]n overwhelming majority of our readers admitted that they did get ideas about how to conduct their personal romances from watching the soaps, and that they had, at some point in their lives, dealt with the same kind of problems soap characters have had to deal with."[48]

In December 1988, the magazine ran a feature entitled, "How to Dress Like a Soap Bride," which included instructive "dos and don'ts" from costume designers.[49] The idea of learning from soaps promotes the importance of decoration, personality, and individual behavior (that which is changeable, moldable, extrinsic): atomized solutions. This is in tune with commercials on the soaps for the sweepstakes, press-on nails, diet pills, and the cures for sinus headaches, greasy stains, boring dinners, and bad breath. It's also compatible with the many advertisements in soap opera fan magazines for self-improvement products that promise you "stronger, thicker hair," "a golden tan overnight," "the perfect bottom," a "round sexy bosom," or "surgery-free facelifting." Or the numerous weight-loss plans and training offers (such as computer-based paralegal training or home art instruction); or Dale Bronner's videotape, "How to Find and Keep a Husband in One Year or Less. Guaranteed!!!"; or moneymaking schemes involving home work or door-to-door marketing ("Get a LOT of Spare Cash for a LITTLE Spare Time" and "How to start your own big-profit home import business").[50] Our lives, too, are always at the intersection of uncompleted stories.

Many of the articles, photographs, and recipes in *Soap Opera Digest* could educate us on how to look like, eat like, or furnish our homes like a soap opera performer—a person who may have more visibility and a higher income than we have, but does not seem to have richer tastes. These "celebrities" are seldom pictured in more than fantasizable middle-class luxury. The performers in the photo sessions, and perhaps even more importantly, the characters on the screen, generally wear ready-made clothing, purchased off the rack and available to the viewer as well.[51]

The same is true of many of the home furnishings and accessories. The scenic designer of *All My Children* told me that the show often gets letters from viewers inquiring where a particular lamp or piece of furniture might be purchased.[52] *Soap Opera Digest*'s "How to Dress Like a Soap Bride" feature included the name of a store in Brooklyn where many of the television bridal gowns are selected, with the whispered assurance that the actresses sometimes return to the store to purchase gowns for their own weddings.[53] Comments such as this, plus the magazine's personality profiles, and the backstage stories in the "news" columns remind us that the performers (even more than the characters) are people like us, or people we know, not only subject to wages, contracts, negotiations, and competition in the workplace, but to the vicissitudes of home life, as well. In a January 1983 interview in *Magazine & Bookseller,* Marc Liu, then the new president and publisher of *Soap Opera Digest,* said that the magazine's "entire treatment of the soap opera field treats people as people. . . . We don't treat the characters and actors as *stars.*"[54] How we relate to a show certainly must depend on how it connects not only to our dreams and dissatisfactions but to what's available.

An ad in the February 1989 issue of *Daytime TV* offered, "THE ULTIMATE FANTASY TRIP BE A SOAP STAR" (a networking enterprise where participants can "design your own character and determine what he or she does," interacting by mail with other participants for an ongoing narrative).[55] *Another World* placed a two-page advertisement in the October 4, 1986, *TV Guide* inviting viewers to audition to be members of a jury for an on-screen murder trial and to actually participate in the decision on the guilt or innocence of the defendant.

Sigmund Freud, in a somewhat ominous tone, has written of the "unfulfilled but possible futures to which we still cling in phantasy, all those strivings of the ego which adverse external circumstances have crushed, and all our suppressed acts of volition which nourish us in the illusion of Free Will."[56] He reminds us that our fantasies *are* a reality of sorts, a psychical reality, plainly not the same as material reality, but nonetheless worthy of investigation.[57] Fantasy and reality are not opposed dualities, but coexist in a dialectic, as differentiations. In trying to come to terms with our lives we are always trying out new possibilities. If new information makes any of our beliefs problematic, the displaced beliefs do not cease to exist; they continue as mutual complements of the new. Difference, as Trinh T. Minh-hà notes, is an ongoing process.[58] New positions, new "authenticities," need displaced ones as oppositions that give meaning. Perhaps, then, the notions of fiction and truth are more useful when they are viewed "not in terms of dualities or conflicts but in terms of degrees and movements within the same concept," always interrelating.[59]

There has been much scholarly consideration (and concern) for how what we watch on television shapes the way we perceive reality, but less for how our perceptions of reality shape how we view our fictions. Our opinions and convictions may be partially formed by those fictions we imagine; however, our fictions are equally infused by our opinions and convictions. New understanding exists within and because of our previous knowledge and experience (even if it opposes them). We know our fictions through our histories, so there is necessarily a truth in every fiction. Our truths and our fictions can only be analyzed as a network of reciprocating processes.

We often attribute to characters a range of feelings and thoughts, passions, and sometimes even actions that we might never allow ourselves. To many, the oppositions, the transgressions, and the glittery and breathless excesses in soaps seem to bear special and often powerful symbolic charges. But I wonder, is it that the characters do what we would want to do but cannot or dare not do; that is, the appeal of an imaginary world where all is permitted? Or, instead of a specific act, belief, or attitude, is it the *idea* of transgression itself that is appealing? Just as dissatisfaction is often displaced into a desire for the ideal,[60] perhaps it may also be displaced into a desire to go beyond the limit.

Are the divisions and discriminations in the home structured, supported, or dissolved by the symbolic transgressions of hierarchy and order that operate in soaps? By the symbolic transgression of hierarchy and order of the viewing situation? Can these "transgressions" reveal the contradictions in the political construction of domestic life? The way that we understand our lives and the way that we understand our fantasies and our pleasures imply creative choices, responsibilities, and clarities that can be tested and threatened by ideology, whether spoken or not.

Maybe we watch soaps, not to discover what we are but to refuse what we are.[61] Hanni chuckled when she told me, "I *like* rich people. My husband always says I should have married a Rockefeller!" When a few of us were talking about the thrill of seeing soap opera performers in person on the street in New York City or at a guest appearance, Marilyn excitedly said, "I would like to meet Jack [on *All My Children*]. And I'd like to be looking *real* good!" Another woman (a single mother on public assistance), in a slightly more serious tone, tried to rationalize how Dixie used her pregnancy to break up Brooke's marriage to Adam (*All My Children,* spring–summer 1989) by assuring herself that "Any woman—if they had the opportunity to marry a millionaire, they're going to go for it." We are bound not only by verisimilitude, but also by the might be, could be, perhaps should be. Must we reconcile the mixed comforts of the familiar with the temptations of the possible?[62] (This may be an insight into the many virtual identities generated on-line.)

In what ways do we gain pleasure, strength, and support from these fantasies? Do they nourish the tangle of longings, feelings, and imaginings that we have inside us? Do we set ourselves off against these fantasies, using them as a sort of underground self?[63] Do we come to depend psychologically upon precisely those fantasies that are rigorously opposed and excluded on the social level? Perhaps our own "civilization" is most perceivable against a backdrop of "inappropriate" behavior. If so, isn't repression at work not only in the rejection of devalued social practices, but also in marking out our own superiority? The blandness that makes a soap opera character appear "unrealistic," the decorum that is nerve wracking, is in fact nothing other than the critical negation of the "outrageousness," the "colorfulness," and the "madness" upon which our legitimacy is partially dependent. Do we use soap operas as our own *Petit Guignol,* the very attributes and actions that horrify us becoming exotic costumes we can try on in order to play out the disorders of our own situation?[64] Remember Dorothy Richardson's coworkers in the box factory—"I don't see what's the use putting things like that in books. . . . They sound just like real, live people."[65] Plausibility in fiction may be overrated. Fictional characters should be allowed to do things that people would never do. And while fiction may begin on familiar ground, it projects beyond it, into the realm of the possible, the what if, the could have been, the ought to be.[66]

If we *do* fear the "yes" within ourselves, if our desire impels us toward self-denial, then watching soap operas offers us the possibility, not only to affirm our existence, but also to sense the exquisite tension between our own finiteness and our longing to push our limits. Perhaps this is the fissure that pleasure makes possible. Our finiteness may be outlined in the paradoxical form of the endless. "Finitude answers itself; it is both the identity and the difference . . . within the figure of the *Same.*"[67]

Pleasure is, by definition, always carried to its limits. But these limits are not stable. And through them we can sense, as though on their blank reverse sides, all that they make possible. If we see fantasy and pleasure as critical practices or as creative self-expression (although not always fully voluntary, immediate, positive, or unambiguous), if we see them as part of a process of questioning that can be both challenging and supportive, then we can understand the importance of the role of fantasy and pleasure in the dialectic of experience and consciousness and in the formation of subjectivity. In other words, it is not that watching soaps is simply ideologically inflected; it is also an ideological act.

In this sense, the activity and entertainment are both exploitative and to some degree utopian. That is, we invent imaginary resolutions to social contradictions, making the existing order more palatable and comfortable and, at the same time, in reacting to those same social contradictions, express collective fantasies.[68] However, we might also consider the possibility that these collective fantasies, besides being the solutions that let us go on, may function to mediate the contradictions of the social order. They might be seen as doubly complicit: papering over contradictions and at the same time building an imaginary world where the oppressed are important, comforted, and comfortable. This may be the kernel of utopian fantasy in soap operas, a utopian fantasy that may negate any radical potential.

However, the repression of fantasy, like the repression of the erotic, can lead to a crippling, deadening life. Although few of the women with whom I spoke would define themselves as active, politically adventurous feminists, they all had a clear idea of their material situation. Even if we accept our oppression, we are still critical of it. And many seem to find representations of their misfortune moving.

But recognizing one's situation is not the same as challenging or confronting it. It is even possible to recognize a situation, yet refuse to accept the feelings that indicate unhappiness. Ordinary life is structured through domination and subordination at its most intimate and banal levels. Although many of us are bored and uneasy with our lives, we have devised resistances in order to survive the experience of living contradictions. This often makes it difficult to understand our situation politically—or to put it to work. As Sheila Rowbotham has reminisced about 1960s women's groups, "How could you organize around a sense of emptiness?"[69]

Depression and torpor are not necessarily concrete enough to be discussed; yet they hang like an umbrella of confusion over much of our lives and many of our activities. Although few of the women I spoke to directly addressed the need for something of their own, many of their descriptions implied it. Marilyn watches *All My Children* when she's at home during the day but says that she doesn't worry too much if she misses a broadcast, and would never think of videotaping it. However, when she does watch it, she sends her six-year-old son away. "I tell him that's my time, don't talk to me, that's my time, I'm watching it. Go play with legos or watch the other TV. After two is your time." Charlotte told me, "It's *my* nighttime thing to do, when everything else is done for the day, and every bit of other television that I might want to see is over with, then it's time for *[General Hospital]* and that's when I watch it" and, "I look forward to it at night . . . it's a soporific . . . it's really for me." Or as one woman who lives in a two-room apartment with her husband and three-year-old daughter put it, "Maybe even more important than what I'm watching is the fact that I've set time aside and I'm by myself and I'm doing something just with me." Like many of Janice Radway's informants, many of the women I interviewed suggested that part of their enjoyment was exercising their right to time for themselves.

ABC's fall 1988 promotion spoke to this use in a comic spot that showed a bride, still in wedding gown, distracted by a mini-television, ignoring her groom in their bedchamber, intercut with scenes from one of ABC's soap operas, with an upbeat chorus of women singing, "My time for me / something to do / something to see / my time, don't talk to me / my time for me / watching my soaps on ABC."

Numerous commercials also try to capitalize on this need. One for Carefree pantiliners, for example, shows several sharp long shots of a woman in various outdoor activities (bounding down the steps of a brownstone, hailing a cab, relaxing in a park), each activity/identity represented by a different style of dress; then, in her bedroom, in a filtered close shot, she directly addresses the camera and confides that Carefree is "something I do for me."[70] Another, for Betty Crocker Sweet Rewards fat-free double-fudge brownies, opens with a mother and her two small children at a mall, shot through foreground chaos and with overlapping sound. The children run off, she stops to rest for a moment on a bench, and a male voice offers, "Hey, how about a little reward?" "How often do you do something for yourself?" asks Mon Cheri chocolates.

Stimulating desire and promising pleasure, such ads count on producing a would-be buyer interested in purchasing a continuous supply of the product. The logic of commodity culture is itself a serial process: of accumulation, consumption or obsolescence, and more accumulation. While we must not, as Lauren Rabinowitz reminds us, "neglect how pleasure itself is subjected to and regulated through the interests of commodity consumerism,"[71] and while the ads need to be perceived as having some measurable effect in the marketplace (or the agency loses their account), must we impose a linear model of influence? Are individuals so easily manipulated? Why is it that critics think of commercials as indoctrination, whereas soaps can more easily be understood as fantasy?

Rather than thinking of such advertisements as merely in the spirit of a consumerist impulse for constant and immediate satisfaction, perhaps we need to think of them as addressing moments in people's lives, moments that might provide us with a position from which to question—or actively struggle against—certain social formations. Can't we read commercials and soap operas' own marketing strategies as we do soaps: for their potential ideological effects and in the context of the viewers' concrete political realities? For the discursive connections forged between our fantasies and our daily lives? It's not a coincidence that Marilyn quoted the ABC commercial. How often *do* we do something for ourselves?

These daily dramas transform household desires (the despair of their context) into the possibility of embracing pleasure or perhaps even a reminder of our capacity for pleasure. Even though soaps themselves, like the products advertised, cannot dispel our despair or satisfy our desire, the power of pleasure cannot altogether be dismissed. The feeling of magic remains, even if it cannot be connected to the search for an absolute, unshakable truth or to restructuring change. Pleasure implies the simple possibility of a need met. What's threatening is not soaps, it's what those needs portend. And what those needs tell us about the organization of work in the home, social relations in the family, social resources, and entitlements. And that these pleasures might offer a window onto other, potentially more destabilizing, political and social forms of gratification. This can be frightening in a world where men have more social power than women, and the upper and upper-middle classes have more social power than the lower-middle or working classes.[72] What pleasure means politically, as Laura Kipnes reminds us, is a question worth thinking about, especially in the absence of any official political discourse that seriously entertains the subject.[73]

Seen in this way, are these fantasies an escape or an attempt to give meaning and value to the historical moment? It may be best to consider the politics involved in watching soaps—and talking about soaps—as grounded in the tension between the wish to celebrate meaning and value, and the wish to evade them.[74] It is possible that the fact that there is no reconciliatory balance, no finality to any solution, no death of the story, allows us to enjoy this tension.

A great many of contradictory experiences and ideas are integrated and accommodated in soap operas. Dissatisfaction and discontent are responded to within and without threatening existing social structures and conventions. Perhaps this helps to explain women's resilience (and how, in the face of disaffection, the existing power relations are so easily maintained). As Raymond Williams points out, any period has a central, dominant, and effective system of practices, meanings, values, and expectations that must be understood as "more substantial and more flexible than any abstract imposed ideology." Because it is "active and adjusting," this system is elastic enough to tolerate and even assuage much of our discontent.[75]

The soap opera ethos, though ambiguous and sometimes contradictory, does not threaten traditional family roles. The self-sufficient women of soaps generally legitimate their independence by either sharing their lives with men and children or working toward doing so. The stories may express the need for more liberated relationships between men and women and may confront women's need for companionship and emotional support within the family; however, the family is ultimately redeemed, precisely because family roles are only roles and not innate attributes. Soaps may be redefining those roles, and perhaps even revolting against certain traditions, but within conservative structures. Soaps pose few threats to the valorization of the family and the re-evaluation of the political, socioeconomic, and cultural position of women that accompanied the hegemony of the Republican Party and the rise of the New Right in the 1980s and continue to this day. Oppositional, or even alternative, images of this world are seldom pictured on, or provoked by, the shows or the commercials. Many aspects of the woman's role in the home may be questioned, but in a way that precludes radical change. But even as soap operas give prominence to and support the centrality of marriage and the sanctity of the family, their insistent, repetitious returns to the fantasy of the family out of control do harbor, and sometimes even deviously celebrate, contrary and conflicting feelings.

The maternal ambivalence that is often expressed in the soap operas' dramatic sequences is generally remedied by the commercials: here an idealized maternal (and a fantasized omnipotence) is associated with the specific products (Jif peanut butter, "Being a mom is doing the best for your kids always and all ways," for example, or Instant Quaker oatmeal, "for moms who have a lot of love but not a lot of time"), so that even (properly informed, modern, and progressive) men can dispense the maternal (as a young father does in a Chef Boyardee ravioli commercial).[76] In the commercials, psychological conflicts and needs are inscribed upon the surface of our bodies and our households; depths are displaced onto surfaces that are easily cared for, enhanced, or cured. To realize our dreams, we must simply try harder, search harder, be patient—and purchase more.[77]

These commercials (along with the form and content of the soap opera stories) venerate the family by validating certain kinds of experience that are important to domestic responsibilities. But the responsibilities of the family have often been accompanied by the collapse of other projects and aspirations and demand that the individual put off the realization of her personal ambitions until a utopian tomorrow.[78] If the outrageousness of soap operas permits women to produce that "other domestic," it is a structural inversion of, and has an ambivalent dependence upon, this ordinary everyday life. If Max Horkheimer and Theodor Adorno are right that "amusement under late capitalism is the prolongation of work. It is sought after as an escape from the mechanized work process, and to recruit strength in order to be able to cope with it again,"[79] then, for the homemaker and caregiver, watching soaps with its unacceptable, improper, transgressive form and content, may be a crucial political space which ultimately looks a lot like an "after-image" of that work.[80]

This conservative thrust, working with and within the family, may play with departure, disruption, and even dissolution, but soaps only destroy in order to reconstitute, so that they ultimately comply with established middle-class pieties. Horkheimer's conclusion in "Authority and the Family" warns us that "the means of protecting the cultural totality and developing it further have increasingly come into conflict with the cultural content itself. Even if the form of the family should finally be stabilized by the new measures, yet, as the importance of the whole bourgeois middle class decreases, this form will lose its active power which is grounded in the free vocational activity of the male. In the end everything about the family as we have known it in this age will have to be supported and held together in an ever more artificial fashion."[81]

If we agree with Horkheimer's perspective, we might ask if watching soaps has the radical potential that Modleski and others claim[82] or whether it is a way to survive the squalor of insignificance? Is it a way to buttress the family in times of uncertainty and change? The appeals of soaps are certainly not opposed to the dominant culture, but are located within its cracks, in the points where meaning itself waivers and where values are questioned. By infusing the system, however temporarily, with the fantasies of the domestic and the personal, there is a certain reversal in status, a displacement of positive and negative values from one term to another. The home, private life, and the individual are accorded dominance, importance over the power and rules of the public sphere, but this is effected without ever disrupting the artificial separation between the culturally constructed domains.

Even if watching soap operas helps us to explore the desires that exceed our social possibilities, and even if the very act of imagining helps us to produce such desires, watching soaps cannot, in itself, dislodge organization within and between the public and private spheres. There is no breakdown in the repressive dichotomy and no suggestion of how we might transcend the opposition—or even how we might formulate a less polarized relationship between the two spheres. We are still within—and even revalorizing—the hierarchical oppositions that define each. There is a change of status, not a crisis in hegemony.

These are transgressions that find their specificity in the dominant order, disturbing, but not destroying, the overdeterminations that organize our perceptions of our lives. Michel Foucault writes that a transgression's relation to the limit "takes the form of a spiral which no simple infraction can exhaust."[83] Contracts and transgressions are inseparable; one generates and affirms the other and they depend upon each other for their intensity.

The soap opera apparatus is a machine that constantly inflects our emotional life by mapping out its own vectors of desire, producing itself anew by assuring our affective existence. It is an interaction that transforms both parties, but without rechanneling the dissatisfactions (the experience of boredom, alienation, powerlessness, and, yes, even loneliness) upon which it depends. If soaps give us strength to negotiate the constraints of our roles, they do so with a personalization and depolitization of desire that may be even more oppressive than that of the hegemony.[84] They both address our fantasies and at the same time rein them in.[85] They are simultaneously adventure and security. Like Nabisco Cafe Cremes, they furnish "a cozy little place in your day."

Freud elaborated a triple time frame in fantasy: the present (some current impression that has "the power to rouse an intense desire"), the past of our childhood (when this desire was fulfilled), and the future (a situation in which the desire can be fulfilled).[86] "So past, present and future are threaded, as it were, on the string of the wish that runs through them all."[87] Our fantasies and the vicissitudes of daily life may also be threaded on the string of the wish that runs through them. Our longings are steeped in traces of the insignificance of the everyday, the occasions that engender them and that have the power to rouse intense desires. Our pleasures, too, are imbedded in the experiences of the present, transcend them, but coexist with them, a mediating agent between remembered aspirations and the reality of exploitation. We are, in the words of Matthew Arnold, "Wandering between two worlds, one dead, / The other powerless to be born."[88]

Watching soaps may be one of the ways we live and function in a world that does not always meet our needs; the flickering iridescence of the television can be an active site in which our dreams impinge on the isolation and fragmentation of our daily life. We are able to provide ourselves with our own space, a space hollowed out by the yawning of desire, an "elsewhere" of our own pleasure and will. Rather than denying values and feelings, watching soaps is the act that carries them to their limits, where the "yes" inside us reverberates, in a scintillating world, a world without shadow and twilight, a world where the divine functions, a world where dreams once destined to be stillborn begin to grow.

But doesn't this radical "elsewhere" deny the bind of the present imperfect? Isn't it the cleverness of the weak, the act of those with little actual power? Far from liberating, these rebellions against the kingdom of the quotidian are a way of coping. I think of soaps as a site for raveled spirits to knit themselves back together, a form of resistance that may even have the potential to subjugate: we run the risk of remaining endlessly a spectator. Watching soaps, then, can be seen as being strategic or transgressive without being progressive.

Marketed as relief, instruction, and reward, the culture of pleasure is circularly related to the culture of oppression. This network of reciprocating processes advances us toward the region where our Other becomes the same as our Self,[89] and where our "elsewhere" is an elsewhere-within-here that may offer us the strength or space to negotiate the constraints of the domestic role, but neither the violence nor the sweet rapture of defiance. These social spaces can never fulfill our dreams of intimacy—or even our dreams of autonomy—because they cannot break the patterns of daily life.

Appendix 1

Flow of Sequences

The Young and the Restless, November 27, 1981

SEGMENT DURATION (minutes, seconds)	SUBJECT MATTER
3'17"	*Dorothy and Bobbi, re: April*
40"	*Wayne at April's, interior monologue, re: Bobbi*
60"	*Teaser with Nikki and Jonas*
Total: 4'57"	
30"	titles
30"	dog food
30"	telephone
30"	trash bags
Total: 2'00"	
4'15"	*Continuation of sequence with Nikki and Jonas, re: Victor*
30"	*Teaser with Patty and Mrs. Williams*
Total: 4'45"	
30"	bath powder (harried mother)
30"	decaffeinated coffee
30"	dog food
30"	network advertisements
Total: 2'00"	

SEGMENT DURATION (minutes, seconds)	SUBJECT MATTER
4'30"	*Continuation of sequence with Patty and Mrs. Williams, re: Jack*
55"	*Victor and Servant, re: Nikki*
40"	*Teaser with Nikki (Cash enters)*
Total: 6'05"	
30"	cold medicine
30"	toothbrushes
30"	hemorrhoid medicine
30"	network advertisements
Total: 2'00"	
2'55"	*Continuation of sequence with Nikki and Cash, re: Victor*
25"	*Teaser with Wayne and Dorothy, re: Bobbi*
60"	*Patty at Jack's office, sees him embracing someone else*
Total: 4'20"	
30"	toys
30"	skin moisturizer
30"	women's laxative
30"	network advertisements
30"	local department store sale
30"	canned tomatoes
10"	cookies
10"	network and title filler
Total: 3'20"	
4'47"	*Continuation of sequence with Wayne and Dorothy, re: Bobbi*
45"	*Teaser: Jonas recognizes Bobbi at bar*
1'05"	*Patty, Jack, and Lover meet in hall*
Total: 6'37"	
30"	sauce and recipe
30"	drain opener
30"	coffee
Total: 1'30"	

SEGMENT DURATION (minutes, seconds)	SUBJECT MATTER
3'35"	*Continuation of sequence with Jonas and Bobbi, re: Dorothy, April, Wayne*
2'20"	*Continuation of sequence with Dorothy and Wayne, re: Bobbi*
30"	*Teaser: Cash visits Victor*
Total: 6'25"	
30"	women's stockings
30"	toys
30"	bacon
Total: 1'30"	
4'05"	*Continuation of sequence with Cash and Victor, re: Nikki*
36"	*Teaser: Patty confronts Jack*
Total: 4'41"	
30"	cough medicine
30"	skin moisturizer
30"	department store sale items (oven)
30"	network advertisements
Total: 2'00"	
5'30"	*Continuation of sequence with Patty and Jack*
Total: 5'30"	
30"	tomato sauce
30"	batteries (for toys)
30"	air freshener
55"	credits with network voice-over
Total: 2'25"	

Twenty narrative sequences (running time: 43'03")
Thirty-four commercial sequences (running time: 16'45")
Total: fifty-four sequences (59'48")

Appendix 2

Outline of Dialogue

Ryan's Hope, August 6, 1986

The situation from previous episodes: Rick Hyde, a police officer, had been planning an undercover mission with the District Attorney, Frank Ryan. Part of the subterfuge included Rick separating from his wife, Frank's niece, Ryan Hyde. Rick was supposed to "shoot" Frank with blanks and Frank would pretend to be injured. Unbeknown to Rick (but on screen, so the home audience was aware), the blanks were replaced by real bullets and Frank was critically injured.

Scene 1. Frank's hospital room, Frank (unconscious) and Jill (his ex-wife). Dakota (Jill's current lover) walks in: "Jill, it's time for us to go. There's nothing more you can do for Frank."

Scene 2. Ryan and Rick kissing: "If I live to be a hundred, I could never be as happy as I am now."

Scene 3. Max Dubujak (a gangster and wife of Frank's sister) speaking on a video phone to five underlings: "Did you order the hit on Ryan? . . . Who among you is the traitor?" *(Fade to black)*

Opening credits
Block of commercials

Scene 4. Frank's hospital room, continuation, Dakota pulls Jill into the hallway: "Do you know what Frank needs? He needs some rest and you need some rest. He doesn't know whether you're here or not." Jill, "I don't believe that." Dakota, "Well, believe it."

Scene 5. Diana (Frank's current friend) arrives, greets Jill and Dakota, and enters Frank's hospital room. Frank regains consciousness and says, "Jill. . . . Jillian?" Diana replies, "No Frank. It's me; it's Diana." Jill re-enters and Diana says, "He opened his eyes." Jill asks if he said anything and Diana responds, "No." *(Fade to black)*

Block of commercials

Scene 6. Exterior of hospital room. Max Dubujak enters and greets his wife, Det. Shioban Ryan: ". . . Believe me, who ever shot Frank will be punished." Shioban replies, "Well unfortunately, justice is not always as sure or as swift as it should be." Max: "Well, in this case, it will be . . . You are the best detective on the force. . . . I am sure that you will have this killer fall right into your hands."

Scene 7. Jack Fenelli (father of Ryan Hyde) and Maeve Ryan (mother of Frank Ryan and mother-in-law to Jack) re: Ryan, "Where did she go and why isn't she here?" "It's possible that she just wanted to be alone." "But you don't think that do you?" "No, I don't think so, I think she would go look for Rick." "In the state she's in, Rick is the last person in the world she should be with."

Scene 8. Shioban and Max, continuation. They are joined by Jack Fenelli's friend who requests that Shioban help to find Ryan.

Scene 9. Ryan and Rick, continuation: Rick, "I think that you should go to the hospital. . . . Don't tell anyone that you saw me or that you know anything." He gives her the telephone number of a phone booth to call him when she arrives at the hospital and knows that everything is O.K. *(Fade to black)*

Block of commercials

Scene 10. Dakota and Jill, outside Frank's room: "Jill, what's happening to us?" She answers, "I'm sorry; I'm really sorry. The only thing I can think of right now is Frank. Dakota, if you can't handle that, I think it would be best if you went home." He replies firmly, "Not without you!" Jill, "While I was out here dealing with your insecurities, Frank came to for a moment . . ." Dakota, "You know something, I think you should go back in there, because I certainly wouldn't want you to miss it if he called out your name." Dakota exits.

Scene 11. Dakota joins Melinda in the waiting room and they discuss his fears that Jill is falling back in love with Frank.

Scene 12. Dakota joins Diana outside Frank's room: "Jill said he opened his eyes. I'm sure that he was happy to see you." Diana replies, "Well, actually—" Dakota interrupts, "I'm sure that you're a big comfort to him right now." "I'd like to believe that." "It's true, believe me. When I was here in the hospital in pretty bad shape, I always could feel Jill's presence. It makes a big difference . . . From what I heard, you really turned his life around." Diana with doubt in her voice, questions, "Frank talked to you about that?" There is some discussion and Dakota ends with, "I'm really happy that you're here with him. You stick by him, OK?"

Scene 13. Ryan enters the waiting room where her father and grandmother are standing vigil; there is much excitement and hugging: "Where the hell have you been?" "Just working things out." "Well, we're just happy that you're here safely." "Aren't you going to ask about your Uncle Frank?" There's a new emergency with Frank in the ICU and Ryan asks, "Dad, what's going on?" "Your uncle might die, Ryan."

Scene 14. Rick by the telephone box impatiently waiting for Ryan's call. *(Fade to black)*

Block of commercials
End logo.

Notes

Chapter 1. Life's Little Problems . . . and Pleasures

1. When I first started studying soaps, in 1981, the television industry estimated that, on average, six and a half million people were watching daytime soap operas on a typical weekday afternoon, 72 percent of them women over eighteen (Nielson Media Research, based on thirteen network soaps, May 1981); by the late 1980s, even with the heavy availability of VCRs (58 percent penetration in 1988), the audience was still estimated to be almost six and a half million, 70 percent women. In 2000, with many more non-network choices (the Lifetime cable channel, for example, and SoapNet) and only ten soaps on air, Nielson estimated that, at any one moment, over four million people are tuned in to a daytime soap, 72 percent of them women. While the near steady percentage of women is impressive, there are important limitations to these statistics. They do not measure people who watch TV outside the home (in college dorms, for example), or account for people "watching" a show that they did not select or taping a show that they may never watch. This makes it unwise to try to extrapolate trends or patterns from the data. And the figures, of course, cannot tell us much at all about the viewing behavior, the practices, and experiences of actual viewers.

2. "Beyond the Pleasure Principle" (1920) *The Standard Edition of the Complete Psychological Works of Sigmund Freud,* vol. 18, James Stachey, ed. (London: The Hogarth Press, 1964), p. 7.

3. *Movie-Radio Guide,* vol. 12, no. 6 (November 14–20, 1942); pp. 19–22 and the page facing p. 40. Subsequent page references will appear in the text. The fifteen-minute radio soap, *Lonely Women,* began in 1942. At the end of 1943, the title was changed to *Today's Children* (a title Phillips revived from her 1933–38 NBC serial). The show continued for five years.

4. *Worlds Without End: The Art and History of the Soap Opera,* Ron Simon and Ellen O'Neill, eds. (New York: Abrams, in conjunction with the Museum of Television and Radio, 1997), p. 16.

5. "Every Woman's Life Is a Soap Opera," March 1965, p. 116.

6. "What Do We Really Know About Daytime Serial Listeners?" *Radio Research, 1942–43,* Paul Lazarsfeld and Frank Stanton, eds. (New York: Duell, Sloan and Pearce, 1944). The volume was reprinted by Arno Press in 1979. Subsequent page references will appear in the text.

7. "Mass Communication and Para-Social Interaction: Observation on Intimacy at a Distance," *Psychiatry,* vol. 19, no. 3 (August 1956); reprinted in *Inter/Media: Interpersonal Communication in a Media World, Third Edition,* Gary Gumpert and Robert Cathcart, eds. (New York: Oxford University Press, 1986). The article emphasizes how the direct address of the quizmaster, news announcers, and the variety host creates the illusion of the performer talking intimately and personally, but then goes on to include fictional programs. The authors point out that the media themselves have recognized the existence of "a marginal segment of the lonely" with specially designed offerings such as the radio program "Lonesome Gal." Cathcart, in "Our Soap Opera Friends" (which we will explore presently), extends Horton's and Wohl's argument specifically to soap operas.

8. George Comstock, et al., *Television and Human Behavior* (New York: Columbia University Press, 1978), p. 309.

9. "Our Soap Opera Friends," in *Inter/Media: Interpersonal Communication in a Media World,* 3rd ed. Gary Gumpert and Robert Cathcart, eds. (New York: Oxford, 1986), pp. 217–18.

10. In *Watching Television,* Todd Gitlin, ed. (New York: Pantheon, 1986), p. 45. Subsequent page references will appear in the text.

11. *Why Viewers Watch* (Thousand Oaks, Calif.: Sage, 1992), p. 58, pp. 168–69. Robert C. Allen, from a slightly different point of view, notes that researchers have seldom granted soap viewers the capacity for aesthetic distance (*Speaking of Soap Operas* [Chapel Hill: University of North Carolina Press, 1985], p. 29).

12. This, for example, is a part of the Sari Thomas study discussed in the next chapter.

13. See Peter Stallybrass and Allon White's *The Politics and Poetics of Transgression* (Ithaca: Cornell University Press, 1986), chapters one and five.

14. There has been some recent discussion, following Pierre Bourdieu (*Distinction: A Social Critique of the Judgement of Taste* [Cambridge, Mass.: Harvard University Press, 1984], pp. 11–96), of soap operas as the naive gaze against which the aesthetic gaze is constructed. (See, for example, Charlotte Brunsdon, "Television: Aesthetics and Audiences," in *Logics of Television,* Patricia Mellencamp, ed. [Bloomington: Indiana University Press, 1990], reprinted in *Screen Tastes: Soap Opera to Satellite Dishes* [New York: Routledge, 1997].) Bourdieu observes that such displays of taste, the business of discriminating between approved pleasures and those considered more base, are a manner of establishing a social distinction, of positioning oneself in a social hierarchy. His thesis underlies much of what you will be reading in this book.

15. "Afterward: The Material of Rhetoric," in *Rhetorical Bodies,* Jack Selzer and Sharon Crowley, eds. (Madison: University of Wisconsin Press, 1999), p. 363.

16. The general idea of various programs as interchangeable options is Jim Collin's in "Watching Ourselves Watch Television, or Who's Your Agent?" *Cultural Studies* 3:3 (October 1989): p. 264.

17. See Joli Jenson's "Fandom as Pathology: The Consequences of Characterization," in *The Adoring Audience: Fan Culture and Popular Media,* Lisa Lewis, ed. (New York: Routledge, 1992), pp. 9–29, especially p. 14. Discussions of the mass media's relation to the dehumanization of culture go back to the nineteenth century.

18. Nancy Chodorow argues that women tend to see themselves in relation to and in connection with other people in *The Reproduction of Mothering: Psychoanalysis and the Sociology of Gender* (Berkeley: University of California Press, 1978), pp. 159–170.

19. Barbara Welter, "The Cult of True Womanhood: 1820–1860," *American Quarterly,* 17 (Summer 1966).

20. Lynne Joyrich has called this "pathologizing femininity through an emphasis on woman as problem and object of concern" in *Re-viewing Reception: Television, Gender, and Postmodern Culture* (Bloomington: Indiana University Press, 1996), p. 13.

21. Joli Jenson, "Fandom as Pathology," pp. 25–27.

22. See, for example, Ruth Rosen's "Soap Operas: Search for Yesterday," pp. 44–45.

23. *Paula* (New York: HarperCollins, 1994), pp. 118–19 and 122. Even Susan Willis in her Marxist/feminist analysis of consumer culture and daily life, commenting on Tania Modleski's discussion of waiting as soap operas structuring presence, writes, "The housewife who comes to waiting as pleasure hardly has access to another, more active and affirming mode of getting through the day." *A Primer for Daily Life* (New York: Routledge, 1991), p. 6.

24. *Television and New Media Audiences* (New York: Oxford University Press, 1999), p. 25.

25. *Crossroads: The Drama of a Soap Opera* (London: Methuen, 1982), p. 169.

26. This comment was lifted from the bulletin board in 1993 by C. Lee Harrington and Denise D. Bielby and appears in *Soap Fans: Pursuing Pleasure and Making Meaning in Everyday Life* (Philadelphia: Temple University Press, 1995), p. 84.

27. This is quoted by Russel Nye, *The Unembarrassed Muse* (New York: Dial, 1970), p. 414, from an interview in the Toronto *Globe and Mail* (June 11, 1969). Nye, however, somehow misquotes Robert Aaron and has him describing the viewer as middle-class. Aaron later co-created the soap opera *Another Life* for the Christian Broadcasting Network.

28. *Eight Years in Another World* (New York: Atheneum, 1981), p. 34.

29. Since this work began in 1980, several others have begun similar work. I will be discussing these more recent studies, many of which are responses to some of the same concerns I mention above, as they relate to the theoretical issues in Chapter 2.

30. Wide-ranging agreement among respondents is not necessarily evidence of a similarity of interpretation; it may indicate the prevalence of a conventional belief (see Paul Messaris, "Biases of Self-Reported 'Functions' and 'Gratifications' of Mass Media Use," *Et cetera,* vol. 34, no. 3 [September 1977]: p. 326).

31. Some communications studies that refer to an active viewer are talking about activities such as making selections and choices, coming to the media event with certain expectations, motives, or needs, or deciding the "acceptability of a

text," not actively making meaning. See, for example, the essay by Elihu Katz and Tamar Liebes on their study of the multicultural reception of *Dallas,* "Mutual Aid in the Decoding of *Dallas:* Preliminary Notes from a Cross-Cultural Study," *Television in Transition: Papers from the First International Television Studies Conference,* Phillip Drummond and Richard Paterson, eds. (London: BFI, 1986). Katz and Liebes have observed several groups of viewers watching an episode of *Dallas* and questioned them afterward about their understandings of the show. This conception of viewer activity is also operating in Sari Thomas's dissertation, discussed in Chapter 2.

32. Much of the work in *Screen* in the 1970s is exemplary of this somewhat idealist perspective.

33. "Women's Genres," *Screen,* vol. 25, no. 1 (January/February 1984). Kuhn's article, a theoretical explication of many of the issues that inspired my study, argues that a feminist cultural politics should explore the relation between the social audience and the spectator/subject (p. 28). Louis Althusser's notion of interpellation, which was influential in the 1970s and 1980s, describes the ways in which ideology functions: As social subjects, we are addressed or "recruited" by dominant ideologies and, often unconsciously, subscribe to them. See *Lenin and Philosophy* (New York: Monthly Review Press, 1971), pp. 173–77.

34. Specific recent studies will be discussed in Chapter 2.

35. "Feminism, Postmodernism, and Gender Skepticism," in *Feminism/Postmodernism,* Linda J. Nicholson, ed. (New York: Routledge, 1990), pp. 136–37.

36. Angela McRobbie, "The Politics of Feminist Research: Between Talk, Text and Action," *Feminist Review,* 12 (October 1982): p. 52.

37. The idea of the analyst's account being an interpretation is indebted to the work of Clifford Geertz. See *The Interpretation of Culture* (New York: Basic Books, 1973), especially p. 15.

38. See "From *Capital* to Marx's Philosophy" in *Reading Capital* (London: New Left Books, 1970).

39. For a discussion of post-Althusserian ethnographic methods, see James Clifford's "On Ethnographic Authority," *Representations* 1:2 (spring 1983), and Steven Webster's "Dialogue and Fiction in Ethnography," *Dialectical Anthropology,* vol. 7, no. 2 (November 1982).

40. This perspective is an essential part of much literary reception theory, especially Stanley Fish. See *Is There a Text in the Class?: The Authority of Interpretive Communities* (Cambridge, Mass.: Harvard University Press, 1980), p. 9. The idea of an active audience will be discussed further in the following chapter.

41. Stuart Hall has discussed this in "Encoding/decoding" in *Culture, Media, Language: Working Papers in Cultural Studies, 1972–79* (London: Hutchinson, 1981), pp. 129–30.

42. The phrase is from Pierre Macherey's interview in *Red Letters,* no. 5 (summer 1977): p. 7.

43. Following Gérard Genette's distinction between "histoire," "récit," and "narration," I will be discussing the story, the text, and the narration, respectively. It is mainly from the text (the sounds and images observed from the television) that the viewer constructs his or her knowledge of the story and of the way the

story is being told (the perspective of the narrative content or the narration). The narrative discourses are produced through the action of telling. See *Narrative Discourse: An Essay in Method* (Ithaca: Cornell University Press, 1980), pp. 25–32.

44. "Television: Aesthetics and Audiences," p. 68.

45. Raymond Williams, in his essay "Base and Superstructure in Marxist Cultural Theory," suggests that we look "not for the components of a product but for the conditions of a practice." See *Problems in Materialism and Culture* (London: Verso Editions, 1980), p. 48.

46. Quoted in Dorothy Hobson's "Housewives: Isolation as Oppression," in *Woman Take Issue: Aspects of Women's Subordination,* by the Women's Studies Group, Centre for Contemporary Cultural Studies, University of Birmingham (London: Hutchinson, 1978).

47. "Talking Back," *Discourse,* 8 (fall/winter 1986/87): pp. 123–128. The quote is from p. 126.

48. Quoted in Ernest Mandel's *Delightful Murder: A Social History of the Crime Story* (London: Pluto Press, 1984), p. 50. See also Tillie Olsen's essay "Silences" in *Silences* (New York: Delta, 1980).

49. See "The 900 Number as Audience Pollster," *New York Times,* July 6, 1987.

50. *Soap Opera Digest* was published biweekly, now weekly, and is sold by subscription, in supermarket checkout racks, and at newsstands. With a 1989 circulation of almost a million and a half (December, Audit Bureau of Circulation), it was, at the time, the most widely read of the soap opera fan magazines. More recently, they have begun sponsoring websites for the daytime shows. In December 2002, with fewer daytime soaps to cover and competition from myriad websites, circulation was still nearly a million copies (Audit Bureau of Circulation).

51. August 5–9, 1991. I am grateful to Krin Gabbard for drawing my attention to these episodes. In the New York City area, the spot was included among such other 900 enterprises as your personal daily horoscope.

52. According to Michael Logan, *TV Guide*'s soap columnist, the contest had no effect, as NBC had already decided on the name. (*TV Guide,* January 2, 1993).

53. C. Lee Harrington and Denise D. Bielby, *Soap Fans: Pursuing Pleasure and Making Meaning in Everyday Life* (Philadelphia: Temple University Press, 1995), p. 162.

54. *Soap Opera and Women's Talk: The Pleasures of Resistance* (Thousand Oaks, Calif.: Sage, 1994), p. 177.

55. "Daytime Utopias: If You Lived in Pine Valley, You'd Be Home" in *Hop on Pop: The Politics and Pleasures of Popular Culture,* Henry Jenkins, Tara McPherson, and Jane Shattuc, eds. (Durham, N.C.: Duke University Press, 2002).

56. Different disciplines have different views on naming informants, although the assumptions of the traditions are seldom fully examined. Issues of privacy, confidentiality, and rapport are involved along with the political aspects of identity. Although others share many of the ideas and feelings that were expressed by the women that I interviewed, I have not assumed that they wished them openly conveyed. In the formal interviews, I asked the interviewee if I happened to refer to her or quote her in my writing, whether she would like me to use her name or not. Some blushed, others proudly consented, one even persisted to make sure

that I knew the correct spelling. I have conformed to their wishes and used names where they requested and left out names where they preferred. In some instances, where I have referred several times to someone who wished to remain anonymous, I have used a pseudonym so that it is easier to follow. Over the years many people have volunteered their experiences to me when they heard that I was interested in people who watch soap operas. In those more informal cases, since they did not always know that they might be part of a written report, if I could no longer reach them to get their permission, I have not used their names. When I finished with the manuscript, I sent those with whom I was still in touch a copy for their comments and to see if it was still acceptable to use their name. I am satisfied that this method meets my needs and my informants' interests; however, I regret that it has prevented me from thanking each of them, individually, in this book.

57. "'Don't Treat Us Like We're So Stupid and Naive': Toward an Ethnography of Soap Opera Viewers," Ellen Seiter, Hans Borchers, Gabriele Kreutzner, and Eva-Maria Warth, eds., in *Remote Control: Television, Audiences and Cultural Power*. (London: Routledge, 1989), p. 233.

58. *Women and Soap Opera: A Study of Prime Time Soaps* (London: Polity Press, 1991), pp. 122–23.

59. See, for example, John G. Cawelti's *Adventure, Mystery and Romance* (Chicago: University of Chicago Press, 1976) and Janice Radway's *Reading the Romance: Women, Patriarchy and Popular Literature* (Chapel Hill: University of North Carolina Press, 1984).

60. "Soap Operas Provide Meaningful Communication for the Elderly," *Feedback* vol. 19, no. 3 (1977): p. 6.

61. James Carey, *Communication As Culture* (New York: Routledge, 1992), p. 18.

62. Steven G. Jones, "Understanding Community in the Information Age," in *CyberSociety: Computer-Mediated Communication and Community,* Steven G. Jones, ed. (Thousand Oaks, Calif.: Sage, 1995), p. 11.

63. Jones asks this question (in another context) in "Understanding Community in the Information Age," p. 15.

64. Nancy K. Baym tells of monthly luncheons of one board's contributors in her hometown and sometimes viewing *All My Children* together, "The Emergence of Community in Computer-Mediated Communication," in *CyberSociety: Computer-Mediated Communication and Community,* Steven G. Jones, ed. (Thousand Oaks, Calif.: Sage, 1995), p. 157.

65. See Sean Griffith, "All My Gay Children? Soaps, Sexuality and Cyberspace," paper presented at Console-ing Passions Conference, Montreal, May 1997.

66. Cited in C. Lee Harrington and Denise D. Bielby's *Soap Fans: Pursuing Pleasure and Making Meaning in Everyday Life* (Philadelphia: Temple University Press, 1995), p. 31.

67. Nancy K. Baym, "The Emergence of Community in Computer-Mediated Communication," p. 145.

68. "All My Computers: The Electronic World of Reception in Soap Opera Nets," paper presented at the Console-ing Passions Conference, Tucson, Arizona, April 1994.

69. Bulletin board posting quoted in C. Lee Harrington and Denise D. Bielby, *Soap Fans: Pursuing Pleasure and Making Meaning in Everyday Life* (Philadelphia: Temple University Press, 1995), p. 150.

70. *Rabelais and His World* (Cambridge, Mass.: MIT Press, 1968), p. 10.

71. B. Reid, "Usenet readership report for July 1993," Newsgroup: news.lists, cited in Baym, "The Emergence of Community," pp. 138, 144, and 148. Rec.arts.tv.soaps began in 1984 when it spun off from the television newsgroup.

72. See Baym, "The Emergence of Community," pp. 155–56. Baym is actually writing about rec.arts.tv.soaps, before the division; however, the same seems to be true for rec.arts.tv.soaps.abc. In 1993, she estimated that the board was 72 percent female.

73. See Baym, "Interpreting Soap Operas and Creating Community: Inside a Computer-Mediated Fan Club," *Journal of Folklore Research,* vol. 30, nos. 2/3 (May/December 1993): pp. 168–69.

74. "Interpreting Soap Operas and Creating Community," p. 158.

75. Laura Stempel Mumford, "AOL My Children: Meta-Discourse in the Cyber-Soap Community," paper presented at the Console-ing Passions Conference, Madison, Wisconsin, April 1996. Mumford notes that this "elaborate system of metadiscourse" is almost completely absent from the AOL *All My Children* board, which is supervised by both AOL and ABC.

76. The notion of television as strip is Horace Newcomb and Paul M. Hirsch's in "Television as a Cultural Forum" in *Television: The Critical View,* pp. 509–10.

77. *Life on the Screen: Identity in the Age of the Internet* (New York: Touchstone, 1995).

78. *On the Margins of Discourse: The Relation of Literature to Language* (Chicago: University of Chicago Press, 1978), p. 109.

79. Dana Kiehl, August 18, 1995, post to r.a.t.s.a., quoted in Sean Griffith's "All My Gay Children?"

80. Mumford, "AOL My Children."

81. Griffith, "All My Gay Children?" The rewriting of current storylines seems to be a tradition that predates the 1995 gay story. Baym quotes a 1991 e-mail correspondence with a r.a.t.s. participant that talks about posts turning "into creative writing sessions" ("Interpreting Soap Operas and Creating Community," p. 147). In the summer of 2003, *http://members.aol.com/soap_links/index.html* listed fifteen on-line soaps, nine original soaps and six alternative versions to network soaps (three alternatives to *General Hospital,* two to *The Guiding Light,* and one to *Days of Our Lives*). Not all were active at the time, but the archives were available.

82. *Textual Poachers: Television Fans and Participatory Culture* (London: Routledge, 1992), p. 23.

83. Quoted in C. Lee Harrington and Denise D. Bielby, *Soap Fans: Pursuing Pleasure and Making Meaning in Everyday Life* (Philadelphia: Temple University Press, 1995), p. 167.

84. "Interpreting Soap Operas and Creating Community," p. 155.

85. This is especially the case on the *All My Children* boards, perhaps because of the use of humor (sometimes almost self-mocking) on the show itself. I hope I

have captured some of the wit in my descriptions throughout this book. Jennifer Hayward, who follows *All My Children* and *One Life to Live,* more directly addresses the use of humor, irony, and self-reflexive parody on these programs. See *Consuming Pleasures: Active Audiences and Serial Fictions from Dickens to Soap Operas* (Lexington: University Press of Kentucky, 1997), pp. 185–89.

86. There is a parallel here with the power individual viewers have over scheduling: if you have a VCR, you can shift the time you view your soap, but you cannot affect the broadcast structure of the day, week, or season. Brad Chisholm compares the cognitive processes of watching TV with playing a chess game and notes the limitations of a television spectator's power to influence the outcome of a screen narrative. See "Difficult Viewing: The Pleasures of Complex Screen Narratives," *Critical Studies in Mass Communication,* 8:4 (December 1991): p. 401.

Although networks and producers have been known to download, photocopy, and distribute Internet discussions, stories are determined so far in advance that changes are unlikely. They often dismiss letters as from a fringe element or as an indication that fans "are watching." Ken Corday, executive producer of *Days of Our Lives,* was quoted by *Soap Opera Weekly,* "When they say 'I hate what you're doing with X, Y and Z,' you know parenthetically they're saying, 'I'll watch to see what they're up to'" (August 31, 1993). Producers are also suspicious of some fan activity as being generated, or encouraged, by individual performers wishing larger roles or more prominent stories. However, it should be noted that some soaps receive over one thousand letters a month, have personnel devoted to opening them, and sometimes tabulate the amount of mail a particular performer or storyline gets. Jennifer Hayward discusses some of these letters and fan talk on the Internet, and puts more emphasis on the power viewers have to shape and reshape soap narratives through fan mail, on-line dialogues, ratings, and audience fora. (Her letters were preselected by an anonymous former ABC viewer mail employee.) See *Consuming Pleasures,* pp. 145–96. Stories of fan campaigns to save popular couples or characters rival those of prime-time rescues such as *Cagney and Lacey.* Hayward tells of fans expressing their disappointment when Billy Husfey left *One Life to Live* (due to contract disputes) to the tune of forty-five thousand letters to ABC. Husfey was quickly rehired and "affirmation of viewer power soon splashed across soap magazine headlines" (p. 165).

87. One r.a.t.s. form of expression, the acronym IWLSHEKIWW ("I was laughing so hard everyone knew I wasn't working") in response to humorous postings, would seem to indicate that a substantial number of people are accessing r.a.t.s. through student accounts or places of employment.

88. This characterization of the period is indebted to Robert N. Bellah, Richard Madsen, William M. Sullivan, Ann Swidler, and Steven M. Tipton's *Habits of the Heart: Individualism and Commitment in American Life* (Berkeley: University of California Press, 1985).

89. *Television Culture* (London: Methuen, 1987), p. 239.

90. John Markoff, "A Newer Lonelier Crowd Emerges in Internet Study," *New York Times,* February 16, 2000. The study on "societal impact of the Internet" was co-authored by Norman Nie, of Stanford Institute for the Quantitative Study of Society, and Lutz Erbring of the Free University of Berlin.

91. *Love and Ideology in the Afternoon: Soap Opera, Women, and Television Genre* (Bloomington: Indiana University Press, 1995).

92. Elizabeth Wilson suggests this about vulnerabilities in *Hidden Agendas: Theory, Politics, and Experience in the Women's Movement,* written with Angela Weir (London: Tavistock, 1986), p. 181.

93. Laura Kipnes, *Bound and Gagged: Pornography and the Politics of Fantasy in America* (Durham, N.C.: Duke University Press, 1999), p. 196.

94. "Street of Crocodiles," in *Street of Crocodiles* (New York: Penguin, 1977 [1934]), p. 109.

95. "Every Woman's Life IS a Soap Opera," March 1965, p. 117, emphasis as such in original.

96. *The Savage Mind* (Chicago: University of Chicago Press, 1966), pp. 16–21.

97. *The Rape of Clarissa: Writing, Sexuality, and Class Struggle in Samuel Richardson* (Minneapolis: University of Minnesota Press, 1986), p. 12.

98. *Bound and Gagged,* pp. 122–60. Recent reality dating shows and sex-charged cable programming, such as *Sex and the City,* have stretched tolerance for the risqué so that soaps no longer seem so raunchy. We've come far from Dr. Johnson's refusal to name the private parts in his dictionary.

99. Jean-Louis Comolli, "Historical Fiction: A Body Too Much," *Screen,* vol. 19, no. 2 (summer 1978): p. 46.

100. "The Relation of the Poet to Day-Dreaming," *On Creativity and the Unconscious* (New York: Harper & Row, 1958), p. 47.

101. Most spots for soap operas are clips from the shows or close-ups of a character with a voice-over entreating the viewer to watch.

102. See Laura Kipnes, "Aesthetics and Foreign Policy," *Social Text,* 15 (fall 1986): p. 93.

103. Vol. 13, no. 2 (January 26, 1988): p. 98. *Soap Opera Digest* covers all network daytime serials as well as prime-time serials. I am differentiating between television series and serials. Series generally have continuing characters and continuing settings but different stories in each episode. The sequence of episodes in a series is generally interchangeable. Stories are usually resolved at the end of each program, though some situations may continue. Some series have stories that continue over two episodes but these are generally marked as "Part 1" and "Part 2." Serials, on the other hand, have continuing characters, settings, and stories in ongoing stories delivered in successive parts. In serials, each episode follows or continues the next. (Of course, as Mimi White points out, compared to film texts, even series are more serial-like than not, entertaining the same characters over a period of time in many of the same situations. [*Tele-Advising: Therapeutic Discourses in American Television* (Chapel Hill: University of North Carolina Press, 1992), p. 17.]) *Murder She Wrote* and *The Cosby Show* are series. *Dallas, Falcon's Crest, Dynasty, Knots Landing,* WB's *Dawson's Creek,* MTV's *Real World,* Fox's *24,* and HBO's *The Sopranos* are prime-time serials. I concentrate on daytime serials but suggest further parallels and contrasts where applicable. See Laura Stempel Mumford's "What Is This Thing Called Soap Opera?" for a helpful review of the debates over what defines soap opera as a genre (in *Love and Ideology in the Afternoon: Soap Opera, Women, and Television Genre* [Bloomington: Indiana University Press, 1995], pp. 14–46).

104. Cora Kaplan notes that romantic and sexual fantasies shouldn't be seen simply as the mark of our subordination, because they are always simultaneously the mark of our humanity. See "*The Thorn Birds:* Fiction, Fantasy, Femininity" in *Formations of Fantasy,* Victor Burgin, James Donald, and Cora Kaplan, eds. (London: Methuen, 1986), pp. 149–50.

105. Alison Light, "'Return to Manderley'—Romance Fiction and Female Sexuality," *Feminist Review,* 16 (April 1984): p. 7.

106. "Psychoanalysis and the Polis," *The Politics of Interpretation,* W. J. T. Mitchell, ed. (Chicago: University of Chicago Press, 1983), p. 84.

107. On love songs, see Simon Frith, *Performing Rites: On the Value of Popular Music* (Cambridge, Mass.: Harvard University Press, 1996), p. 165.

Chapter 2. The Theoretical Matrix

1. *The Serials: Suspense and Drama by Installment* (Norman, Oklahoma: University of Oklahoma Press, 1977), p. 238.

2. *Speaking of Soap Operas* (Chapel Hill: University of North Carolina Press, 1985), pp. 26–27. Allen's book has a fine opening chapter that reviews the social constructions of "soap opera" in broadcasting, aesthetic, and social science discourses. My work is certainly indebted to Allen's study, but concentrates more on the viewer's construction of meanings and pleasures.

3. Quoted in Ellen Seiter, "'To Teach and To Sell': Irna Phillips and Her Sponsors, 1930–1954," *Journal of Film and Video,* vol. 41, no. 1 (spring 1989); p. 32.

4. Quoted in Seiter, "'To Teach and To Sell'," pp. 31–32.

5. Quoted in Seiter, "'To Teach and To Sell'," p. 31.

6. "The Television Executive's View of Daytime Serials: An Interview with Robert E. Short," *Life on Daytime Television: Tuning-In American Serial Drama* (Norwood, N.J.: Ablex, 1983), p. 182. Short worked with Phillips on *The Guiding Light, As the World Turns,* and *Another World.*

7. Agnes Nixon Seminars at the Museum of Broadcasting, New York, January 26, 27, 28, and 29, 1988. The quote is from p. 26 of the transcript but the sentiment was repeated often during the four seminars. See, for example, pages 24, 38–39, 44, 58, and 66–68.

8. T. J. Jackson Lears, "From Salvation to Self-Realization: Advertising and the Therapeutic Roots of the Consumer Culture" in *Culture of Consumption: Critical Essays in American History, 1880–1980,* Richard Wrightman Fox and T. J. Jackson Lears, eds. (New York: Pantheon, 1983), pp. 3–38. See also Stuart Ewen's *Captains of Consciousness: Advertising and the Social Role of Consumer Culture* (New York: McGraw-Hill, 1976).

9. See Marita Sturken and Lisa Cartwright, *Practices of Looking: An Introduction to Visual Culture* (New York: Oxford University Press, 2001), p. 197.

10. October 31, 1989, p. 15.

11. The issue of being "good for you" (something educational and therefore worthwhile) seems important to many women today. The social prestige of learn-

ing justifies the time spent. The current advertising line, "Learn something new every day on *Ask Martha* [Stewart]," capitalizes on this importance.

12. American businesses have been interested in the homemaker as the organizer of family life since the last decades of the nineteenth century. But the interest seems to have bloomed in the 1920s with their use of household efficiency experts and publicists to promote and celebrate the centrality of the housewife in her role as the modern manager of family consumption. Interestingly, this seems to have been concomitant with the beginning of radio serialized drama (which Stedman, in *The Serials,* pp. 226–27, dates with *The Smith Family* in 1925). How daytime broadcasting and the scientific management of the home are related to the promise of personal fulfillment, to hegemonic power structures, and to desire would make an interesting historical study and should certainly include such television shows as ABC's *Home,* from the mid–1980s, and, more recently, CBS's *Martha Stewart Living.*

13. "What Do We Really Know about Daytime Serial Listeners?" *Radio Research, 1942–43,* Paul Lazarsfeld and Frank Stanton, eds. (New York: Duell, Sloan and Pearce, 1944), pp. 11–12. Subsequent page references will appear in the text.

14. Although her listener seems to use the soap operas in creative ways, Herzog's model of communication is still a linear one, where a simple manifest message, although mediated by the listener's needs, brings forth some response. Herta Herzog was still interested in the "effects" of the serials and their influence on audience behavior. But can such quantitative methods, which emphasize shared characteristics, ever deal with internal inconsistencies, conflicts, contradictions, or even the process of change? Her positivism, by limiting its attention to the measurable, can only reify (rather than transform) the existing order.

15. The Office of War Information had made an effort to use radio serials as a vehicle for such war messages as urging conservation, vigilance, information on emergency medical treatment, and so on. See Stedman's discussion in *The Serials,* pp. 329–39.

16. See Gitlin's "Media Sociology: The Dominant Paradigm," *Theory and Society,* 6 (1978), p. 231. See also Allen, *Speaking of Soap Operas,* pp. 18–28, on the relationship of the ascendancy of behaviorism in American social science research and the American advertising industry.

17. *The Relationship Between Daytime Serials and Their Viewers,* Ph.D. thesis, Mass Communications, University of Pennsylvania, 1977. Subsequent page references will appear in the text.

18. "Uses and Gratifications Research: A Critique and a Sociological Alternative," in *The Uses of Mass Communications: Current Perspectives on Gratifications Research,* Jay G. Blumler and Elihu Katz, eds. (Beverly Hills: Sage, 1974), p. 258.

19. Thomas herself raises some doubts about how such a method might implicitly support the existing structure in her reflections on stimulus-response models in her later essay "Some Problems of the Paradigm in Communication Theory," *Philosophy of the Social Sciences,* 10, 1980.

20. "Uses and Gratifications Research and the Study of Social Change," in D. L. Paletz, ed. *Political Communications Research: Approaches, Studies, Assessments*

(Norwood, N.J.: Ablex, 1987), p. 195, cited in *Television and New Media Audiences* (New York: Oxford University Press, 1999), pp. 11–12. This paradigm continues to be used by mass communications scholars to study soap opera audiences. (See, for example, the articles in the summer 1985 special edition of *Journal of Broadcasting and Electronic Media* [vol. 29, no. 3] entitled, "A Soap Opera Symposium.") As a theoretical method, the uses and gratifications approach is somewhat circular and self-serving. Since there does not seem to be any independent way to measure "need," it is measured by the use or effects of the media. The needs are then inferred from the supposed gratifications. Or measured effects are imputed as needs. Or media use is linked to an assumed need or configuration of needs and then the media are explained in terms of those needs. Likewise, there is no way to measure the direction of the influence between needs and use. (See Denis McQuail, "With the Benefit of Hindsight," *Mass Communication Review Yearbook,* vol. 5, 1985, p. 130.) Is there any independent evidence for the intervening mental or emotional states and processes or can they only be indirectly assessed? Are they proved by the method or are they artifacts of the method?

21. *Loving with a Vengeance: Mass-Produced Fantasies for Women* (Hamden, Conn.: Archon, 1982). Subsequent page references will appear in the text. Modleski's chapter on soaps appeared in two abbreviated articles published in *Film Quarterly* in the fall of 1979 and in *Tabloid* in the summer of 1981. It is in the book, however, that the full complexity of her theoretical argument becomes evident. The book also includes chapters that analyze mass-marketed romances and Gothics.

22. Martha Nochimson, too, laments the lack of respect that soaps are accorded. And she, like Modleski, celebrates the multiple perspectives and absence of closure as a "feminine" form (diverging from the dominant Hollywood filmic model). See *No End to Her: Soap Opera and the Female Subject* (Berkeley: University of California Press, 1993).

23. Although they were making the serial for lesbian audiences and thus didn't feel they had to dilute issues or "explain" lesbianism, the show did have the educational advantage of showing lesbians and gay men living and interacting in established communities and showing that you don't have to give up intimacy and personal relationships to be a lesbian. However, the serial never challenges the "patriarchal core" of soaps, the codes of the personal and the relational that express and reinforce the socially constructed lives of women in domestic situations. One might ask if *Two in Twenty,* like broadcast soaps, doesn't continue to address female subjectivity as a self built in relation to others? But perhaps they meant to ridicule this. The videos include clearly satirical commercials that mock not only the products being advertised, but also the representation of women and femininity in broadcast commercials.

The serial also raises interesting questions about the differences between public and private reception of television. Would reception be different if one views the show in a room full of politically involved lesbians than if one views it alone? Is there a different sense of laughter?

Lynn Spigel takes issue with Modleski's suggestion that feminists might incorporate the pleasure soaps afford into their artistic practice, noting that the use of a realist aesthetic works against any radical dislocation or decentering of the viewing subject. "Detours in the Search for Tomorrow: Tania Modleski's *Loving with a Vengeance: Mass-Produced Fantasies for Women,*" *Camera Obscura,* 13–14 (spring/summer 1985): p. 229.

24. See Annette Kuhn's "Women's Genres," *Screen,* vol. 25, no. 1 (January/February 1984): p. 24.

25. "Women Watching Television," in *MedieKultur,* 4 (November 1986): p. 105.

26. "Crossroads: Notes on a Soap Opera," *Screen,* vol. 22, no. 4 (1981), reprinted in *Screen Tastes: Soap Opera to Satellite Dishes* (New York: Routledge, 1997). Subsequent page references from the *Screen* article will appear in the text. See also "Writing About Soap Opera" in *Television Mythologies: Stars, Shows and Signs,* Len Masterman, ed. (London: Comedia, 1984), reprinted in *Screen Tastes.*

27. Op. cit., p. 26.

28. Brunsdon's recent book, *The Feminist, the Housewife, and the Soap Opera* (New York: Oxford University Press, 2000), includes a very useful academic survey of soap opera audience studies from 1975–1986.

29. "Introduction to Ethnography at the Centre," by Roger Grimshaw, Dorothy Hobson, and Paul Willis, in *Culture, Media, Language: Working Papers in Cultural Studies, 1972–1979,* Stuart Hall et al., eds. (London: Hutchinson, 1981), p. 73.

30. Many interesting studies of media and other popular culture have come out of the Centre for Contemporary Cultural Studies. Several of them have informed my work. I will mention them individually as they are relevant; however, here I will limit my discussion to those studies that specifically look at television audience activity.

31. "Overcoming Resistance to Cultural Studies," *Mass Communication Review Yearbook,* vol. 5 (1985), p. 7, emphasis in original.

32. See Stuart Hall's "Cultural Studies: Two Paradigms" in *Culture, Ideology and Social Process: A Reader,* Tony Bennett et al., eds. (London: Open University Press, 1981), pp. 26–27.

33. Stuart Hall, "Introduction to Media Studies at the Centre," in Hall et al., eds., *Culture, Media, Language,* p. 118 and p. 121.

34. Which is not to say that they constitute a program for political action. See Hall's "The Rediscovery of 'Ideology': Return of the Repressed in Media Studies," *Culture, Society and the Media,* Michael Gurevitch, Tony Bennett, James Curran and Janet Woolacott, eds. (London: Methuen, 1982).

35. Stuart Hall, "Encoding/decoding," in *Culture, Media, Language,* pp. 128–38.

36. Hall, "Encoding/decoding," pp. 136–38.

37. *The 'Nationwide' Audience* (London: BFI, 1980). Subsequent page references will appear in the text.

38. Although most of the groups consisted of men or boys, two of the twenty-nine groups were all women and a few groups had men and women. However, Morley does not look at how gender inflects the process.

39. *Family Television: Cultural Power and Domestic Leisure* (London: Comedia, 1986), p. 43. Subsequent page references will appear in the text. Morley's 1981 critique of the *Nationwide* study ("*The 'Nationwide' Audience*—A Critical Postscript," *Screen Education,* 39, reprinted in his collection of essays *Television, Audiences and*

Cultural Studies [London: Routledge, 1992]) suggested that Hall's concept of decoding model might have collapsed a number of processes and experiences into one action. A more complex notion of decoding seems to be operating in the newer study. His more recent essay, "Towards an ethnography of the television audience," in *Television, Audiences and Cultural Studies,* discusses quantitative and qualitative audience studies (and the literature on them) and ethnography as an empirical method, and expresses many of my own concerns.

40. Ann Gray's empirical study of thirty British (predominantly working-class) women with children at home and their use of their VCRs and rental videos appeared as an article, "Behind closed doors: video recorders in the home," in *Boxed-In: Women and Television,* Helen Baehr and Gillian Dyer, eds. (London: Pandora, 1986). The research has since been published in an expanded form in *Video Playtime: The Gendering of Leisure Technology* (London: Routledge, 1992). Neither Morley nor Gray discusses textual interpretation (neither their informants' nor their own). They also find less contradiction in gender roles and family relations than I have found. Whereas they find gender roles and family hierarchy determine media usage in the home, I will be arguing that soap opera usage and interpretations also inflect our consciousness and therefore gender identity and family relations. Gender roles and family hierarchy are less static in my formulation. This will be discussed further at the end of this chapter.

41. Morley's research was funded by the Independent Broadcasting Authority. This may be inherent in any such funded study. In a subsequent essay, written with Roger Silverstone, Morley comes out strongly for investigating audiences in their "natural" setting, the domestic environment, but, again, his main interest is how television (and other communication and information technologies) "acquire meaning." See "Communication and context: ethnographic perspectives on the media audience," in Klaus Bruhn Jensen and Nicholas W. Jankowski, eds., *A Handbook of Qualitative Methodologies for Mass Communication Research* (New York: Routledge, 1991), p. 150.

42. *Crossroads: The Drama of a Soap Opera* (London: Methuen, 1982). Subsequent page references will appear in the text. The research was begun as a part of her Ph.D. thesis. Excerpts from her M.A. thesis, "A Study of Working-Class Women at Home: Femininity, Domesticity, and Maternity," which looks at housewives' use of radio and TV, is excerpted in the "Ethnography" section of *Culture, Media, Language,* pp. 105–15.

43. A theory that sees the viewer as completely self-consistent or unified would have to be founded on a pre-Freudian notion of subjectivity.

44. Paul Willis, "Notes on Method," *Culture, Media, Language,* p. 90. Concerns about realism were not unique to Hobson. Mary Ellen Brown, for example, also asked her respondents whether they thought soap characters are like real people and whether the stories are like real life or not (*Soap Opera and Women's Talk: The Pleasures of Resistance* [Thousand Oaks, Calif.: Sage, 1994] pp. 189–90).

45. *Watching* Dallas: *Soap Opera and the Melodramatic Imagination* (London: Methuen, 1985). Subsequent page references will appear in the text. The original Dutch study was conducted in 1982 as a thesis in General Social Sciences at the University of Amsterdam.

46. "Blurred Genres: The Refiguration of Social Thought," *Local Knowledge: Further Essays in Interpretive Anthropology* (New York: Basic Books, 1983).

47. Op. cit., p. 34.

48. Ang questions how textual features of the program organize the viewer's experience and in what ideological context these experiences acquire meaning. She is speaking about concrete viewers, not "audiences," and her conceptualization of their activity and their relation to the television show seems close to British cultural studies. The structure of a text stimulates the emotional and cognitive involvements of the viewer, but the viewer also brings cultural knowledge of the "specific codes and conventions in order to be able to have any grasp what a text is about" (p. 27). "A text functions only if it is 'read'. Only in and through the practice of reading does the text have meaning (or several meanings) for the reader. In the confrontation between *Dallas* and its viewers the reading activity of the latter is therefore the connecting principle" (ibid.).

49. See his review of *Watching Dallas, Journal of Communication,* vol. 36, no. 4 (autumn 1986).

50. Her letter writers have no context other than the show and the competing popular discourses about the show. We are not even given any information about the magazine in which she placed the advertisement and which her respondents presumably read.

51. Chapel Hill: University of North Carolina Press, 1984. Subsequent page references will appear in the text. Radway's study parallels many of my own concerns and was a great encouragement to me. I am grateful to Robert Sklar for recommending her work, while it was still in press, at a time when I was formulating my own study.

52. "Romance and the Work of Fantasy: Struggles Over Feminine Sexuality and Subjectivity at Century's End," in Jon Cruz and Justin Lewis, eds., *Viewing, Reading, Listening: Audiences and Cultural Reception* (Boulder: Westview Press, 1996), p. 214.

53. For the variety of approaches see the essays in Jane P. Tompkins's *Reader Response Criticism: From Formalism to Post Structuralism* (Baltimore: Johns Hopkins University Press, 1980), especially her review, "The Reader in History: The Changing Shape of Literary Response" (pp. 201–32), and Susan B. Suleiman and Inge Crosman, eds., *The Reader in the Text: Essays on Audience and Interpretation* (Princeton, N.J.: Princeton University Press, 1980).

54. "Identifying Ideological Seams: Mass Culture, Analytical Method, and Political Practice," *Communication,* vol. 9 (1986): p. 98.

55. *The Practice of Everyday Life* (Berkeley: University of California Press, 1984), p. 30. For deCerteau, marginality is not limited to a minority, but seems to be becoming a universal condition. See p. xvii. Henry Jenkins's work on textual poachers applies deCerteau's theories to television fans and their response to and reworking of the media. See *Textual Poachers: Television Fans and Participatory Culture* (London: Routledge, 1992).

56. Loc. cit.

57. Radway met each of the women through their bookstore advisor. It should be noted, however, that there is no indication that the women had known each

other before Radway began interviewing them in small groups or that they had seen themselves as a community before being introduced to her project. Nor is there any reflection on the extent her interest may have built "a community" or "a culture" or even whether any friendships or social interactions grew out of her discussion groups.

58. Chapel Hill: University of North Carolina Press. Subsequent page references will appear in the text.

59. The viewer that is invoked is a theoretical construct. "Actual" viewers enter his discussion only as demographic information or as references to his own experiences as a viewer. As Allen puts it, "The implicit challenge is to relate these constructed [viewer] positions to the experiences of actual soap opera [viewers]" (p. 182).

60. Although the complexity and ambiguities of soaps are an important part of his perspective, Allen's rather mechanical imposition of Iser and narrative theory onto soaps leaves many aspects unanalyzed (much like a cookie cutter eliminates the dough on the outside of the form) and points to some of the difficulties in applying literary theory to television.

61. *The Promise of Melodrama: Recent Women's Films and Soap Operas,* Ph.D. thesis, Northwestern University, 1981. Seiter has also published articles using a similar methodology. See "The Role of the Woman Reader: Eco's Narrative Theory and Soap Operas," in *Tabloid,* 6 (1981) and "Men, Sex and Money in Recent Family Melodramas," in *Journal of the University Film and Video Association,* vol. 35, no. 1 (winter 1983).

62. "'Don't Treat Us Like We're So Stupid and Naive': Toward an Ethnography of Soap Opera Viewers," written with Hans Borchers, Gabriele Kreutzner, and Eva-Maria Warth, in *Remote Control: Television, Audiences and Cultural Power.* Seiter, Borchers, Kreutzner, and Warth, eds. (London: Routledge, 1989). They found, for example, that middle-class, educated informants more readily took up the position of ideal mother than did the working-class ones, and that position was "vehemently rejected" by most (p. 237). (Andrea Press, however, in "Class, Gender and the Female Viewer: Women's Responses to *Dynasty,*" in *Television and Women's Culture: The Politics of the Popular,* Mary Ellen Brown, ed. [Thousand Oaks, Calif.: Sage, spring 1990] came to different conclusions from the audiences she studied.) In an interesting essay ("Making Distinction in TV Audience Research: Case Study of a Troubling Interview," *Cultural Studies,* vol.4, no. 1, 1990), Seiter discusses some of the methodological difficulties they encountered interviewing, especially the problems in adhering to their resolution to be nondirective when there are a lack of rapport and differences in "cultural capital." On "cultural capital," see Pierre Bourdieu's *Distinction: A Social Critique of the Judgement of Taste* (Cambridge, Mass.: Harvard University Press, 1986).

63. She presented part of her research in a paper, "Reading/Resisting: Teenagers, Adults and Their Soaps," at the Society of Cinema Studies Conference, University of Iowa, Iowa City, April 15, 1989.

64. *Soap Opera and Women's Talk.* Although American daytime soaps are now seen abroad (sometimes in prime time) and although some of what I say about American daytime soaps may be generalizable to those audiences or to prime-time American serials, such as *Dallas* or *Dynasty,* or foreign-made soaps, such as

Coronation Street or *East Enders,* or even to 1950s Hollywood family melodramas, I am not making those claims in this study. The viewing context (the family, the role of women in the family, and the distribution of work in the family) as well as the narrative discourses and textual practices would need to be examined and are clearly beyond the scope of this book.

65. *Television and New Media Audiences* (New York: Oxford University Press, 1999). After the major part of my research was completed several broader ethnographic studies of popular culture were published. These are reviewed in *Television and New Media Audiences.* I am limiting my discussion here to studies of television soap opera viewing and works such as Radway's that have been a part of my own quest for methods.

66. Celeste Michelle Condit points out that "polysemy" may not be as accurate a description of the television text as "polyvalent." "It is not that text routinely features unstable denotation but that instability of connotation requires viewers to judge texts from their own value systems." "The Rhetorical Limits of Polysemy," *Critical Studies in Mass Communications,* June 1989, reprinted in Horace Newcomb's *Television: The Critical View,* 5th edition (New York: Oxford University Press, 1994). The quote is from p. 431.

67. "Complexity and Contradiction in Mass-Culture Analysis: On Ien Ang's *Watching Dallas,*" *Camera Obscura,* 16 (January 1988).

68. As, for example, in Sandy Flitterman-Lewis's essay, "All's Well That Doesn't End: Soap Operas and the Marriage Motif," *Camera Obscura,* 16 (January 1988), in which an audience of ideal viewers constructed by the text allows her to privilege her own understanding. There are other variations. For instance, in literary theory, Stanley Fish proposes himself as an informed reader who is "neither an abstraction, nor an actual living reader, but a hybrid—a real reader (me) who does everything within his power to make himself informed," including "suppressing, in so far as that is possible . . . what is personal and idiosyncratic . . . in my response." (*Is There a Text in This Class?: The Authority of Interpretive Communities* [Cambridge: Harvard University Press, 1980] p. 49.)

69. *Local Knowledge,* p. 69.

70. Ibid.

71. This term is inspired by the French journal *Actes de la recherche en science sociales.*

72. Sari Thomas's research, for example, attempts a value-free and quantitative treatment of matters that are inherently evaluative, subjective, and qualitative. No research plan is uncontaminated with a priori assumptions. The questions she asked were fairly directed and although all responses were considered in the codifying process, they were taken at face value. That is, they were not problematized by the interviewer/analyst. For instance, to determine where the respondents fell on her "dedication-scale," Thomas asked them questions about what they might do if their viewing were interrupted (or had the potential to be interrupted). She found that the less educated were more "dedicated" (pp. 34–36); however, she never questioned whether the college-educated group might assume that the highly educated researcher might value personal interaction more, or whether they might be aware of personal interaction as a value. That is, the concept might

have a different social meaning and social value for them. In other words, Thomas takes the answers as "truth," without considering the answers as behavior or her role in the dialogue.

73. Elaine Showalter's "Feminist Criticism in the Wilderness," in *Feminist Criticism: Essays on Women, Literature and Theory,* Showalter, ed. (New York: Pantheon Books, 1985), p. 244. *The Authority of Experience* is the title of a 1977 anthology edited by Arlyn Diamond and Lee R. Edwards (Amherst: University of Massachusetts Press).

74. Op. cit., p. 252.

75. Tania Modleski, in the introduction to *Studies in Entertainment: Critical Approaches to Mass Culture* (Bloomington: Indiana University Press, 1986), argues that ethnographic audience studies run the risk of a perilous "collusion" with consumer society because the mass culture critic cannot maintain a "critical distance" (p. xii). It seems to me that one does need to maintain a critical stance in relation to both consumer society and one's own research plan; however, a critical *distance* may not be necessarily helpful, as it implies the researcher may be aiming to construct an objective, monologic truth. (Ian Ang concurs; see *Living Room Wars: Rethinking Media Audiences for a Postmodern World* [New York: Routledge, 1996], pp. 99–100.)

76. James Clifford, "Introduction: Partial Truths," *Writing Culture: The Poetics and Politics of Ethnography,* James Clifford and George E. Marcus, eds. (Berkeley: University of California, 1986), p. 8.

77. The films and writing of Trinh T. Minh-há, as well as post-structuralist literary theorists, come to mind as an example of this strategy.

78. See Raymond Williams's discussion of "structures of feeling" in *Marxism and Literature* (Oxford: Oxford University Press, 1977), pp. 128–35.

79. *Kinesics and Context: Essays on Body Motion Communication* (Philadelphia: University of Pennsylvania Press, 1970), p. 191.

80. Ronald J. Grele, "Movement Without Aim" in *Envelopes of Sound,* Ronald J. Grele, ed. (Chicago: Precedent Publishing, 1975), p. 137.

81. "Travels in Nowhere Land: Ethnography and the 'Impossible' Audience," *Critical Studies in Mass Communication,* 9 (1992): p. 252.

82. Some of Janice Radway's informants cited the social legitimacy of reading, yet seemed to need to apologize for reading romances. Even to them, romances were understood to be a deprecated and devalued genre. Does this undercut their pleasures, as Brunsdon argues ("Women Watching Television," p. 109), or does it add to them?

83. Even though some men certainly watch soap operas, and although several of the women I spoke to mentioned watching with their daughters, none mentioned watching with their sons.

84. None of the women I spoke to, for example, expressed any doubt in the validity of my project.

85. *The Use of Pleasure: The History of Sexuality, Vol. 2* (New York: Pantheon, 1985), p. 10.

86. Elihu Katz and Tamar Liebes, in their study of viewers of an episode of the prime-time serial *Dallas,* began with the assumption that television viewing is a social event often involving family members and friends, including talk during

commercials and afterwards, and therefore observed groups of people watching *Dallas* and talking about their interpretations. ("Mutual Aid in the Decoding of *Dallas:* Preliminary Notes from a Cross-Cultural Study," *Television in Transition: Papers from the First International Television Studies Conference,* Phillip Drummond and Richard Paterson, eds. ([London: BFI, 1986]). This is not the case with most of the daytime viewers with whom I spoke. Interestingly, even though Candy spoke about the men she convinced to watch soaps, all of her examples were of watching alone (often having to wait until other family members were asleep in order to get the time to watch). Watching alone is also reported as the typical state of the daytime viewer in Madeline Edmondson and David Rounds's *The Soaps: Daytime Serials of Radio and TV* (New York: Stein and Day, 1973), p. 184. Robert E. Short, while Manager of Daytime Programs for Procter and Gamble Productions, was also of the opinion that the majority of the audience is women who watch alone. See "The Television Executive's View of Daytime Serials" in Mary Cassata and Thomas Skill, op. cit., p. 175.

87. Walter Benjamin points out that our educational privilege has given us a means of production which we can adapt for the purposes of political struggle; however, the solidarity of the intellectual and the proletariat can only be a mediated one. "The Author As Producer," *Reflections* (New York: Harcourt Brace Jovanovich, 1978), p. 237. James Clifford describes modern ethnography as "a state of being in culture while looking at culture," but he also discusses it as "a pervasive condition of off-centeredness." *The Predicament of Culture: Twentieth-Century Ethnography, Literature, and Art* (Cambridge, Mass.: Harvard University Press, 1988), p. 9.

88. *Outline of a Theory of Practice* (Cambridge: Cambridge University Press, 1977), p. 10.

89. "Dialogue and Fiction in Ethnography," *Dialectical Anthropology,* vol. 7, no. 2 (November 1982): pp. 95–96.

90. *On Deconstruction* (Ithaca: Cornell University Press, 1982), p. 35.

91. *The Practice of Everyday Life* (Berkeley: University of California Press, 1984), pp. xii–xiii. One fine example of this is the African Brazilians' productive use of the colonizer's Catholicism.

92. Many studies have analyzed the manifest content of soap operas. See, for example, Bradley S. Greenberg, Robert Abelman, and Kimberly Neuendorf, "Sex on the Soap Operas: Afternoon Delight," *Journal of Communication,* vol. 31, no. 3 (summer 1981); Mary Cassata and Thomas Skill, *Life on Daytime Television;* R. Arnheim, "The World of the Daytime Serial," in *Radio Research, 1942–1943,* P. Lazarfeld and F. Stanton, eds. (New York: Duell, Sloan and Pearce, 1944); and Mildred Downing, "Heroine of the Daytime Serials," *Journal of Communication,* vol. 24, no. 2 (spring 1974).

93. *Journal of Communication,* vol. 31, no. 3 (summer 1981).

94. See Stanley Fish, *Is There a Text in the Class?,* p. 9.

95. "The Death of an Author," *Music Image Text* (New York: Hill and Wang, 1977), p. 148.

96. "History in Ruins: Television and the Triumph of Culture," in *The Postmodern Scene: Excremental Culture and Hyper-Aesthetics* (New York: St. Martins Press, 1986), p. 269.

97. Op. cit., p. 275.

98. *The Poetics of Space* (Boston: Beacon Press, 1969), p. 4.

99. Op. cit., pp. 5, 6, 10, 72, passim.

100. *The Second Sex* (New York: Bantam, 1965), p. 425. I thank Robert Stam for reminding me of this passage.

101. *Cuentos: Stories by Latinas,* Alma Gómez, Cherríe Moraga, Mariana Romo-Carmona, eds. (New York: Kitchen Table: Women of Color Press, 1983), p. 17.

102. Dorothy Hobson suggests this repetitiousness and lack of escape intensify the compulsion we experience in trying to manage our duties in "Housewives: isolation as oppression," in *Women Take Issue: Aspects of Women's Subordination,* Women's Studies Group, Centre for Contemporary Cultural Studies, University of Birmingham, eds. (London: Hutchinson, 1978), p. 89.

103. "Housewives and Their Work Today," in *Woman's Work: The Housewife, Past and Present* (New York: Vintage Books, 1976), p. 95. There are, of course, also many extradomestic influences that suggest that a rationalized organization of work in the home is more scientific or progressive.

104. Loc. cit. One is reminded of the question that Jewish American women of the post–World War II generation would use when speaking to their contemporaries: Do you "go to business?" They were asking about work outside the home, but the expression implicitly acknowledged that housework is a job, too.

105. James C. Carmine, quoted in Boddy's "'The Shining Centre of the Home': Ontologies of Television in the 'Golden Age,'" in *Television in Transition,* p. 132. See also Lynn Spigel's *Make Room for TV: Television and the Family Ideal in Postwar America* (Chicago: University of Chicago Press, 1992), pp. 75, 78. Leo Bogart's 1956 study, *The Age of Television: A Study of Viewing Habits and the Impact of Television on American Life* (New York: Frederick Ungar, 1972), reports on surveys that attempted to measure the housewife's attention to the set—and how much time she was stealing away from her housework. See especially pp. 111–13.

106. *Television Audience Research,* quoted in Boddy, p. 132.

107. Quoted in Allen, *Speaking of Soap Operas,* p. 123.

108. "DuMont Skeds 7 A.M. to 11 P.M.," *Variety* 22 (September 1948), cited in Spigel, *Make Room for TV,* p. 78.

109. "NBC-TV Gets Daytime Bug as Full Hour Dramas Bow in Tint," November 2, 1955.

110. "Sitcoms and Suburbs: Positioning the 1950s Homemaker," *Quarterly Review of Film and Video,* vol. 11, no. 1 (1989).

111. DeCerteau, *The Practice of Everyday Life,* p. 29.

112. "Leisure Time of the American Housewife," by J. Roy Leevy in *Sociology and Social Research,* vol. 35, no. 2 (November/December 1950).

113. *Make Room for TV,* pp. 73, 74, 89.

114. *North British Review,* May 3, 1845. The author was concerned about the consequences of the serial form. Quoted in Jennifer Hayward's *Consuming Pleasures: Active Audiences and Serial Fictions from Dickens to Soap Operas* (Lexington: University Press of Kentucky, 1997), p. 26.

115. See, for example, Ann Gray's "Behind Closed Doors: Video Recorders in the Home," in *Boxed-In: Women and Television,* Helen Baehr and Gillian Dyer,

eds. (London: Pandora, 1986); Rick Altman's "Television/Sound" in *Studies in Entertainment: Critical Approaches to Mass Culture,* Tania Modleski, ed. (Bloomington: Indiana University Press, 1986); Dorothy Hobson's "Housewives: Isolation as Oppression," in *Women Take Issue;* and David Morley's *Family Television.*

116. Many of the women in David Morley's study also tended to do chores while watching television (*Family Television,* p. 150) as did some of those in Ellen Seiter, et al.'s study ("'Don't Treat Us Like We're So Stupid and Naive,'" p. 231). They also quoted one woman who is careful to finish up *before* she sits down to watch, "What I try to do is get everything I want to do done before that time. Then I don't feel guilty if I sit down and watch them. . . . I like to get up in the morning and get done what I figure I should do and then that's my relaxing time" (p. 230).

117. Rick Altman (ibid.) discusses the responsibility of the soundtrack to keep "viewers" informed and attentive even when they are only listening or intermittently watching, and thus encouraging them to keep their sets on and allowing them to be counted by the rating services. The sound track alone is "in contact with the audience for fully half the time that the set is on." He argues that "television must be organized in such a way as to harmonize with the household flow on which it depends," and with which, in many ways, it is in competition (p. 44). William Boddy has pointed out that early discussions of television often debated the amount of attention and concentration that would be needed to enjoy the medium. It was sometimes assumed that television would be watched in darkness or semi-darkness and that the eyestrain ensuing might limit the amount of viewing that would be comfortable. ("'The Shining Centre of the Home,'" p. 131.)

118. Though Tania Modleski, Carol Lopate, and others argue that the very flow of daytime television reflects the flow of the household activity that distracts the spectators from concentrating on the television (Modleski's *Loving with a Vengeance* and Carole Lopate's seminal article, "Daytime Television: You'll Never Want to Leave Home," in *Radical America,* vol. 11, no. 1 [January/February 1977] directly address this), some researchers (Sari Thomas, for example) measure spectator "loyalty" (couched in high-minded and reformist language) by her very refusal to be distracted by other activities.

119. See, for example, Fiske's essay in *Channels of Discourse* (the quote is from p. 286) and his book *Television Culture* (London: Methuen, 1987), p. 83; p. 255; et passim. David Sholle aptly points out that such resistance studies are based on an unspoken social theory of liberal pluralism in "Reading the Audience, Reading Resistance: Prospects and Problems," *Journal of Film and Video,* vol. 43, no. 1–2 (spring/summer 1991): p. 83.

120. *Power/Knowledge: Selected Interviews and Other Writings, 1972–1977,* p. 145.

121. "Who Communicates What to Whom, in What Voice and Why, About the Study of Mass Communication?" *Critical Studies in Mass Communication,* 7 (1990): p. 192. See also, "The Affirmative Character of U.S. Cultural Studies," by Mike Budd, Robert M. Entman, and Clay Steinman, in the same issue of *Critical Studies in Mass Communication.*

122. See Pierre Bourdieu, *Distinction.*

123. *Textual Poachers,* p. 17. Jenkins is speaking of television fan culture in general, not specifically about soap fans. Martha Nochimson brings her own experience in

the industry, as writer, editor, or consultant on five soap operas, to her analysis, but, interestingly, also writes as a fan. She introduces the notion of quality and artistic value to the discussion of particular productions and the form's uniqueness. Her terms and strategies are the same as those used by soap critics, even though she reverses their aesthetic assessments. (See especially the epilogue to *No End to Her.*) This is an example, to use Audre Lorde's metaphor, of trying to dismantle the master's house by using the master's tools. How much more radical would it be to consider soaps without the question of excellence!

124. "The problems of being popular," *New Socialist,* 41 (September 1986): p. 15.

125. "The In-Difference of Television," *Screen,* vol. 28, no. 2 (spring 1987): p. 38.

126. Op. cit., pp. 38–39. I, however, would stop short of Grossberg's contention that television situates the subject "within an affective democracy." Grossberg sees television's "in-difference" as a part of a democratizing effect, ultimately negating the power of affect itself. He sees this as an empowering economy for many viewers "precisely because it is not ideological" (pp. 44–45).

127. See Simon Watney's discussion of processes of identification in *Policing Desire: Pornography, AIDS and the Media* (Minneapolis: University of Minnesota Press, 1987), pp. 22–37, et passim.

128. *Making Stories: Law, Literature, Life* (Cambridge, Mass.: Harvard University Press, 2002), p. 64.

129. "Watching Ourselves Watch Television, or, Who's Your Agent?" *Cultural Studies,* vol. 3, no. 3 (October 1989): p. 265; emphasis as such in original.

130. Stanley Fish, *Is There a Text in the Class?* p. 335.

131. See Jacques Leenhardt's "Toward a Sociology of Reading," in Susan B. Suleiman and Inge Crosman, eds., *The Reader in the Text: Essays on Audience and Interpretation* (Princeton, N.J.: Princeton University Press, 1980).

132. Sean Griffith's "All My Gay Children? Soaps, Sexuality and Cyberspace," paper presented at the Console-ing Passions Conference, Montreal, May 1997.

133. I am not making a formalist distinction between story and discourse here; that is, the story, in this usage, does not exist independently of (or prior to) its constitution in discourse.

134. January 19, 1996 post to r.a.t.s.a., cited in Griffith's "All My Gay Children?"

135. *S/Z* (New York: Hill and Wang, 1974), p. 90.

Chapter 3: The Narrative Discourses of Soap Operas

1. Robert C. Allen, writing in 1981, asked similar questions and did an elaborate multiplication of the number of hours that would be necessary to view the, then, entire television run of *The Guiding Light* and concluded that it would take one month of continuous viewing, but at the end we would still have waiting the sixteen hours broadcasted during our marathon screening session. See "The Guiding Light: Soap Opera As Economic Product and Cultural Document," in *American History/American Television,* John E. O'Connor, ed. (New York: Frederick Ungar, 1983), p. 314.

2. "Text and Audience," in *Remote Control: Television, Audiences and Cultural Power,* Ellen Seiter, Hans Borchers, Gabriele Kreutzner, and Eva-Maria Warth, eds. (London: Routledge, 1989), p. 123. Discussing recent soap opera audience studies, Brunsdon points to the necessity of retaining a notion of text, to construct a "televisual object of study" (p. 125). She also discusses this in a later version of the essay in "Television: Aesthetics and Audiences," in *Logics of Television,* Patricia Mellencamp, ed. (Bloomington: Indiana University Press, 1990), p. 63, reprinted in *Screen Tastes: Soap Opera to Satellite Dishes* (New York: Routledge, 1997).

3. Ibid.

4. *Bond and Beyond: The Political Career of a Popular Hero* (London: Methuen, 1987), pp. 90–91; Bennett's and Woollacott's work has influenced my approach to intertextual "encrustations."

5. Fredric Jameson, in the preface of *The Political Unconscious,* says that we never really confront a text as a fresh thing because "texts come before us as the always-already-read." (*The Political Unconscious: Narrative As a Socially Symbolic Act* [Ithaca, N.Y.: Cornell University Press, 1981], p. 9). Roland Barthes calls this the "déjà-lu" (see "From Work to Text," in *Image/Music/Text* [New York: Hill and Wang, 1977], p. 160).

6. This argument is indebted to Umberto Eco's in "The Myth of Superman," in *The Role of the Reader: Explorations in the Semiotics of Texts* (Bloomington: Indiana University Press, 1979), p. 109. Charlotte Brunsdon makes this point about watching British soap operas in "Writing About Soap Opera" in *Television Mythologies: Stars, Shows and Signs,* Len Masterman, ed. (London: Comedia, 1984), reprinted in *Screen Tastes: Soap Opera to Satellite Dishes* (New York: Routledge, 1997).

7. This began with the Reagan-era push for deregulation that inaugurated a period of intense competition among new technologies and delivery systems, and, more recently, massive mergers.

8. *Making Stories: Law, Literature, Life* (Cambridge, Mass.: Harvard University Press, 2002), p. 30.

9. "The Myth of Superman," p. 120.

10. Jameson, loc. cit.

11. *The Role of the Reader: Explorations in the Semiotics of Texts* (Bloomington: Indiana University Press, 1979), p. 5.

12. *S/Z* (New York: Hill and Wang, 1974), p. 160 and again in "From Work to Text," in *Image/Music/Text,* p. 159.

13. Some of this work on intertextuality overlaps with John Fiske's in his book, *Television Culture* (London: Methuen, 1987).

14. The concept of individual works manifesting, rather than belonging to, a genre is Tzvetan Todorov's. See *The Fantastic: A Structural Approach to a Literary Genre* (Ithaca, N.Y.: Cornell University Press, 1975), p. 17.

15. Jameson (in *The Political Unconscious,* p. 105) points out that the concept of genre has a strategic function for the analyst, allowing the critic the possibility of coordinating an immanent analysis of an individual text with a diachronic perspective on the history of forms and social life.

16. Jameson describes literary genres as essentially "institutions, or social contracts between a writer and a specific public, whose function is to specify the

proper use of a particular cultural artifact" (op. cit., p. 106). Stephen Neale describes film genres as "systems of orientations, expectations and conventions that circulate between industry, text and subject" in *Genre* (London: BFI, 1980), p. 6. John G. Cawelti, in *Adventure, Mystery and Romance,* writes of the emotional security that familiar formulas offer (Chicago: University of Chicago Press, 1976), p. 9.

17. New soaps are generally heavily advertised during other soap operas.

18. For a while in 2000, ABC soaps experimented by beginning with a video recap from the previous day's show, going right into the titles, and ending with clips from the next day's show. Recently, all three networks have been ending with previews of coming scenes. And some have been superimposing production credits over the opening pre-title sequences.

19. Among longtime viewers, the idea of authorship also encourages viewing the next soap; the same creator's, or creative team's, newest work is generally scheduled adjacent to a previous one. For instance, in most markets Agnes Nixon's most recent soap, *Loving,* was followed by her very popular *All My Children.* Likewise, *The Bold and the Beautiful* (a newer soap opera from William J. Bell and Lee Phillip Bell) is usually scheduled following (and is very much like) *The Young and the Restless,* created by the same team and a staple on CBS since 1973.

20. In *Reading the Romance* (Chapel Hill: University of North Carolina Press, 1984), p. 23.

21. Meredith Brown, "The Making of Soap Operas: A Special Report" (vol. 7, no. 18): p. 26.

22. "ABC Hopes Its Daytime Bubble Won't Burst," August 19, 1983.

23. Mary Alice Kellogg, for example, claims that in 1981 daytime television accounted for $1.4 billion of a total of $5.6 billion of the networks' advertising revenues and that in 1982, when the three top-rated soap operas were owned by ABC, 50 percent of ABC's network profits came from its daytime programming ("High Noon for Soaps: All the Intrigue Isn't on the Screen," *TV Guide* [February 26, 1983] p. 6).

24. Cobbett Steinberg, *TV Facts* (New York: Facts on File, 1980), p. 136. Peter Boyer, in the 1983 *Los Angeles Times* article cited above, gave a weekly budget for an hour-long soap as $300,000 to $400,000 (that is, for five one-hour shows), whereas a prime-time drama cost between $660,000 and one million dollars per hour.

25. Michael James Intintoli, *Taking Soaps Seriously: The World of* Guiding Light (New York: Praeger, 1984), p. 63. This study gives a detailed description of the production process.

26. See, for example, the interview with Robert E. Short, manager of daytime programs for Procter & Gamble Productions in Mary Cassata and Thomas Skill's *Life on Daytime Television: Tuning-In American Serial Drama* (Norwood, N.J.: Ablex, 1983), pp. 175 and 179.

27. Stuart Ewen discusses a 1944 article in *Architectural Record* about mass-produced suburban housing that speaks of the possibility of taking a single floor-plan and varying it with such changes as reversing the plan, rotating the garage, and changing the surface of the facade in order to produce seventy-two marketable combinations. *All Consuming Images: Politics and Style in Contemporary Culture* (New York: Basic Books, 1988), p. 229. One could imagine a mathematically

minded student of soap operas being able to construct a handbook that lists seventy-two variations on each of the fifteen most popularly used storylines, 1,080 combinations of at once familiar and dissimilar stories. Jean Rouverol's amicable *Writing for the Soaps* (Cincinnati: Writer's Digest Books, 1984) includes a chapter called "The Assembly Line," which discusses the distribution of writers' chores and the chain of command, but does not discuss the standardization of stories or even where the ideas for stories come from. She does note, however (in a back-handed acknowledgment of story similarities), that producers return unsolicited story projections unopened, fearing future plagiarism suits (p. 25).

28. Although I know of no detailed study that looks at the stylistic differences or idiosyncrasies of specific soaps, the fans seem quite informed on this (and one would assume that the networks, the production companies, and the advertising agencies are also). One could certainly trace the use of humor in Agnes Nixon's soaps, the glamour of the L.A.-produced William J. Bell soaps, the penchant for almost gothic intrigue on *As the World Turns,* and so on. This would make an interesting historical study involving important research on production and marketing. There is also much that could be said about the appeal of the differences. This will be discussed further where it is relevant, though any systematic comparison is still awaited. (Martha Nochimson's *No End to Her: Soap Opera and the Female Subject* [Berkeley: University of California Press, 1993] does pay admirable attention to these differences, tracing many of them back to the different producing goals of, for example, Gloria Monty [*General Hospital*], Bridget and Jerry Dobson [*Santa Barbara*], and Al Rabin [*Days of Our Lives*].)

Because I focus on the audience and interpretation, I give little attention to the current institutional matrix of soap operas, changes in the shows over time, the way soaps are shaped by the demands of serial production, or the connections between soaps and other daytime programs and between soaps and the feminist films and videos that reflect on and deconstruct romance, or that use soap opera as a trope for understandings of gender, sexuality, and the family, or that scrutinize the ideological character of soaps. These are all valuable projects that are only alluded to here.

29. Shlomith Rimmon-Kenan lists this as one of the paradoxes of repetition in "The Paradoxical Status of Repetition," *Poetics Today* (vol. 1, no. 4, 1980): pp. 152–53.

30. The interest in Muybridge's photographs among the conceptual artists of the late 1960s and early 1970s may be an interesting case in point. That is, it may be that Muybridge's photographs were not only instances of rationalization and systematic process but also an indication of how accumulation changes conditions and affects perception.

31. "'What sort of things do *you* remember best?' Alice ventured to ask. 'O, things that happened the week after next . . . ,'" *Through the Looking Glass,* Lewis Carroll, p. 248 in Martin Gardner's *The Annotated Alice* (New York: Bramhall House, 1960).

32. Cited in *Soap Fans: Pursuing Pleasure and Making Meaning in Everyday Life* (Philadelphia: Temple University Press, 1995), p. 77, emphasis in original.

33. As quoted in the *New York Times,* "They Spin the Tales for Soap Operas," by Kathy Henderson, July 6, 1986.

34. These are often scheduled during the four yearly "sweeps" when audience ratings are calculated to determine advertising rates (February, May, August, and November). Both of the above examples were during or just before the fall 1986 "sweeps." As Lauren Rabinowitz points out, weddings are also popular during "sweeps." ("Soap Opera Bridal Fantasies," *Screen*, vol. 33, no. 3 [autumn 1992]: p. 278.) In general, these periods are more spectacular than ordinary soaps.

35. "Innovation and Repetition: Between Modern and Post-Modern Aesthetics," *Daedalus*, vol. 114, no. 4 (fall 1985): p. 164.

36. p. 35.

37. *S/Z*, p. 19.

38. Brooks is referring to literary manifestations of repetition. See *Reading for the Plot: Design and Intention in Narratives* (New York: Random House, 1984), p. 101.

39. See, for example, the gothic overtones (and moral and psychic atmosphere) of *General Hospital*'s Summer 1996 set for Stefan's island home, "Wyndemere."

40. See his discussion of the "semic" and "cultural" codes in *S/Z*, especially pages 67–68, 181–84, and 190–97.

41. *Speaking of Soap Operas* (Chapel Hill: University of North Carolina Press, 1985), pp. 70–71.

42. "The Culture Industry: Enlightenment As Mass Deception," *Dialectic of Enlightenment* (New York: Seabury Press, 1972), p. 125. Robert LaGuardia, in *The Wonderful World of TV Soap Operas*, writes about this redundancy—the repetitiveness in soaps—as slowing down modern life so that there is time for reflection. (New York: Ballantine Books, 1974), p. 4.

43. *Feminist Theory: From Margin to Cente*r (Boston: South End Press, 1984), p. 45.

44. What fun to discover *Les Feux de l'Amour* on French television, *The Young and the Restless* with stories four years behind those in the United States!

45. Raymond Williams noted, in a 1983 essay, that as stage melodrama became more popular in the 1820s, "its plots increasingly resembled events reported in the popular press: sensational crimes and seductions." "British Film History: New Perspectives," in *British Cinema History*, James Curran and Vincent Porter, eds. (London: Weidenfeld and Nicolson, 1983), p. 16.

46. The episode is remarkable not only for its high emotion, but also for its sense of closure. The August 31st end-of-the-summer broadcast concluded with a three-minute montage of clips from the Billy and Andrew summer story and included the credits for the entire cast and staff. For further discussion of the implications of the storyline, see Joy V. Fuqua, "'There's a Queer in My Soap!': The Homophobia/AIDS Story-line of *One Life to Live*," in Robert C. Allen, ed., *To Be Continued: Soap Operas Around the World* (New York: Routledge, 1995), pp. 199–212. In an interview in *Soap Opera Digest* ten years later, writer Michael Malone said that he was "deeply proud" of the story (December 24, 2002, p. 46).

47. "Will All My Children Search for Tomorrow?" by Connie Passalacqua, *New York Times*, June 23, 1991, p. 27. Christine Geraghty traces such social issue stories in British soaps back to the beginning of *Coronation Street* in 1960 during the "new wave" of social realism (especially around questions of class and region)

in British theater, literature, and film in "Social Issues and Realist Soaps: A Study of British Soaps in the 1980s/1990s," in *To Be Continued: Soap Operas Around the World,* Robert C. Allen, ed. (New York: Routledge, 1995).

48. February 9, 1988.

49. January 21–27, 1989.

50. See James Carey, *Communication as Culture* (New York: Routledge, 1992) for a discussion of the two views of communication, the transmission view and the ritual view (pp. 13–36).

51. The metaphor is borrowed from Terry Eagleton, *The Rape of Clarissa: Writing, Sexuality, and Class Struggle in Samuel Richardson* (Minneapolis: University of Minnesota Press, 1986), p. 40.

52. See Susan Suleiman's discussion of "exemplary" narratives in *Authoritarian Fictions: The Ideological Novel As a Literary Genre* (New York: Columbia University Press, 1983), pp. 25–45, especially p. 35.

53. Even separate television rooms still look like the other rooms in our home, often with framed pictures of the family decorating the top of the TV set.

54. August 22, 1987; Rogers plays Maggie Horton. Publicity sometimes assures viewers that performers do not have some of the less than admirable traits that their characters exhibit. The December 26, 1987, *TV Guide,* for example, noted that Ilene Kristen who played the flighty, childish, manipulative, outrageous Delia on *Ryan's Hope* was more caring off-camera and spent three days a week visiting children in welfare hotels. Jeremy Butler discusses many of these issues in "'I'm Not a Doctor, But I Play One on TV': Characters, Actors, and Acting in Television Soap Opera," *Cinema Journal* 30:4 (summer 1991).

55. See, for instance, *TV Guide*'s August 29, 1987, issue, which announced that the two were married and suggested, "Maybe that's why their love scenes seem so convincing" (p. 28).

56. "*As the World Turns*'s Scott Bryce Says Farewell to Daytime," *Soap Opera Digest,* June 16, 1987, p. 131.

57. In the New York City area, 1996 daytime network television had twenty minutes and five seconds of commercials and promotions, "clutter," in an average hour (as reported by the 1997 Commercial Monitoring Report, *New York Times,* 3/21/97). On "flow," see Raymond Williams, *Television: Technology and Cultural Form,* pp. 86–96; Nick Browne's "supertext" ("The Political Economy of the Television [Super] Text"); Jane Feuer's "dialectic of segmentation and flow" ("The Concept of Live Television: Ontology As Ideology" in *Regarding Television,* p. 16); Horace Newcomb and Paul M. Hirsch's "strip" ("Television As a Cultural Forum" in *Television: The Critical View,* pp. 509–10); and Rick Altman's discussion of television sound as continuity ("Television/Sound" in *Studies in Entertainment: Critical Approaches to Mass Culture*). On sound insuring continuity of attention, see also Robert Deming's "The Television Spectator-Subject," *Journal of Film and Video,* vol. 37, no 3 (summer 1985). Recent critics (John Thornton Caldwell, for example, in *Televisuality: Style, Crisis, and Authority in American Television* [New Brunswick, N.J.: Rutgers University Press, 1995], p. 264) have argued that the widespread use of the VCR and the remote control has seriously challenged the notion of "flow." However, in order to fast forward through the commercials, promos, and

newsbreaks and stop when the show reappears, it is necessary to watch the screen. Although you cannot hear the audio, you *do* see the image. Some commercials have taken advantage of this with prolonged shots of the product near the end of the spot.

58. *Variety,* July 1, 1987.

59. As advertised in *Soap Opera Digest,* May 19, 1987, p. 33.

60. Some individuals also appear at political rallies and charity events.

61. Mimi White elaborates the idea of an all-encompassing television text (a "heterogeneous totality") in "Crossing Wavelengths: The Diegetic and Referential Imaginary of American Commercial Television," *Cinema Journal* (vol. 25, no. 2, winter 1986). The phrase quoted is on p. 62.

62. See, for instance, Karl-Lorimar Home Video's "Shades of Love" series, eighty-minute taped productions made expressly for the home video consumer.

63. "Heart Light City: A New and Different Kind of Soap Opera," by Toby Goldstein, *Soap Opera Digest,* August 30, 1985, pp. 136–37.

64. Patrice Petro has elaborated the thematic similarities between soap operas and daytime law shows, which she describes as providing narrative order and closure to soap opera's complications and frustrated endings in "Criminality or Hysteria? Television and the Law," *Discourse* 10.2 (spring/summer 1988).

65. Jennifer Hayward, *Consuming Pleasures: Active Audiences and Serial Fictions from Dickens to Soap Operas* (Lexington: University Press of Kentucky, 1997), p. 166.

66. *Re-viewing Reception: Television, Gender, and Postmodern Culture* (Bloomington: Indiana University Press, 1996), p. 58. Joyrich gives other examples of the phenomenon, including one where actors who once played siblings appeared as lovers on another soap; however, her concern for the postmodern dissipation of memory and history and its relation to consumer fantasies is different from mine here.

67. March 21, 1988.

68. A history of character endorsements would certainly want to refer to the "payola" scandals of the late 1950s. Until the 1980s, ABC refused to allow soap performers to appear in commercials that would play on their network.

69. See the interview with Pierre Macherey in *Red Letters,* 5 (summer 1977): p. 7.

70. The metaphor is Tony Bennett and Janet Woolacott's in *Bond and Beyond: The Political Career of a Popular Hero* (London: Methuen, 1987), p. 91.

71. Tony Bennett, "Text and Social Process: The Case of James Bond," *Screen Education* 41 (spring/smmer 1982): p. 13. I am not too happy with Bennett's term "activation" which it seems to me (like "decoding") has the unfortunate implication that meaning is in the text and is acted upon by the viewer. This, of course, is not Bennett's intention. See also his discussion in "Texts, Readers, Reading Formations," *Bulletin of the Midwest Modern Language Association,* vol. 16, no. 1 (spring 1983).

72. Besides viewing tapes from the '50s, '60s, and early 1970s, I have followed (during various times from 1980–1990) *The Young and the Restless, All My Children, The Guiding Light, Ryan's Hope, As the World Turns, Search for Tomorrow, The Bold and the Beautiful, Loving,* and *Generations* (for the short period it was on). I have also watched, for a lesser period of time, *Santa Barbara, One Life to Live,*

Capitol, Days of Our Lives, and, very briefly, *General Hospital.* I tuned in only sporadically from 1990 to 1999 while I was working on another project, generally when someone called to tell me that I *must* watch a particular storyline. I did watch for a few weeks when *Sunset Beach* debuted and after *Another World* announced it would be going off the air, and began to watch *The Young and the Restless* and *All My Children* again with my sabbatical in 2000.

73. John G. Cawelti uses this expression in describing the overarching structure of best-selling literary melodramas in *Adventure, Mystery and Romance* (Chicago: University of Chicago Press, 1976), p. 266.

74. Eli Zaretsky, *Capitalism, the Family and Personal Life* (New York: Harper & Row, 1976), p. 17.

75. Nancy Chodorow, *The Reproduction of Mothering: Psychoanalysis and the Sociology of Gender* (Berkeley: University of California Press, 1978), p. 179. Much of my discussion of the family is indebted to Chodorow and Zaretsky.

76. Ibid., pp. 159–70.

77. *Loving with a Vengeance: Mass-Produced Fantasies for Women* (Hamden, Conn.: Archon Books, 1982), pp. 107–08.

78. This, of course, is not unique to soap operas. Richardson's *Clarissa* was issued in installments in the eighteenth century and serial narratives have been popular on the radio and in film, as well. John Ellis argues that even episodic television is premised on ongoing dilemmas, never really reaching a final closure. See *Visible Fictions: Cinema: Television: Video* (London: Routledge & Kegan Paul, 1982), p. 156. For a history of serial narratives, see Roger Hagedorn's "Doubtless to Be Continued: A Brief History of Serial Narrative," in Robert C. Allen, ed., *To Be Continued: Soap Operas Around the World* (New York: Routledge, 1995), pp. 27–48. See also Jennifer Hayward's *Consuming Pleasures.*

79. During the seminar celebrating the Silver Anniversary of *One Life to Live,* for example, Museum of Television and Radio, New York, July 8, 1993. The line is generally attributed to Wilkie Collins.

80. Roland Barthes, *S/Z* (New York: Hill and Wang, 1974), p. 76.

81. Some of the alternations are quite discordant. For example on the July 1, 1986, episode of *All My Children,* Erika and Brooke's kidnapping by terrorists is intercut with Charlie and Julie's teenage flirting.

82. *Loving with a Vengeance,* p. 100. Arguing from Modleski, John Fiske, along with others, has discussed this endless deferment as an articulation of a specifically feminine conception of desire and pleasure (*Television Culture,* p. 183). Annette Kuhn's psychoanalytic reading, however, complicates this. She writes of both mastery (in solving the plot's enigmas) and masochism (in the endlessly held off resolutions); she also designates these as masculine and feminine subject positions. "Women's Genres," *Screen,* vol. 25, no. 1 (January/February 1984): p. 27.

83. About two-thirds of the commercials are aimed specifically at homemakers, parents, or women. See Appendix I.

84. By comparison, prime-time serials running at the time tended to be slightly less fragmented. The plot in the episode of *Dallas* aired the same day as the episode of *The Young and the Restless* under examination, for example, covered four days, each divided by a commercial break. There were twenty-four story sequences

and twenty-three commercials, station breaks, and title breaks; there were longer blocks of story, less commercial time, and fewer blocks of commercial interruptions.

85. Sandy Flitterman elaborates this (pp. 93–94) and points out that, in 1983 (and it still seems to be the case), the type of commercial that expounds a theme, rather than a chronological narrative, generally appears on prime time. See: "The *Real* Soap Opera," in *Regarding Television,* E. Ann Kaplan, ed. (Los Angeles: The American Film Institute, 1983), p. 90.

86. The average shot duration in the episode of *Dallas* discussed above was six and a quarter seconds.

87. Some soaps, and indeed some episodes of *The Young and the Restless,* have a somewhat ironic relationship implied between some of the segments. In the September 3, 1985, episode of *The Young and the Restless,* for example, Lauren is talking to her mother-in-law about her marriage and says that nothing will ever come between her and her husband again. The next sequence shows one of her enemies preparing to give Lauren's husband some news that will surely cause a rift.

88. *The Melodramatic Imagination: Balzac, Henry James, Melodrama and the Mode of Excess* (New Haven, Conn.: Yale University Press, 1976), p. 48. Jane Feuer, writing about the prime-time soap operas, *Dynasty* and *Dallas,* remarks how they followed the convention of daytime soaps by also holding a close-up on screen after the dialogue has ended, leaving "a residue of emotional intensity" just prior to the scene change or commercial break. ("Melodrama, Serial Form and Television Today," *Screen,* vol. 25, no. 1 [January/February 1984] pp. 10–11.) I will be pointing out many similarities between Brooks' descriptions of popular stage melodramas of the early nineteenth century and my understanding of U.S. daytime soap operas. Brooks, however, might object; he uses soap opera as the bad object, "cheap and banal melodrama," in order to justify the worthiness of scholarly attention to nineteenth-century stage melodrama (*The Melodramatic Imagination,* p. 12).

Comparisons might also be made with the grandiose expression and elevated feelings of nineteenth-century Italian opera, but, as Christine Gledhill's "Speculations on the Relationship Between Soap Opera and Melodrama" (*Quarterly Review of Film and Video,* vol. 14, nos. 1–2 [July 1992]: p. 104) points out, such projects run the risk of constructing static genres, and, as Brooks and others have pointed out, the Manichaean oppositions of melodrama characterized much nineteenth-century thought (p. 20).

89. "Narrative Analysis: Oral Versions of Personal Experience," *Proceedings of the Annual Spring Meeting of the American Ethnological Society* (1966): pp. 12–44. See also William Labov and Joshua Waletzky, "Natural Narratives" in *Essays on the Verbal and Visual Arts,* June Helm, ed. (Seattle: University of Washington Press, 1967).

90. They showed the entire text of the ceremony in real time, according to Mary Ellen Brown, *Soap Opera and Women's Talk: The Pleasures of Resistance* (Thousand Oaks, Calif.: Sage, 1994), p. 157.

91. Soaps that go off the air seldom end their stories, thus leaving themselves open to being revived or picked up by another network. During the final week of *Capital,* CBS promotional spots invited viewers to tune in to the "exciting conclusion" of the serial; however, the final week's episodes continued to introduce new

characters, new plot convolutions, and new possibilities. In the next-to-last episode (March 19, 1987), for example, Sam's first wife, who has finally recovered from twenty-seven years of catatonia, arrives in town disguised as the new nanny of the little boy who is thought to be her son Trey's child, but is really Sam's own child by Trey's wife. The final sequence of the last telecast ended on an extreme close-up of the Queen of Baracq's eyes as the guns of her execution squad are cocked and her recently arrived brother-in-law, the new King of Baracq, is beginning to broadcast a plea for her life.

Ryan's Hope advertised extensively their final weeks' episodes and invited viewers to say farewell. The final broadcast (one which I am sure was preserved by many video-tapers) was the day of Jack Fenelli's wedding. The occasion of his marrying out of the Ryan family called for many reminiscences, good-byes, and good lucks. Even though the writers attempted to tidy up several of the stories (shipping two members of two separate triangles to Australia, having another character win the lottery), when Maeve sings her last touching rendition of "Danny Boy," Patrick still does not know if Grace is his child and Maggie is still threatening to break up Roger and Delia's marriage (January 13, 1989).

While the producers of *Another World,* again with great publicity, forecasted a happy ending for their show, and did manage to cram several weddings into the final few weeks' broadcasts, the producer also reminded readers of *Soap Opera Digest* that, should the show move to another network, marriages can always be broken up (May 18, 1999). Although many fans I spoke with were adamant that stories were resolved when the show went off the air on June 25, 1999, the fact that four characters moved to *As the World Turns* somewhat mitigates the idea of an ending.

92. *The Sense of an Ending: Studies in the Theory of Fiction* (New York: Oxford University Press, 1966), p. 7.

93. Ibid., p. 23.

94. *Television Culture* (London: Methuen, 1987), p. 180.

95. "Soap Time: Thoughts on a Commodity Art Form," *College English* (vol. 38, no. 8, April 1977): p. 788.

96. William J. Bell, co-creator of *The Young and the Restless,* at a 1997 seminar at the Museum of Television and Radio, Los Angeles, told of the fifty-five page treatment for the new show that he brought to CBS's programming and business executives, twenty pages of which was backstory, before the show began, and thirty-five pages projected the story through the next two years. (University Satellite Series, *Worlds Without End: The Art and History of the Soap Opera: The Making of a William J. Bell Soap Opera:* The Young and the Restless [Museum of Television and Radio, 12/11/97].)

97. *Reading for the Plot,* p. 21.

98. See Christian Metz (*Film Language: A Semiotics of the Cinema* [New York: Oxford University Press, 1974], p. 18) on the "doubly temporal sequence" of narrative which "invents one time scheme in terms of another," and Gérard Genette (*Narrative Discourse: An Essay in Method* [Ithaca, N.Y.: Cornell University Press, 1980], p. 34) on the "pseudo-time" of the text, which metonymically borrows "with a combination of reservation and acquiescence" from the reading time.

99. Even if one is able to time-shift by preserving an episode with a videotape recorder, one still has to be attentive to the scheduled urgency of the telecast in order to capture the event.

100. Unless the pre-emption has been scheduled in advance and carried by all the affiliates, the episode that would have been broadcast is not shown at all. The gap in the continuity is generally minimized by the high redundancy customary to soaps; however, the change in the routine and what seems to many like an arbitrary exercise in scheduling power seems to offend some viewers and the popular press often carries stories of the objections. See, for instance, "Fans of Soap Operas Protest Iran Hearings," *New York Times,* December 11, 1986, or Warner Wolf's laughter on ABC radio, April 6, 2002, about the complaints CBS received when their Friday schedule was disrupted for the opening game of the Yankees' season.

The televising of "vintage soaps" has occurred recently. ABC, for instance, in 1997 aired some old episodes of *General Hospital* as they were about to debut their new soap, *Port Charles.* The cable network SoapNet was showing 1975 episodes of *Ryan's Hope* in the spring of 2000 and has been rescreening current ABC soaps in the evenings and weekends. NBC has now made clips from recent episodes available on their web page and some fans also host sites with video clips or episode archives. There are also weekend marathon sessions in some markets. ABC Home Video has merchandized compilation tapes of wedding scenes from their daytime serials and fans also often circulate tapes with their own compilations of favorite characters, storylines, or scenes. And, of course, those who travel might find ancient episodes of their soap playing abroad.

101. Occasionally, the daytime soap operas have exterior scenes taped out of the studio (the AIDS quilt in Llanview on *One Life to Live,* August 31, 1992, for example). Though great publicity is associated with infrequent remote shooting, especially those in exotic locations, it is much more costly (the simplest remotes cost approximately three times what it does to shoot in the studio) and represents a very small percentage of screen time. Lately, some shows, *All My Children* under production designer Boyd Dumrose, for example, have been using more prominent windows and exterior sets shot in the studio (on *All My Children,* the summer of 2000, a porch, a park, a beach).

102. Interestingly, dialogue situations are seldom used in the title scenes. *Ryan's Hope*'s titles in the late 1980s, for example, included fourteen shots of the characters with the theme music over. All out-of-doors, uncharacteristically showing the characters in some physical activity (which is otherwise seldom shown on screen), none of them show the characters in dialogue, which is the dominant image for the rest of the show.

103. *Signs Taken for Wonders* (London: Verso, 1983), p. 162. Moretti, however, is writing about adolescent literature, not soap operas.

104. Gaye Tuchman, in *Making News: A Study in the Construction of Reality* (New York: The Free Press, 1978), distinguishes scale in television newscasts as social distances and notes that an intimate distance (extreme close-up) is seldom used because it expresses emotion, not objectivity.

105. This is assuredly partially due to the large number of close shots. However,

the shows do, when necessary, picture two characters in close-up, one behind the other, both obliquely facing the camera (see frontispiece). In an attempt to put this in some perspective, I monitored episodes of both *M*A*S*H* and *Hill Street Blues* (both dialogue-centered dramas involving a large number of people in concurrent stories) and found that 37 percent and 31 percent, respectively, of the total shots had a single person in the frame. There does, however, seem to be a continuity between daytime and prime-time serials: in the episode of *Dallas* that was aired the same day as the episode of *The Young and the Restless* under examination, 70 percent of the shots had a single person in the frame.

106. *Brecht on Theatre,* John Willett, trans. and ed. (New York: Hill and Wang, 1977), p. 197.

107. Op. cit., p. 33.

108. Peter L. Berger and Hansfried Kellner, "Marriage and the Construction of Reality," in Rose Laub Coser, ed., *The Family: Its Structures and Functions* (New York: St. Martin's Press, 1974), p. 158, emphasis in original.

109. Ibid., p. 169.

110. *Love and Ideology in the Afternoon: Soap Opera, Women, and Television Genre* (Bloomington: Indiana University Press, 1995), p. 92.

111. Agnes Eckhard Nixon, "In Daytime TV the Golden Age Is Now," *Television Quarterly* (fall 1972): p. 51.

112. Op. cit., p. 45.

113. *A Theory of Literary Production* (London: Routledge & Kegan Paul, 1978), p. 85.

114. Christa Wolf, *The Quest for Christa T* (New York: Farrar, Straus & Giroux, 1970), p. 23.

115. Mumford argues that soaps have an obsession with paternity in "Plotting Paternity: Looking for Dad on the Daytime Soaps," *Love and Ideology in the Afternoon,* pp. 94–116. Certainly, as others have pointed out, women often use pregnancy, real or feigned, as power over the father of the unborn child.

116. See James B. Twitchell, *Forbidden Partners: The Incest Taboo in Modern Culture* (New York: Columbia University Press, 1987), pp. 147–62.

117. Ibid., p. 149.

118. September 9, 1986, p. 45.

119. *Soap Opera and Women's Talk,* p. 127.

120. Twitchell notes that in Gothic novels where the incestuous man is in a position of power or authority, the girl's weakness is often exaggerated by her being orphaned, abandoned, or at least motherless (p. 153).

121. "Family Romances," *The Sexual Enlightenment of Children* (New York: Collier Books, 1963), pp. 41–45. The date is noted by editor Philip Rieff to be the probable date of composition.

122. See Jessica Benjamin, *The Bonds of Love: Psychoanalysis, Feminism, and the Problem of Domination* (New York: Pantheon, 1988), p. 151.

123. *The History of Sexuality, Vol. 1.* (New York: Vintage Books, 1980) pp. 108–9.

124. The phrase is Jacqueline Rose's as she describes the dimension of risk in sexuality in the introduction to *Sexuality in the Field of Vision* (London: New Left Books, 1986), p. 3.

125. Michel Foucault, "Preface to Transgression," in *Language, Counter-Memory, Practice* (Ithaca, N.Y.: Cornell University Press, 1980), pp. 33–36.

126. See Sandra Gilbert's and Susan Gubar's, *The Madwoman in the Attic* (New Haven, Conn.: Yale University Press, 1979).

127. I am indebted to Christopher Schemering's *The Soap Opera Encyclopedia* for this description of Niki Smith (New York: Ballantine, 1985). The double roles are generally interpreted by the same player and are considered an opportunity for bravura performance. Erika Slezak won a 1985–1986 Daytime Emmy Award for her Niki/Viki interpretation.

128. An exception is often made with the death of a performer associated with a role for a long time. For example when Kay Campbell, who had played Kate Martin on *All My Children* (1970–1985), died, her character passed away in her sleep offscreen. The discovery of her death by members of her family was also offscreen but most of the cast came together at her on-screen funeral to eulogize an important tent-pole character (and a longtime castmate). The death of Chris Hughes on *As The World Turns* (who was played by Don MacLaughlin from the time the show began in 1956 until he died in 1986) and Mackenzie Cory (played by Douglass Watson for fifteen years) on *Another World* were handled similarly. Jeremy Butler discusses the MacLaughlin tribute in "'I'm Not a Doctor, But I Play One on TV.'" *Another World* managed to revive Mac in the final shot of the show's final broadcast with a still image of him looking into the camera toasting the home audience (June 25, 1999).

129. Mary Cassata, Thomas Skill, and Samuel Osei Boadu have done a demographic study of the instances of sickness, accidents, and death found in the 1977 soap operas summarized by *Soap Opera Digest.* (See "Life and Death in the Daytime Television Serial: A Content Analysis," in *Life on Daytime Television: Tuning-In American Serial Drama,* by Mary Cassata and Thomas Skill, [Norwood, N.J.: Ablex, 1983].) The study classifies and counts instances of illness, accidents, and death and compares the soap opera instances with statistics from real life. However, it doesn't discuss how these instances are represented or how they function in the serial. This type of analysis would not be able to explain much about the unnamed disease that broke up Nikki Newman's husband's affair with Ashley Abbott and cemented her foundering marriage (*The Young and the Restless,* 1986–1987). The article does not mention the numerous cases of people who have returned from "death."

130. When Joe reappeared as Siobhan's chauffeur he was played by Walt Willey. In the fall of 1988, when Roscoe Born (who had played Joe from 1981 to 1983) returned to the role, the face change was forgotten.

131. Anthony Herrera, the performer who plays Stenbeck, had spent the past couple of years in a very similar role on *Loving.* The character he played on that show was driven out of town, so it almost seems as though he returned to Oakdale from *Loving*'s Corinth. In a related phenomenon, a performer will sometimes return to a role, replacing his or her replacement (as in the case of Roscoe Born mentioned above). Grant Aleksander, for example, was recast in the role of Phillip Spaulding on *The Guiding Light* in January 1987, replacing John Bolger who had played the role for almost two years. Brenda Dickson also returned to the role of

Jill Foster Abbott on *The Young and the Restless* in 1983 after a hiatus of several years. The effect is a bit disorienting, colliding the player and the role, almost as though they had been raised from the dead. Sometimes, as with Taylor Miller's return as Nina Cortlandt Warner (*All My Children,* 1986), the character will leave town or otherwise be offscreen for a short time to ease the transition.

132. *The Edge of Night* (1956–1984), originally a late afternoon serial, was based on stories of mystery and crime. Detection and policing have become more popular on other soap operas since the late 1970s. In this discussion, I am speaking about how detection and policing function in these other shows.

133. I consider such shows as *Hill Street Blues, Crime Story, 24,* and *The Sopranos* serials, not series, and they obviously do not follow my description.

134. Soap operas are not the only television genre where the criminal is generally known to the viewer and not to the detective. *Columbo,* for example, a 1970s detective series, opened with a murder scene and ingenious attempts by the murderer to cover up his or her guilt. The rest of the show involved Lt. Columbo's masterly maneuvers to uncover the criminal.

135. Laura Stempel Mumford argues that because soaps' stories are highly formulaic, the answer to the basic question that propelled the narrative or the explanation of a central enigma is somewhat predictable. Therefore when an individual storyline resolves, even though ramifications on other storylines may continue, there is some element of closure-like satisfaction. See "How Things End: The Problem of Closure," *Love and Ideology in the Afternoon,* pp. 64–93. In my opinion, however, the commercial necessity to emphasize the ongoing nature of stories and the power of viewers' prescient knowledge may actually be stronger than any sense of closure. As Robert C. Allen points out, soaps' "series of overlapping 'mini-closures,'" which may resolve particular narrative questions, are not understood as moving the overall story toward a potential end (*Speaking of Soap Operas,* p. 75).

136. Quoted in Moretti, *Signs Taken for Wonders,* p. 142.

137. See for example, her interview in the 1993 ABC Daytime Home Video, *All My Children, Behind the Scenes.*

138. I am not attempting a demographic description of characters based on an analysis of the shows' content. Mildred Downing's "Heroine of the Daytime Serials," in the *Journal of Communications* (vol. 24, no. 2, 1974) is a good example of this type of work, which is quite popular in television studies.

139. The characters in *General Hospital*'s alien and science fiction stories in the 1980s are exceptions.

140. The viewers I have been interviewing overwhelmingly mention how "real" the characters are and often compare them favorably to the characters on prime time. Interestingly, they seldom compare them to the real people on other daytime genres, such as talk shows, court shows, or, in earlier days, game shows.

141. Ernest Mandel makes a similar argument for the detective in detective novels. See *Delightful Murder: A Social History of the Crime Story* (London: Pluto Press, 1984), p. 48.

142. Propp and Greimas's functional taxonomies, with their emphasis on verbs of action and agency, don't seem appropriate to soap opera characters. If we used the analogy of narrative as a sentence writ large (as Todorov does), we would find

that there are few verbs (action). Soap operas are predicated with adjectives (states of being).

143. This polarization is especially tense when it occurs, as it often does, in a married couple. See, for example, Tina and Cordero Roberts (*One Life to Live*) or Jill and John Abbott (*The Young and the Restless*).

144. Interesting exceptions are the members of organized crime, who are often represented as just plain crazed, or just plain sadistic, with no other clear motives. Mr. Anthony, the syndicate boss of *The Young and the Restless* (fall–spring 1985–1986), though somewhat softened in the end by his love for his daughter, is an example of this type of representation, as is Vinnie Vincent on *Ryan's Hope* (summer 1986). However, these characters are generally secondary and not long-lasting.

145. There seems to have been a predominance of rich villains in the mid-1980s (probably influenced by prime-time serials), but this has not always been the case.

146. This description of adolescent risk was suggested by Moretti's chapter on adolescent literature, "Kindergarden," in *Signs Taken for Wonders,* pp. 157–81.

147. *Madness and Civilization: A History of Insanity in the Age of Reason* (New York: Vintage Books, 1965) p. 106.

148. Ibid.

149. Until the late 1980s, such issues in sexual attraction as race, religion, and sexual preference were much more seldom treated. In 1988 a couple of the soaps were exploring interracial dating. Homosexuality (as a structure of desire and as a form of political practice) is not generally explored on daytime soaps (an exception was a limited 1983 story on *All My Children* that was attended by much publicity including an article in the *New York Times*). A gay character was introduced on *As the World Turns* (1988), but his lover and his love life were kept offscreen. Eventually he was written off the show by sending him to care for a sick friend who lived in another city. The gay man in *One Life to Live*'s summer of 1992 homophobia storyline was dead before the story began and the gay adolescent, Billy, faded away after the homophobia story ended. (I thank Becky Cole for filling me in on episodes I missed.) Joy Fuqua discusses the conditions that delimit and proscribe the representations of gay sexuality and the lives of gay couples in "'There's a Queer in My Soap!'" op. cit.

150. In the late 1980s, probably because of the publicity about AIDS, it seems to me that eroticism became more watered down by sentimental love. Although, at the time, there was seldom any discussion about safer sex or even birth control. Fears and responsibility seem to have been translated into an ethic where sensation without feeling was frowned upon.

151. Ellen Seiter, Hans Borchers, Gabriele Kreutzner, and Eva-Maria Warth. "'Don't Treat Us Like We're So Stupid and Naive': Towards an Ethnography of Soap Opera Viewers," *Rethinking Television Audiences,* Seiter, Borchers, Kreutzner, and Warth, eds. (London: Routledge, 1989), p. 240.

152. Tania Modleski, writing about the feminized male in 1940s melodramas, suggests that the appeal to women watching is that of a certain freedom: "freedom to get in touch with and to act upon her own desire and freedom to reject patriarchal power." See "Time and Desire in the Woman's Film," in *Cinema Journal,* vol. 23, no. 3 (spring 1984): pp. 26–27. Carole Lopate suggests that by "playing down

men's domination over women (and children) the soaps . . . make the family palatable." "Daytime Television: You'll Never Want to Leave Home," *Radical America,* vol. 11, no. 1 (January/February 1977): pp. 50–51.

153. More mature (i.e., longer) marriages also generally allow a good deal of companionship and a reciprocate sense of duty.

154. Cora Kaplan makes this point about the security of the disruptive sexuality in *Gone with the Wind.* See "*The Thorn Birds:* Fiction, Fantasy, Femininity," in *Formations of Fantasy,* Victor Burgin, James Donald, and Cora Kaplan, eds. (London: Methuen, 1986), p. 164. Seiter and her collaborators suggest that viewers find that stories of female transgression "destroy the ideological nucleus of the text: the priority and sacredness of the family." ("'Don't Treat Us Like We're So Stupid and Naive,'" p. 240.) But the fact that relationships generally break up to form new relationships challenges such an interpretation. What interests me is how the overall narrative structure of soaps both satisfies feelings of unrest and makes, to use Lopate's words once again, "the family palatable" (op. cit.).

155. "'Return to Manderley'—Romance Fiction, Female Sexuality and Class," *Feminist Review* 16 (April 1984): p. 20.

156. *Television Culture* (New York: Methuen, 1987), p. 181.

157. "Our Soap Opera Friends" in *Inter/Media: Interpersonal Communication in a Media World,* 3d Ed., Gary Gumpert and Robert Cathcart, eds. (New York: Oxford, 1986), p. 213.

158. *Soap Opera and Women's Talk,* p. 96. This is certainly a legacy from radio serials. Soap opera conversations may have more in common with nineteenth-century American domestic fiction than the relatively nonverbal stage melodrama. See the discussion in Robert C. Allen's *Speaking of Soap Operas,* pp. 140–41.

159. Peter Brooks, *The Melodramatic Imagination,* p. 4.

160. The characterization of the demands of daily life is Brooks's, op. cit., p. 41.

161. For this discussion of dialogue when I refer to the "listener," I am speaking of the fictional recipient of talk and when I refer to the "viewer," I am speaking of the home audience member. My terminology is a bit imprecise as the two are obviously involved in both listening and looking activities.

162. Mimi White discusses the importance of cures on 1980s television in *Tele-Advising: Therapeutic Discourses in American Television* (Chapel Hill: University of North Carolina Press, 1992).

163. Maternal working-class women are sometimes excepted from this. Both Maeve Ryan and Kate Rescott (on *Ryan's Hope* and *Loving,* respectively) are often seen dispensing well-worn advice while performing household chores, though the camera generally moves in quickly to a head shot, omitting the dust rag or the beans.

164. This discussion of the disparity between dialogue and popular spoken utterances is indebted to Lennard J. Davis's discussion of dialogue in novels. See *Resisting Novels: Ideology and Fiction* (New York: Methuen, 1987), pp. 162–76.

165. Admittedly, the idea of "unique" or "original" is always somewhat strained in language, since words have generally been used before and the structures are conventionalized and rather formulaic. Roland Barthes in "The Death of the Author" (*Music/Image/Text,* p. 146) writes, "[t]he text is a tissue of quotations drawn from innumerable centers of culture." And, according to Mikhail

Bakhtin, texts do not begin in the present with a speaker or a story but inherit part of the historical consciousness and social matrices of their authors and their audiences (*The Dialogic Imagination* ([Austin: University of Texas Press, 1981]), pp. 288, 293, et passim).

166. Nochimson's interview with Rabin, July 26, 1990, quoted in *No End to Her: Soap Opera and the Female Subject,* p. 195.

167. Barthes quotes J.-P. Vernant on this point on Greek tragedy in "The Death of the Author," p. 148.

168. Brian Winston used this apt description of soap opera performance style in a lecture at New York University, February 6, 1985.

169. This is adapted freely from Roland Barthes's discussion of wrestling performances in "The World of Wrestling," *Mythologies* (New York: Hill and Wang, 1972) pp. 15–25. Barthes is discussing live, not televised, wrestling.

170. Although my discussion here centers on dialogue, the same dynamic occurs in the wider narrative. In his discussion of the "hermeneutic code" (*S/Z,* pp. 75–76), Barthes outlines a useful taxonomy of mechanisms (evasive answers, partial answers, suspended answers, etc.) that function to delay the forward thrust of the narrative. These delays, however, by frustrating, also inscribe a desire for "the truth." Modleski, too, writes about the charms of postponement when she notes that the narrative, "by placing ever more complex obstacles between desire and its fulfillment, makes anticipation an end in itself." She concludes that soaps, by transforming experience into a form, make waiting, "a central condition of a woman's life," enjoyable (*Loving With a Vengeance,* p. 88).

171. See his discussion in *The Melodramatic Imagination,* pp. 48–49.

172. Collection of The Museum of Television and Radio, New York City. I am grateful to Ron Simon for calling my attention to this episode.

173. *The Desire to Desire: The Woman's Film of the 1940s* (Bloomington: Indiana University Press, 1987), p. 97.

174. *Soap Opera Digest* frequently prints requests from viewers about the origin and availability of the love themes and compilations of love themes have been commercially issued on tape and CD. See, for example, *Soap Opera's Greatest Love Themes,* released by Scotti Bros. Records in 1992.

175. *The Melodramatic Imagination,* pp. 56–57.

176. Todd Gitlin discusses this simultaneity as an aspect of American culture in "Hip-Deep in Post-modernism," *The New York Times Book Review* (November 6, 1988): p. 36.

177. Susan Lucci seems to play Erica as if she knew that everyone was watching her.

178. "Emphasis Added: Plots and Plausibility in Women's Fiction," in *The New Feminist Criticism: Essays on Women, Literature and Theory,* Elaine Showalter, ed. (New York: Pantheon, 1985), p. 339.

179. On the phenomenon in seventeenth-century and early eighteenth-century novels, see Lennard J. Davis's "A Social History of Fact and Fiction: Authorial Disavowel in the Early English Novel," in *Literature and Society,* Edward W. Said, ed. (Baltimore: Johns Hopkins, 1980).

180. *Selected Letters of Samuel Richardson,* ed. with an introduction by John

Carrol (Oxford, 1964), p. 85, cited in Terry Eagleton, *The Rape of Clarissa: Writing, Sexuality, and Class Struggle in Samuel Richardson,* p. 18.

181. As quoted in Michael Denning's *Mechanic Accents: Dime Novels and Working Class Culture in America* (London: Verso, 1987), p. 200. Denning notes that, although little is known of Richardson, it seems that she is of a middle-class background and doesn't share the culture of the other workers (p. 197). Originally written in 1905, Richardson's *The Long Day: The Story of a New York Working Girl* is reprinted in William O'Neill, ed., *Women at Work* (New York: Times Books, 1972).

182. In a rare reflexive moment, Katherine Chancellor Sterling, a character on *The Young and the Restless,* seemed to express incredulity about the plot in which she was partaking. Held captive with her maid in a rural cabin, she sees a woman who looks exactly like her (played by the same performer) on television accepting an honorary award meant for Katherine and kissing Katherine's husband, Rex Sterling. She comments with astonishment, "It's unreal. It's unbelievable!" (January 12, 1990).

183. Ellen Seiter and her collaborators questioned their respondents more directly about strong "villainesses" and found them to be popular. The "whinier," suffering women, on the other hand, as Marilyn and Awilda expressed, were not as well liked (Seiter et al., pp. 24–26). Mary Ellen Brown also questioned her respondents on villainesses and asked them if they "get pleasure out of hating" them. (p. 190). But since these villainesses act within a framework of moral disapproval and are almost certain to get "what they deserve," I am not sure that "like" and "dislike," "love" and "hate," can be so easily tabulated from either questionnaires or interviews. I am describing a more general excess, which seems to be not only a lot of fun, but essential to soaps—and melodrama in general—and a part of their credibility. Fiske claims that excess is a characteristic of television in general (see chapter 6, *Television Culture,* 1987). Feuer finds that the excess of the 1980s prime-time serials has a radical potential ("Melodrama, Serial Form and Television Today"), whereas Laura Mulvey, in "Notes on Sirk and Melodrama," *Movie* 25–26 (1976–1977), finds that film melodrama's excesses function as a safety valve whose effect is ultimately hegemonic.

184. *Soap Opera Digest,* May 5, 1987, p. 11.

185. October 4, 1988, p. 18.

186. *The Melodramatic Imagination,* p. 60.

187. Moretti is writing about the literature read by adolescent boys in his chapter "Kindergarden," in *Signs Taken for Wonders.* The emphasis is in the original, p. 162. He points out that when the recognition takes place at the point of the protagonist's death, it ends any relationship between the idea of teleology and that of causality. Steve Neale, in "Melodrama and Tears" (*Screen,* vol. 27, no. 16 [November/December, 1986]), elaborates Moretti's thesis in his discussion of film melodramas in order to explore the delays in the coincidence of the spectator's and the character's points of view. For Neale, it is not only that the character's or characters' recognition is often too late, but also that the delay in the recognition produces a position of powerlessness on the part of the film spectator (who cannot influence the narrative). This, combined with the fantasy structure of melodramas,

allows a "degree of separation-in-identification with the characters and the scenario which binds the spectator into the fantasy and generates empathy with the protagonists" (p. 22).

188. The phenomenon of crying is considered further in the following chapter.

189. In discussing the nineteenth century, Foucault writes that "the secret" of sexuality was inscribed in "an economy of pleasure." (*The History of Sexuality, Vol. 1*, p. 69.)

190. "Thickening the Plot," *Journal of Communications*, vol. 29, no. 4 (autumn 1979): p. 83.

191. *Love and Ideology in the Afternoon*, pp. 47–66. The Geraghty quote is on p. 56.

192. Mumford, *Love and Ideology in the Afternoon*, p. 60.

193. It also concealed the actress's maternity leave, as reported in fan magazines and newspaper gossip columns.

194. These women's privatized daily work is seldom negotiated and contracted but generally taken for granted as their personal commitment to their families ("a labor of love").

195. Angela Carter makes this point about the enjoyment of pornographic literature in *The Sadeian Woman and the Ideology of Pornography* (New York: Harper & Row, 1980), pp. 14–15. I am grateful to Melinda Barlow for drawing my attention to Carter's work at an early stage of my writing.

196. *The Melodramatic Imagination*, p. 48.

197. *Re-viewing Reception*, p. 56.

198. "Christine Gledhill on *Stella Dallas* and Feminist Film Theory," *Cinema Journal*, vol. 25, no. 4 (summer 1986): p. 45.

199. *The Melodramatic Imagination*, p. 40.

200. Over the years there have been many actual parodies of soap operas such as the television serials *Soap* (1977–1981) and *Mary Hartman, Mary Hartman* (1976–1978), Carol Burnett's sketch, "As the Stomach Turns," and skits on Nickelodeon and *SCTV*.

201. *Soap Opera and Women's Talk*, p. 127.

202. "Emphasis Added," p. 39.

203. Brooks claims that melodrama is charged with reference to a "moral occult," the locus of intense ethical forces from which we feel cut off, but which we feel have a real existence somewhere beyond the facade of reality and exert an influence on secular life. (*The Melodramatic Imagination*, p. 202, et passim.) The genre "strives to find, to articulate, to demonstrate, to 'prove' the existence of a moral universe which, though put into question . . . does exist and can be made to assert its presence." (p. 20).

204. Daniel Mendelsohn, "The Melodramatic Moment," the *New York Times Magazine*, March 23, 2003, p. 43.

205. *Re-viewing Reception*, p. 56.

Chapter 4. The Power of Pleasure

1. Elaine Showalter, arguing from Edwin Ardener's 1972 essay, "Belief and the Problem of Women," writes that all people generate beliefs and order ideas of social

reality at the unconscious level, but dominant groups control the forms and structures in which consciousness can be articulated. Thus, women are a "muted group," precisely because we must mediate our beliefs through the permitted forms of dominant discourse. For Showalter, this is a problem of both language and power. See "Feminist Criticism in the Wilderness," *The New Feminist Criticism: Essays on Women, Literature and Theory,* Showalter, ed. (New York: Pantheon Books, 1985), p. 262. The term "muted group" is Ardener's.

2. Audre Lorde, *The Uses of the Erotic: The Erotic As Power* (Brooklyn: Out and Out Books, 1982), unpaginated.

3. "The Relation of the Poet to Day-Dreaming," (1908) in *On Creativity and the Unconscious* (New York: Harper & Row, 1958), p. 46.

4. Op. cit., p. 54.

5. Compassionate because, as Alison Light suggests, as feminists, our analysis should try to keep open the spaces of pleasure "whilst rechanneling the dissatisfactions upon which they depend." "'Return to Manderley'—Romance Fiction and Female Sexuality," *Feminist Review* 16 (April 1984): p. 21.

6. *The Uses of the Erotic,* unpaginated.

7. Quoted in Charlotte Brunsdon's *The Feminist, the Housewife, and the Soap Opera* (New York: Oxford University Press, 2000), p. 192.

8. Recently, SoapNet, a cable service, has been rebroadcasting the day's soaps in the evening. The Internet has also made it easier to catch up on lost episodes. However, it is still necessary to be timely, or you see events out of sequence.

9. *Consuming Pleasures: Active Audiences and Serial Fictions from Dickens to Soap Opera* (Lexington: University Press of Kentucky, 1997), p. 6.

10. This aspect of seriality is undoubtedly part of the appeal of *Survivor* and other recent reality programming.

11. Benedict Anderson points out that members of even "the smallest nation" will never know most of their fellow members, "yet in the midst of each lives the image of their communion." It is "the style in which they are imagined" that distinguishes communities. *Imagined Communities: Reflections on the Origin and Spread of Nationalism* (London: Verso, 1983), p. 15.

12. When I asked her, "Why *One Life to Live*?" Heather replied that the TV was already on ABC from the news the night before. Hanni also mentioned that that is why she first started watching CBS serials.

13. *Loving with a Vengeance: Mass-Produced Fantasies for Women* (Hamden, Conn.: Archon Books, 1982), p. 108.

14. *All That Is Solid Melts into Air* (New York: Penguin Books, 1988), p. 15.

15. "Housewives: Isolation as Oppression," in *Women Take Issue: Aspects of Women's Subordination,* Women's Studies Group, Centre for Contemporary Cultural Studies, University of Birmingham (London Hutchinson, 1978).

16. See Julia Lesage's article "Why Christian Television Is Good TV," *The Independent,* 10:4 (May 1987).

17. "Television and the Triumph of Culture," *The Postmodern Scene: Excremental Culture and Hyper-Aesthetics,* by Arthur Kroker and David Cook (New York: St. Martin's Press, 1986), pp. 270–72. In this essay, Kroker draws on Sartre's philosophical meditation on the mass media in general and radio broadcasting in particular in *The Critique of Dialectical Reason* (1960).

18. For more on the organization of fan clubs and the social dynamics of belonging, see C. Lee Harrington and Denise D. Bielby's *Soap Fans: Pursuing Pleasure and Making Meaning in Everyday Life* (Philadelphia: Temple University Press, 1995).

19. Seiter et al. call explanations of how women began watching soaps "initiation stories" in "'Don't Treat Us Like We're So Stupid and Naive': Towards an Ethnography of Soap Opera Viewers," in *Remote Control: Television, Audiences and Cultural Power,* Seiter, Borchers, Kreutzner, and Warth, eds. (London: Routledge, 1989), pp. 233–34.

20. Bulletin board posting quoted in Harrington and Bielby, *Soap Fans,* p. 150.

21. Bulletin board posting quoted in *Soap Fans,* p. 151.

22. Ellen Seiter et al. in "'Don't Treat Us Like We're So Stupid and Naive'" claimed to have found no "explicitly apologetic overtones" in their study of soap opera viewers in Western Oregon and suggest that this "non-defensive position" indicates "significant differences" between the United States and Europe in "the social construction of femininity" and the necessity to look at such views in the context of the specific "social exchange" (pp. 242–43). Although I never directly asked the women I spoke with how they feel about watching soaps, contradictory feelings were evident in many of their statements. I wonder if the lack of conflict that Seiter et al. observed was due to the interview situation (groups brought together by an informant), their method of gathering informants (through ads in the employment section of the local newspaper), or their level of analysis. Their reflections on the power relations in the interview process and gendered discourses used do not account for these differences (pp. 243–44).

23. "Women Watching Together: An Ethnographic Study of Korean Soap Opera Fans in the U.S.," *Cultural Studies* 4 (1990): pp. 30–44.

24. Laura Kipness makes this point about pornography in her insightful book, *Bound and Gagged: Pornography and the Politics of Fantasy in America* (Durham, N.C.: Duke University Press, 1999), p. 150.

25. This, however, is not unique to the already-middle class. One young woman on public assistance mentioned that her mother was so disturbed at how much she had been watching that she had sent her for counseling.

26. Fredric Jameson points out that this differentiation is based on a false dichotomy. See his essay "Pleasure: A Political Issue" in the Formations Editorial Collective's *Formations of Pleasure* (London: Routledge & Kegan Paul, 1983), p. 3.

27. Robert N. Bellah, Richard Madsen, William M. Sullivan, Ann Swidler, and Steven M. Tipton, *Habits of the Heart: Individualism and Commitment in American Life* (Berkeley: University of California Press, 1985), p. 66.

28. Cited in *Soap Fans,* p. 91.

29. Roland Barthes, in an essay that is admirably attentive to the cultural practice of spectatorship, also writes about the darkness of the theater as an important part of the "reverie" of the cinematic experience ("Leaving the Movie Theater," in *The Rustle of Language* [New York: Hill and Wang, 1986]). For Metz's discussions, see *The Imaginary Signifier: Psychoanalysis and the Cinema* (Bloomington: Indiana University Press, 1982). In *Language and Cinema* (The Hague: Mouton, 1974), Metz discusses television as sharing many means of expression with cinema but

having very different "socio-psychological and affective-perceptual" conditions of reception (pp. 235–36). Sandy Flitterman-Lewis contrasts television viewing to the womb-like state of the film viewer in "Psychoanalysis, Film, and Television," in *Channels of Discourse: Television and Contemporary Criticism,* Robert C. Allen, ed. (Chapel Hill: University of North Carolina Press, 1987).

30. Mary Cassata and Thomas Skill, *Life on Daytime Television: Tuning-In American Serial Drama* (Norwood, N.J.: Ablex, 1983), p. 31. Lennard J. Davis also makes this point about the fictional characters in novels in *Resisting Novels: Ideology and Fiction* (New York: Methuen, 1987), p. 104. One of my respondents said that she felt that she knew some of the characters on the show that she had been watching for eighteen years better than she knew herself.

31. Quoted in *The Village Voice,* September 11, 1988.

32. This is what the French call a *volupté des larmes.*

33. See Sheila Page Bayne's *Tears and Weeping: An Aspect of Emotional Climate Reflected in Seventeenth-Century French Literature* (Tübingen: Gunter Narr Verlag, 1981), pp. 55–56.

34. Charlotte Brunsdon, "Women Watching Television," *MedieKultur* 4 (November 1986): p. 110.

35. Soap stars and writers report that viewers often try to give advice, consolation, and gifts to characters. See, for example, Harding Lemay's *Eight Years in Another World* (New York: Atheneum, 1981) and Eileen Fulton and Brett Bolton's *How My World Turns* (New York: Taplinger, 1970). I still remember the involuntary shudder that came over me when an actor who was playing a rapist came in to check the call-board as I was interviewing one of the crew members in the lunchroom of *All My Children.*

36. October 18, 1988; the passages quoted are on pages 13 and 14, respectively. These letters may have been edited "for style and brevity," as the magazine maintains is their right. I quote them not as pure testimony, but as part of the discourse surrounding soap opera viewing, which fan magazines help to create as well as perpetuate.

37. *The Act of Reading* (Baltimore: Johns Hopkins University Press, 1978), p. 70.

38. (New York: Capricorn Books, 1965), pp. 11–12.

39. *Narratology: Introduction to the Theory of Narrative* (Toronto: University of Toronto Press, 1985), p. 10.

40. "Writing about soap opera," in *Television Mythologies: Stars, Shows and Signs,* Len Masterman, ed. (London: Comedia, 1984), p. 83, reprinted in *Screen Tastes: Soap Opera to Satellite Dishes* (New York: Routledge, 1997).

41. See Lawrence Grossberg's "Is There a Fan in the House?: The Affective Sensibility of Fandom," in *The Adoring Audience: Fan Culture and Popular Media,* Lisa Lewis, ed. (New York: Routledge, 1992), p. 61.

42. Jeremy Butler discusses this in "'I'm Not a Doctor, But I Play One on TV': Characters, Actors, and Acting in Television Soap Opera," *Cinema Journal* 30:4 (summer 1991).

43. "The In-Difference of Television," *Screen,* vol. 28, no. 2 (spring 1987): p. 42.

44. See Davis's *Resisting Novels,* p. 2.

45. *Fictional Truth* (Baltimore: Johns Hopkins University Press, 1990). Riffaterre's book investigates how novels establish their illusion of reality.

46. Of course, this elision of fiction and reality is not unique to soap operas or soap opera viewers. The day that I was writing this section, I turned on the radio to get the weather forecast and tuned in to Jeffrey Lyons's review of a Canadian animated film, *The Man Who Planted Trees.* Lyons opened by saying that the film "tells the story, which I hope is true, of a man who . . ." The next piece was an ad for a Channel 2 news special report on Soviet spying which began, "You've seen it in James Bond movies, you've read about it in spy novels, tonight you'll see the real thing, startling undercover footage of a Soviet agent spying in your own backyard." Later, investigative reporter Jack Anderson's novel, *Control,* "a story written from tomorrow's headlines," was advertised with the tagline "based on a truth so frightening it had to be fictionalized to tell it" (CBS radio, November 2, 1988). The implication in all of these examples is that knowledge of life is to be learned from fiction, and that our knowledge of real life contributes to our understanding of fiction. In some cases, the fictions may even throw the very definition of reality into question.

47. P. 70.

48. October 4, 1988, p. 96. The questions included: "Do you ever get ideas about how to conduct your own personal romances from watching the ones on soaps? Have you ever dealt with a problem that a soap couple had to deal with and dealt with it the same way? Do you think you handle your own romantic problems and challenges better than most soap characters? Do you get ideas for romantic settings, clothing, presents, dinners or surprises from watching soaps?" As we saw in Chapter 2, this connection goes back at least to Herta Herzog's 1942 essay, "What Do We Really Know About Daytime Serial Listeners?" where she claimed that the listeners in her study looked to radio soap operas as an important source of advice (*Radio Research, 1942–1943,* Paul Lazarsfeld and Frank Stanton, eds., reprinted [New York: Arno Press, 1979], p. 25).

49. *Soap Opera Digest,* December 13, 1988, pp. 20–24. The same magazine ran a 1992 article: "A Shopper's Guide to Soaps' Most Elegant Wedding Dresses." Lauren Rabinowitz's "Soap Opera Bridal Fantasies" discusses how fan magazines and the tabloid press also link fictional soap weddings to the performers' actual weddings by featuring photographs of each side by side (*Screen,* vol. 33, no. 3 [autumn 1992]: p. 280).

50. All quotes are from the February 1989 issue of *Daytime TV.* Spelling, punctuation, and capitalization thus in original.

51. Some of the wedding gowns are designed especially for the show. In these cases, however, information about the frock is generally leaked to the press in advance so that the dress itself is part of the allure of the wedding. New York's Museum of Television and Radio's 1997 exhibition on soap operas featured many such wedding gowns.

But this is an exception. Jim O'Daniel, *General Hospital*'s costume designer, confessed, "Holly's clothes come from Saks, the waterfront people's from Penney's." ("Surprise! Here's Tony Geary in a Sequined Evening Gown," Mary Alice Kellogg, *TV Guide,* October 22, 1983.)

52. Interview, January 16, 1986. Stories about fans who inquire about wedding and bridesmaid's dresses are legion. See Rabinowitz, op. cit., pp. 280–81.

53. P. 22.

54. P. 16, emphasis in original.

55. P. 45.

56. "The Uncanny" (1919), *Studies in Parapsychology* (New York: Collier, 1971) p. 41.

57. "The Paths to the Formation of Symptoms" (1917), in *Introductory Lectures on Psychoanalysis* (New York: W. W. Norton, 1977), p. 368.

58. "Of Other Peoples: Beyond the 'Salvage Paradigm,'" transcription of a discussion in the Dia Art Foundation's *Discussions of Contemporary Culture,* Hal Foster, ed. (Seattle: Bay Press, 1987), p. 140. Trinh is speaking specifically about the production of differences between the "First" and "Third Worlds."

59. As Trinh suggests about "otherness" and "sameness," loc. cit.

60. Rosalind Coward, *Female Desires: How They Are Sought, Bought and Packaged* (New York: Grove Press, 1985), p. 13.

61. See Michel Foucault's essay "The Subject and Power" in *Art After Modernism: Rethinking Representation,* Brian Willis, ed. (New York: Godine, 1984), p. 424.

62. Jerome Bruner, *Making Stories: Law, Literature, Life* (Cambridge, Mass.: Harvard University Press, 2002), p. 14.

63. Edward W. Said, *Orientalism* (New York: Vintage Books, 1979), p. 3.

64. See Peter Stallybrass and Allon White's *The Politics and Poetics of Transgression* (Ithaca, N.Y.: Cornell University Press, 1986), p. 200.

65. As quoted in Michael Denning's *Mechanic Accents: Dime Novels and Working Class Culture in America* (London: Verso, 1987), p. 200.

66. Bruner, op. cit., p. 13.

67. Michel Foucault, *The Order of Things: An Archeology of the Human Sciences* (New York: Vintage Books, 1973), pp. 312–18; the quote is from p. 315; emphasis as such in the original.

68. For discussions of the utopian aspects of mass culture see Fredric Jameson's "Reification and Utopia in Mass Culture," *Social Text* 1 (Winter 1979), Richard Dyer's "Entertainment and Utopia," *Movie* 24 (Spring 1977), and Hans Magnus Enzensberger's "Constituents of a Theory of the Media," *The Consciousness Industry* (New York: Seabury Press, 1974).

69. *Woman's Consciousness, Man's World* (London: Penguin, 1973), p. 18.

70. I am grateful to Nusreta Kolenovic for calling my attention to this ad. It is an interesting one that gives no information about the product itself, but instead identifies it with the lifestyle of a "modern woman," one that seems to be both independent and in need of self-indulgence.

71. "Soap Opera Bridal Fantasies," *Screen,* vol. 33, no. 3 (autumn 1992): p. 283, emphasis in original. Lynne Joyrich's book *Re-viewing Reception: Television, Gender, and Postmodern Culture* (Bloomington: Indiana University Press, 1996) argues that television, consumerism, and femininity are linked in both the scholarly and popular discourses of postmodern culture. John Fiske also points to the close connection between fan culture and the commercial interests of the culture industries with fan culture itself often involved in accumulation and investment. See "The Cultural Economy of Fandom," in *The Adoring Audience,* pp. 45–47.

72. Raymond Williams notes that, in a society of great disparity, some forms of alternative and directly oppositional culture and politics may be allowed so that other more destabilizing forms are avoided. *Marxism and Literature* (London: Oxford University Press, 1977), pp. 113–14.

73. *Bound and Gagged,* p. 187. My argument here is indebted to Kipnes's discussion of Allan Bloom's invectives against pornography, pp. 186–89.

74. This argument is derived from Lawrence Grossberg's approach in "Another Boring Day in Paradise: Rock and Roll and the Empowerment of Everyday Life," in *Popular Music* 4 (1984). See especially his second hypothesis, pp. 233–36.

75. *Problems in Materialism and Culture* (London: Verso, 1980), pp. 38–39.

76. Lisa Ballou's interesting paper on soap opera commercials read at the 1989 Florida State University Conference on Literature and Film discussed the maternal as situated *in* the products advertised.

77. Elayne Rapping, *The Looking Glass World of Nonfiction TV* (Boston: South End Press, 1987), p. 16.

78. Tillie Olsen writes eloquently about this in the title essay of *Silences* (New York: Delta, 1980).

79. *Dialectic of Enlightenment* (New York: Seabury Press, 1972), p. 137.

80. Loc. cit.

81. *Critical Theory* (New York: Continuum, 1989), pp. 127–28.

82. Jane Feuer, for example, also writes about soaps representing "a radical response to and expression of cultural contradictions" in "Melodrama, Serial Form and Television Today," *Screen,* vol. 25, no. 1 (January/February 1984): p. 16. Feuer is writing about prime-time serials but claims that her conclusions are generalizable to daytime soaps.

83. *Language, Counter-Memory, Practice* (Ithaca, N.Y.: Cornell University Press, 1980), p. 35.

84. Perhaps this contributes to the element of disappointment that many viewers express.

85. While making a very different argument, Lennard Davis makes a similar point about novels in *Resisting Novels: Ideology and Fiction,* p. 225.

86. "The Relation of the Poet to Day-Dreaming," p. 48.

87. Op. cit., p. 49.

88. "Stanzas from the Grande Chartreuse," 1855, in *Matthew Arnold: Selected Poems,* Keith Silver, ed. (Manchester, England: Carcanet Press, 1994), p. 123.

89. Foucault designates this as the trajectory of all modern thought in *The Order of Things,* p. 328.

Author's Note

1. "The Death of an Author," in *Music Image Text* (New York: Hill and Wang, 1977) p. 146.

Selected Bibliography

The following list of references cites books and scholarly articles that are referred to in the text or were useful in formulating some of my positions and interpretations.

Alberti, Giulia. "Conditions of Illusion." *Off Screen: Women and Film in Italy,* edited by Giuliana Bruno and Maria Nadotti. London: Routledge, 1988.

Allen, Robert C., ed. *Channels of Discourse: Television and Contemporary Criticism.* Chapel Hill: University of North Carolina Press, 1987.

———. "The Guiding Light: Soap Opera As Economic Product and Cultural Document." *American History/American Television,* edited by John E. O'Connor. New York: Frederick Ungar, 1983.

———. Review of *Watching* Dallas, *Journal of Communication* 36, no. 4 (autumn 1986).

———. *Speaking of Soap Operas.* Chapel Hill: University of North Carolina Press, 1985.

———, ed. *To Be Continued: Soap Operas Around the World.* New York: Routledge, 1995.

Allende, Isabel. *Paula.* New York: HarperCollins, 1994.

Althusser, Louis, and Etienne Balibar. *Reading Capital.* London: New Left Books, 1970.

Anderson, Benedict. *Imagined Communities: Reflections on the Origin and Spread of Nationalism.* London: Verso, 1983.

Ang, Ien. *Desperately Seeking the Audience.* New York: Routledge, 1991.

———. *Living Room Wars: Rethinking Media Audiences for a Postmodern World.* New York: Routledge, 1996.

———. *Watching* Dallas: *Soap Opera and the Melodramatic Imagination.* London: Methuen, 1985.

Arnheim, R. "The World of the Daytime Serial." *Radio Research, 1942–1943,* edited by P. Lazarfeld and F. Stanton. New York: Duell, Sloan and Pearce, 1944.

Bachelard, Gaston. *The Poetics of Space.* Boston: Beacon Press, 1969.

Bacon-Smith, Camille. *Enterprising Women: Television Fandom and the Creation of Popular Myth.* Philadelphia: University of Pennsylvania Press, 1992.

Baehr, Helen, and Gillian Dyer, eds. *Boxed-In: Women and Television.* London: Pandora, 1986.

Bakhtin, M. M. *The Dialogic Imagination.* Austin: University of Texas Press, 1981.
———. *Rabelais and His World.* Cambridge: MIT Press, 1968.
Bal, Mieke. *Narratology: Introduction to the Theory of Narrative.* Toronto: University of Toronto Press, 1985.
Ballou, Lisa. "The Damsel in Distress: Women's Space in Soap Opera Advertising." Paper delivered at the 1989 Florida State University Conference on Literature and Film, Tallahassee, Florida.
Barrett, Michèle, and Mary McIntosh. *The Anti-Social Family.* London: Verso Editions, 1982.
Barthes, Roland. *Music Image Text.* New York: Hill and Wang, 1977.
———. *Mythologies.* New York: Hill and Wang, 1972.
———. *The Pleasure of the Text.* New York: Hill and Wang, 1975.
———. *The Rustle of Language.* New York: Hill and Wang, 1986.
———. *S/Z.* New York: Hill and Wang, 1974.
Barton, R. L. "Soap Operas Provide Meaningful Communication for the Elderly." *Feedback* 19, no. 3 (1977).
Baym, Nancy K. "The Emergence of Community in Computer-Mediated Communication." *CyberSociety: Computer-mediated Communication and Community,* edited by Steven G. Jones. Thousand Oaks, Calif.: Sage, 1995.
———. "Interpreting Soap Operas and Creating Community: Inside a Computer-Mediated Fan Club." *Journal of Folklore Research* 30, nos. 2/3 (May/December 1993).
Bayne, Sheila Page. *Tears and Weeping: An Aspect of Emotional Climate Reflected in Seventeenth-Century French Literature.* Tübingen: Gunter Narr Verlag, 1981.
Bellah, Robert N., Richard Madsen, William M. Sullivan, Ann Swidler, and Steven M. Tipton. *Habits of the Heart: Individualism and Commitment in American Life.* Berkeley: University of California Press, 1985.
Benjamin, Jessica. *The Bonds of Love: Psychoanalysis, Feminism, and the Problem of Domination.* New York: Pantheon, 1988.
Benjamin, Walter. "The Author as Producer." *Reflections.* New York: Harcourt Brace Jovanovich, 1978.
Bennett, Tony. "Text and Social Process: The Case of James Bond." *Screen Education* 41 (spring/summer 1982).
———. "Texts, Readers, Reading Formations," *Bulletin of the Midwest Modern Language Association* 16, no. 1 (spring 1983).
———, et al. *Culture, Ideology and Social Process: A Reader.* London: Open University Press, 1981.
Bennett, Tony, and Janet Woollacott. *Bond and Beyond: The Political Career of a Popular Hero.* London: Methuen, 1987.
Berger, Peter L., and Hansfried Kellner. "Marriage and the Construction of Reality." *The Family: Its Structures and Functions,* edited by Rose Laub Coser. New York: St. Martin's Press, 1974.
Berman, Marshall. *All That Is Solid Melts Into Air.* New York: Penguin Books, 1988.
Berman, Ronald. *How Television Sees Its Audience: A Look at the Looking Glass.* Beverly Hills, Calif.: Sage, 1987.

Bird, Elizabeth. "Travels in Nowhere Land: Ethnography and the 'Impossible' Audience." *Critical Studies in Mass Communication* 9 (1992).

Birdwhistell, Ray L. *Kinesics and Context: Essays on Body Motion Communication.* Philadelphia: University of Pennsylvania Press, 1970.

Blumler, Jay G., and Elihu Katz, eds. *The Uses of Mass Communications: Current Perspectives on Gratifications Research.* Beverly Hills: Sage, 1974.

Boddy, William. "'The Shining Centre of the Home': Ontologies of Television in the 'Golden Age.'" *Television in Transition: Papers from the First International Televisions Studies Conference,* edited by Phillip Drummond and Richard Paterson. London: BFI, 1986.

Bogart, Leo. *The Age of Television: A Study of Viewing Habits and the Impact of Television on American Life.* New York: Frederick Ungar, 1972. (Originally published 1956.)

Booth, Wayne C. *The Rhetoric of Fiction.* Chicago: University of Chicago Press, 1961.

Bordo, Susan. "Femininsm, Postmodernism, and Gender Scepticism." *Feminism/Postmodernism,* edited by Linda J. Nicholson. New York: Routledge, 1990.

Bourdieu, Pierre. *Distinction: A Social Critique of the Judgement of Taste.* Cambridge, Mass.: Harvard University Press, 1984.

———. *Outline of a Theory of Practice.* Cambridge: Cambridge University Press, 1977.

Bovenschen, Silvia. "Is There a Feminine Aesthetic?" *New German Critique* 10 (winter 1977).

Boyer, Peter. "ABC Hopes Its Daytime Bubble Won't Burst." *Los Angeles Times* (August 19, 1983).

Brooks, Peter. *The Melodramatic Imagination: Balzac, Henry James, Melodrama and the Mode of Excess.* New Haven, Conn.: Yale University Press, 1976.

———. *Reading for the Plot: Design and Intention in Narratives.* New York: Random House, 1984.

Brown, Mary Ellen. *Soap Opera and Women's Talk: The Pleasures of Resistance.* Thousand Oaks, Calif.: Sage, 1994.

———, ed. *Television and Women's Culture: The Politics of the Popular.* Thousand Oaks, Calif.: Sage, 1990.

Browne, Nick. "The Political Economy of the Television (Super) Text." *Quarterly Review of Film Studies* 9, no. 3 (1984).

Bruner, Jerome. *Making Stories: Law, Literature, Life.* Cambridge, Mass.: Harvard University Press, 2002.

Brunsdon, Charlotte. "Crossroads: Notes on a Soap Opera." *Screen* 22, no. 4 (1981).

———. *The Feminist, the Housewife, and the Soap Opera.* New York: Oxford University Press, 2000.

———. "Identity in Feminist Television Criticism," *Media, Culture and Society* 15 (1993).

———. *Screen Tastes: Soap Opera to Satellite Dishes.* New York: Routledge, 1997.

———. "Women Watching Television." *MedieKultur* 4 (November 1986).

Buckman, Peter. *All for Love: A Study in Soap Opera.* Salem, N.H.: Salem House, 1985.

Budd, Mike, Robert M. Entman, and Clay Steinman. "The Affirmative Character of U.S. Cultural Studies." *Critical Studies in Mass Communication* 7 (1990).

Buerkel-Rothfuss, N. C., and S. Mayes. "Soap Opera Viewing: The Cultivation Effect." *Journal of Communication* 31, no. 3 (summer 1981).

Burgin, Victor, James Donald, and Cora Kaplan, eds. *Formations of Fantasy.* London: Methuen, 1986.

Butler, Jeremy. "'I'm Not a Doctor, But I Play One on TV': Characters, Actors, and Acting in Television Soap Opera." *Cinema Journal* 30, no. 4 (summer 1991).

Bybee, Carl. "Uses and Gratifications Research and the Study of Social Change." *Political Communications Research: Approaches, Studies, and Assessments,* edited by D. L. Paletz. Norwood, N.J.: Ablex, 1987.

Caldwell, John Thornton. *Televisuality: Style, Crisis, and Authority in American Television.* New Brunswick, N.J.: Rutgers University Press, 1995.

Camera Obscura Collective. "Feminism and Film." *Camera Obscura* 1 (fall 1976).

Camera Obscura. Special issue on "Television and the Female Consumer" (vol. 16, 1988).

Cantor, Muriel G., and Suzanne Pingree. *The Soap Opera.* Beverly Hills, Calif.: Sage, 1983.

Carey, James. *Communication as Culture.* New York: Routledge, 1992.

Carter, Angela. *The Sadeian Woman and the Ideology of Pornography.* New York: Harper & Row, 1980.

Cassata, Mary, and Thomas Skill. *Life on Daytime Television: Tuning-In American Serial Drama.* Norwood, N.J.: Ablex, 1983.

Cathcart, Robert. "Our Soap Opera Friends." *Inter/Media: Interpersonal Communication in a Media World,* 3rd Ed., edited by Gary Gumpert and Robert Cathcart. New York: Oxford University Press, 1986.

Cawelti, John G. *Adventure, Mystery and Romance.* Chicago: University of Chicago Press, 1976.

deCerteau, Michel. *The Practice of Everyday Life.* Berkeley: University of California Press, 1984.

Chisholm, Brad. "Difficult Viewing: The Pleasures of Complex Screen Narratives." *Critical Studies in Mass Communication* 8, no. 4 (December 1991).

Chodorow, Nancy. *The Reproduction of Mothering: Psychoanalysis and the Sociology of Gender.* Berkeley: University of California Press, 1978.

Cixous, Helene. "The Laugh of the Medusa." *Signs* 1, no. 4 (summer 1976).

Clifford, James. "On Ethnographic Authority." *Representations* 1, no. 2 (spring 1983).

———. *The Predicament of Culture: Twentieth-Century Ethnography, Literature, and Art.* Cambridge, Mass.: Harvard University Press, 1988.

Clifford, James, and George E. Marcus, eds. *Writing Culture: The Poetics and Politics of Ethnography.* Berkeley: University of California Press, 1986.

Collin, Jim. "Watching Ourselves Watch Television, or, Who's Your Agent?" *Cultural Studies* 3, no. 3 (October 1989).

Comolli, Jean-Louis. "Historical Fiction: A Body Too Much." *Screen* 19, no. 2 (summer 1978).

Compesi, Ronald J. "Gratifications of Daytime TV Serial Viewers." *Journalism Quarterly* 57 (1980).

Comstock, George, Steven Chaffee, Natan Katzman, Maxwell McCombs, and Donald Roberts. *Television and Human Behavior.* New York: Columbia University Press, 1978.

Cowan, Ruth Schwartz. *More Work for Mother.* New York: Basic Books, 1983.

Coward, Rosalind. *Female Desires: How They Are Sought, Bought and Packaged.* New York: Grove Press, 1985.

Crowley, Sharon. "Afterward: The Material of Rhetoric." *Rhetorical Bodies,* edited by Jack Selzer and Sharon Crowley. Madison: University of Wisconsin Press, 1999.

Cruz, Jon, and Justin Lewis, eds. *Viewing, Reading, Listening: Audiences and Cultural Reception.* Boulder: Westview Press, 1996.

Culler, Jonathan. *On Deconstruction.* Ithaca, N.Y.: Cornell University Press, 1982.

Curran, James, et al., eds. *Mass Communication and Society.* London: Open University Press, 1977.

Curti, Lidia. "What Is Real and What Is Not: Female Fabulations in Cultural Analysis." *Cultural Studies,* edited by Lawrence Grossbery, Cary Nelson, and Paula Treichler. New York and London: Routledge, 1992.

Davidson, Cathy, and Esther Broner, eds. *The Lost Tradition: Mothers and Daughters in Literature.* New York: Frederick Ungar, 1980.

Davis, Lennard J. *Resisting Novels: Ideology and Fiction.* New York: Methuen, 1987.

———. "A Social History of Fact and Fiction: Authorial Disavowal in the Early English Novel." *Literature and Society,* edited by Edward W. Said. Baltimore: Johns Hopkins University Press, 1980.

Delphy, Christine. *Close to Home: A Materialist Analysis of Women's Oppression.* Amherst: The University of Massachusetts Press, 1984.

Deming, Robert. "The Television Spectator-Subject," *Journal of Film and Video* 37, no. 3 (summer 1985).

Denning, Michael. *Mechanic Accents: Dime Novels and Working Class Culture in America.* London: Verso, 1987.

Derry, Charles. "Television Soap Opera: Incest, Bigamy, and Fatal Disease." *Journal of the University Film and Video Association* 35, no. 1 (winter 1983).

Dittmar, Linda. "Beyond Gender and Within it: The Social Construction of Female Desire." *Wide Angle* 8, nos. 3/4 (1986).

Doane, Mary Ann. *The Desire to Desire: The Woman's Film of the 1940s.* Bloomington: Indiana University Press, 1987.

———. "Film and the Masquerade: Theorizing the Female Spectator." *Screen* 23, nos. 3/4 (September/October 1982).

———. "Misrecognition and Identity." *Cinétracts* 3, no. 3 (fall 1980).

———. "The 'Woman's Film': Possession and Address." *Re-Visions: Essays in Feminist Film Criticism,* edited by Mary Ann Doane, Patricia Mellencamp, and Linda Williams. American Film Institute Monograph. Baltimore: University Publications of America, 1984.

Downing, Mildred. "Heroine of the Daytime Serials." *Journal of Communication* 24, no. 2 (spring 1974).

——. *The World of Daytime Serial Drama.* Doctoral Dissertation, University of Pennsylvania, 1975.

Dyer, Richard. "Entertainment and Utopia." *Movie* 24 (spring 1977).

Dyer, Richard, et al. *Coronation Street.* London: BFI, 1981.

Eagleton, Terry. *The Rape of Clarissa: Writing, Sexuality, and Class Struggle in Samuel Richardson.* Minneapolis: University of Minnesota Press, 1986.

Eco, Umberto. "Innovation and Repetition: Between Modern and Post-Modern Aesthetics." *Daedalus* 114, no. 4 (fall 1985).

——. "The Myth of Superman." *The Role of the Reader: Explorations in the Semiotics of Texts.* Bloomington: Indiana University Press, 1979.

Edmondson, Madeline, and David Rounds. *The Soaps: Daytime Serials of Radio and TV.* New York: Stein and Day, 1973.

Ehrenreich, Barbara, and Deirdre English. *For Her Own Good: 150 Years of the Experts' Advice to Women.* Garden City, N.Y.: Anchor Books, 1978.

Eisenstein, Hester, and Alice Jardine, eds. *The Future of Difference.* Boston: G. K. Hall, 1980.

Ellis, John. *Visible Fictions: Cinema: Television: Video.* London: Routledge & Kegan Paul, 1982.

Elsaesser, Thomas. "Tales of Sound and Fury." *Monogram* 4 (1972).

Enzensberger, Hans Magnus. "Constituents of a Theory of the Media." *The Consciousness Industry.* New York: Seabury Press, 1974.

Ewen, Stuart. *All Consuming Images: Politics and Style in Contemporary Culture.* New York: Basic Books, 1988.

——. *Captains of Consciousness: Advertising and the Social Role of Consumer Culture.* New York: McGraw-Hill, 1976.

Feuer, Jane. "Melodrama, Serial Form and Television Today." *Screen* 25, no. 1 (January/February 1984).

——. "Reading Dynasty: Television and Reception Theory." Paper delivered at the Society for Cinema Studies Convention, New Orleans, April 1986.

——. *Seeing Through the Eighties: Television and Reaganism.* Durham, N.C.: Duke University Press, 1995.

Fine, Marlene G. "Soap Opera Conversation: The Talk that Binds." *Journal of Communication* 31, no. 3 (summer 1981).

Fish, Stanley. *Is There a Text in the Class?: The Authority of Interpretive Communities.* Cambridge. Mass.: Harvard University Press, 1980.

Fiske, John. "Ethnosemiotics: Some Personal and Theoretical Reflection." *Cultural Studies* 4, no. 1 (spring 1990).

——. *Television Culture.* London: Methuen, 1987.

Flitterman-Lewis, Sandy. "All's Well That Doesn't End: Soap Operas and the Marriage Motif." *Camera Obscura* 16 (January 1988).

Flynn, Elizabeth A., and Patrocinio P. Schweickart. *Gender and Reading: Essays on Readers, Texts, and Contexts.* Baltimore: Johns Hopkins University Press, 1986.

Formations Editorial Collective. *Formations of Pleasure.* London: Routledge & Kegan Paul, 1983.

Foster, Hal, ed. *Discussions of Contemporary Culture.* Seattle: Bay Press, 1987.

Foucault, Michel. *The History of Sexuality, Vol. 1.* New York: Vintage Books, 1980.

———. *Language, Counter-Memory, Practice.* Ithaca, N.Y.: Cornell University Press, 1980.

———. *Madness and Civilization: A History of Insanity in the Age of Reason.* New York: Vintage Books, 1965.

———. *The Order of Things: An Archeology of the Human Sciences.* New York: Vintage Books, 1973.

———. *Power/Knowledge: Selected Interviews and Other Writings, 1972–1977.* New York: Pantheon, 1980.

———. "The Subject and Power." *Art After Modernism: Rethinking Representation,* edited by Brian Willis. New York: Godine, 1984.

———. *The Use of Pleasure: The History of Sexuality, Vol. 2.* New York: Pantheon, 1985.

Fox, Bonnie, ed. *Hidden in the Household: Women's Domestic Labor Under Capitalism.* Toronto: The Women's Press, 1980.

Frentz, Suzanne, ed. *Staying Tuned: Contemporary Soap Opera Criticism.* Bowling Green, Ohio: Bowling Green State University Popular Press, 1992.

Freud, Sigmund. "Beyond the Pleasure Principle [1920]." *The Standard Edition of the Complete Psychological Works of Sigmund Freud, vol. 18,* edited by James Stachey. London: The Hogarth Press, 1964.

———. "Family Romances [1908]." *The Sexual Enlightenment of Children.* New York: Collier Books, 1963.

———. "The Paths to the Formation of Symptoms [1917]." *Introductory Lectures on Psychoanalysis.* New York: W.W. Norton, 1977.

———. "The Relation of the Poet to Day-Dreaming [1908]." *On Creativity and the Unconscious.* New York: Harper & Row, 1958.

———. "The Uncanny [1919]." *Studies in Parapsychology.* New York: Collier, 1971.

Frith, Simon. *Performing Rites: On the Value of Popular Music.* Cambridge, Mass.: Harvard University Press, 1996.

Fulton, Eileen, and Brett Bolton. *How My World Turns.* New York: Taplinger, 1970.

Garnham, N., and Raymond Williams. "Pierre Bourdieu and the Sociology of Culture: An Introduction." *Media, Culture and Society* 2, no. 3 (July 1980).

Geertz, Clifford. *The Interpretation of Culture.* New York: Basic Books, 1973.

———. *Local Knowledge: Further Essays in Interpretive Anthropology.* New York: Basic Books, 1983.

Genette, Gerard. *Narrative Discourse: An Essay in Method.* Ithaca, N.Y.: Cornell University Press, 1980.

Geraghty, Christine. *Women and Soap Opera: A Study of Prime Time Soaps.* London: Polity Press, 1991.

Gilligan, Carol. *In a Different Voice: Psychological Theory and Women's Development.* Cambridge, Mass.: Harvard University Press, 1982.

Gitlin, Todd. "Hip-Deep in Post-modernism." *New York Times Book Review* (November 6, 1988).

———. "Media Sociology: The Dominant Paradigm," *Theory and Society* 6 (1978).

———. "Who Communicates What to Whom, in What Voice and Why, About the Study of Mass Communication?" *Critical Studies in Mass Communication* 7 (1990).

Gledhill, Christine. "Dialogue on *Stella Dallas* and Feminist Film Theory." *Cinema Journal* 25, no. 4 (summer 1986).

———. "Recent Developments in Feminist Criticism." *Quarterly Review of Film Studies* 3, no. 4 (fall 1978).

———. "Speculations on the Relationship Between Soap Opera and Melodrama." *Quarterly Review of Film and Video* 14, no. 1/2 (July 1992).

Goffman, Erving. *Forms of Talk.* Philadelphia: University of Pennsylvania Press, 1981.

Goldsen, Rose. *The Show and Tell Machine: How Television Works and Works You Over.* New York: Dial Press, 1977.

Gómez, Alma, Cherríe Moraga, Mariana Romo-Carmona, eds. *Cuentos: Stories by Latinas.* New York: Kitchen Table: Women of Color Press, 1983.

Gray, Ann. *Video Playtime: The Gendering of Leisure Technology.* London: Routledge, 1992.

Greenberg, Bradley S., Robert Abelman, and Kimberly Neuendorf. "Sex on the Soap Operas: Afternoon Delight." *Journal of Communication* 31, no. 3 (summer 1981).

Greimas, A. J. "The Interaction of Semiotic Constraints." *Yale French Studies* 41 (1968).

Grele, Ronald J., ed. *Envelopes of Sound.* Chicago: Precedent Publishing, 1975.

Griffith, Sean. "All My Gay Children? Soaps, Sexuality and Cyberspace." Paper presented at Console-ing Passions Conference, Montreal, May 1997.

Grossberg, Lawrence. "Another Boring Day in Paradise: Rock and Roll and the Empowerment of Everyday Life." *Popular Music* 4 (1984).

———. "The In-Difference of Television." *Screen* 28, no. 2 (spring 1987).

Gurevitch, Michael, Tony Bennett, James Curran, and Janet Woolacott, eds. *Culture, Society and the Media.* London: Methuen, 1982.

Hall, Stuart, et al., eds. *Culture, Media, Language: Working Papers in Cultural Studies, 1972–79.* London: Hutchinson, 1981.

Haralovich, Mary Beth. "Sitcoms and Suburbs: Positioning the 1950s Homemaker." *Quarterly Review of Film and Video* 11, no. 1 (1989).

Harrington, C. Lee, and Denise D. Bielby. *Soap Fans: Pursuing Pleasure and Making Meaning in Everyday Life.* Philadelphia: Temple University Press, 1995.

Hay, James, Lawrence Grossberg, and Ellen Wartella, eds. *The Audience and Its Landscape.* Boulder: Westview Press, 1996.

Hayward, Jennifer. *Consuming Pleasures: Active Audiences and Serial Fictions from Dickens to Soap Operas.* Lexington: University Press of Kentucky, 1997.

Heide, Margaret J. *Television Culture and Women's Lives:* thirtysomething *and the Contradictions of Gender.* Philadelphia: University of Pennsylvania Press, 1995.

Henderson, Kathy. "They Spin the Tales for Soap Operas." *New York Times* (July 6, 1986).

Herzog, Herta. "On Borrowed Experience," *Studies in Philosophy and Social Science.* 9, no. 1 (1941).

———. "What Do We Really Know About Daytime Serial Listeners?" *Radio Research, 1942–1943,* edited by Paul Lazarsfeld and Frank Stanton. Reprinted, New York: Arno Press, 1979.

Hobson, Dorothy. *Crossroads: The Drama of a Soap Opera.* London: Methuen, 1982.

hooks, bell. *Feminist Theory: From Margin to Center.* Boston: South End Press, 1984.

———. "Talking Back," *Discourse* 8 (fall/winter 1986/87).

Horkheimer, Max. "Authority and the Family." *Critical Theory.* New York: Continuum, 1989.

Horkheimer, Max, and Theodor W. Adorno. "The Culture Industry: Enlightenment As Mass Deception." *Dialectic of Enlightenment.* New York: Seabury, 1972.

Horton, Donald, and R. Richard Wohl. "Mass Communication and Para-Social Interaction: Observation on Intimacy at a Distance." Reprinted in *Inter/Media: Interpersonal Communication in a Media World,* 3rd Ed., edited by Gary Gumpert and Robert Cathcart. New York: Oxford University Press, 1986.

Intintoli, Michael James. *Taking Soaps Seriously: The World of* Guiding Light. New York: Praeger, 1984.

Irigaray, Luce. *Speculum of the Other Woman.* Ithaca, N.Y.: Cornell University Press, 1985.

———. *This Sex Which Is Not One.* Ithaca, N.Y.: Cornell University Press, 1985.

Iser, Wolfgang. *The Act of Reading.* Baltimore: Johns Hopkins University Press, 1978.

———. *The Implied Reader: Patterns of Communications in Prose Fiction from Bunyan to Beckett.* Baltimore: Johns Hopkins University Press, 1974.

Jameson, Fredric. *The Political Unconscious: Narrative As a Socially Symbolic Act.* Ithaca, N.Y.: Cornell University Press, 1981.

———. "Reification and Utopia in Mass Culture." *Social Text* 1 (1979).

Jenkins, Henry. "'Going Bonkers!': Children, Play and Pee-wee," *Camera Obscura* 17 (May 1988).

———. "Star Trek Rerun, Reread, Rewritten: Fan Writing as Textual Poaching." *Critical Studies in Mass Communications* 5, no. 2 (1988).

———. *Textual Poachers: Television Fans and Participatory Culture.* London: Routledge, 1992.

Jensen, Klaus Bruhn, and Nicholas W. Jankowski, eds. *A Handbook of Qualitative Methodologies for Mass Communication Research.* London and New York: Routledge, 1991.

Jones, Steven G. "Understanding Community in the Information Age." *CyberSociety: Computer-Mediated Communication and Community,* edited by Steven G. Jones. Thousand Oaks, Calif.: Sage, 1995.

Journal of Broadcasting and Electronic Media 29, no. 3 (summer 1985) Special Edition: A Soap Opera Symposium.

Joyrich, Lynne. *Re-viewing Reception: Television, Gender, and Postmodern Culture.* Bloomington: Indiana University Press, 1996.

Kaplan, E. Ann. *Regarding Television: Critical Approaches—An Anthology.* Baltimore: University Publications of America, 1983.

———. "Theories of Melodrama: A Feminist Perspective." *Women and Performance: A Journal of Feminist Theory* 1, no. 1 (spring/summer 1983).

Katz, Elihu, and Tamar Liebes. "Mutual Aid in the Decoding of *Dallas:* Preliminary Notes from a Cross-Cultural Study." *Television in Transition: Papers from the First International Television Studies Conference,* edited by Phillip Drummond and Richard Paterson. London: BFI, 1986.

Katzman, Natan. "Television Soap Operas: What's Been Going On Anyway?" *Public Opinion Quarterly* 36 (summer 1972).

Kaufman, Helen. "The Appeal of Specific Daytime Serials." *Radio Research, 1942–1943,* edited by P. Lazarfeld and F. Stanton. New York: Duell, Sloan and Pearce, 1944.

Kellogg, Mary Alice. "High Noon for Soaps: All the Intrigue Isn't on the Screen." *TV Guide* (February 26, 1983).

Kermode, Frank. *The Sense of an Ending: Studies in the Theory of Fiction.* New York: Oxford University Press, 1981.

Kipnes, Laura. "Aesthetics and Foreign Policy," *Social Text* 15 (fall 1986).

———. *Bound and Gagged: Pornography and the Politics of Fantasy in America.* Durham, N.C.: Duke University Press, 1999.

Koch, Gertrud. "Ex-Changing the Gaze: Re-Visioning Feminist Film Theory." *New German Critique* 34 (winter 1985).

Kristeva, Julia. *Desire in Language.* New York: Columbia University Press, 1980.

———. "Women's Time." *Signs* 7, no. 1 (autumn 1981).

Kroker, Arthur, and David Cook. *The Postmodern Scene: Excremental Culture and Hyper-Aesthetics.* New York: St. Martin's Press, 1986.

Kuhn, Annette. "Women's Genres." *Screen* 25, no. 1 (January/February 1984).

Kuhn, Thomas S. *The Structure of Scientific Revolutions.* Chicago: University of Chicago Press, 1970.

Labov, William, and Joshua Waletzky. "Narrative Analysis: Oral Versions of Personal Experience." *Proceedings of the Annual Spring Meeting of the American Ethnological Society* (1966).

LaGuardia, Robert. *The Wonderful World of TV Soap Operas.* New York: Ballantine Books, 1974.

de Lauretis, Teresa. *Alice Doesn't: Femininsm, Semiotics and Cinema.* Bloomington: Indiana University Press, 1984.

Lears, T. J. Jackson. "From Salvation to Self-Realization: Advertising and the Therapeutic Roots of the Consumer Culture." *Culture of Consumption: Critical Essays in American History, 1880–1980,* edited by Richard Wrightman Fox and T. J. Jackson Lears. New York: Pantheon, 1983.

Lee, Minu, and Chong Heup Cho. "Women Watching Together: An Ethnographic Study of Korean Soap Opera Fans in the United States." *Cultural Studies* 4 (1990).

Leevy, J. Roy. "Leisure Time of the American Housewife." *Sociology and Social Research* 35, no. 2 (November/December 1950).

Lefebvre, Henri. *Everyday Life in the Modern World.* New York: Harper & Row, 1971.

LeMay, Harding. *Eight Years in Another World.* New York: Atheneum, 1981.

Lesage, Julia "The Human Subject—You, He, or Me?" *Screen* 16, no. 2 (summer 1975).

Levi-Strauss, Claude. *The Savage Mind.* Chicago: University of Chicago Press, 1966.

Lewis, Lisa, ed. *The Adoring Audience: Fan Culture and Popular Media.* New York: Routledge, 1992.

Light, Alison. "'Return to Manderley'—Romance Fiction, Female Sexuality and Class." *Feminist Review* 16 (April 1984).

Lopate, Carole. "Daytime Television: You'll Never Want to Leave Home." *Radical America* 11, no. 1 (January/February 1977).

Lorde, Audre. *The Uses of the Erotic: The Erotic as Power.* Brooklyn: Out and Out Books, 1982.

Lovell, Terry. *Pictures of Reality.* London: BFI, 1980.

Macherey, Pierre. "Interview." *Red Letters* 5 (summer 1977).

———. *A Theory of Literary Production.* London: Routledge & Kegan Paul, 1978.

Magazine & Bookseller. "Interview: Marc Liu, President of *Soap Opera Digest*" (unsigned, January 1983).

Mandel, Ernest. *Delightful Murder: A Social History of the Crime Story.* London: Pluto Press, 1984.

Marcus, George E. *Ethnography Through Thick and Thin.* Princeton, N.J.: Princeton University Press, 1998.

Markoff, John. "A Newer Lonelier Crowd Emerges in Internet Study." *New York Times* (February 16, 2000).

Masciarotte, Gloria-Jean. "'C'mon Girl: Oprah Winfrey and the Discourse of Feminine Talk." *Genders* 11 (fall 1991).

Masterman, Len, ed. *Television Mythologies: Stars, Shows and Signs.* London: Comedia, 1984.

Mayne, Judith. "The Woman at the Keyhole: Women's Cinema and Feminist Criticism." *New German Critique* 23 (spring/summer 1981).

McQuail, Denis. "With the Benefit of Hindsight." *Mass Communication Review Yearbook,* 1985.

McRobbie, Angela. "Dance and Social Fantasy." *Gender and Generation,* edited by Angela McRobbie and Mica Nava. London: MacMillan, 1984.

Mellencamp, Patricia, ed. *Logics of Television.* Bloomington: Indiana University Press, 1990.

Mendelsohn, Daniel. "The Melodramatic Moment," *The New York Times Magazine* (March 23, 2003).

Messaris, Paul. "Biases of Self-Reported 'Functions' and 'Gratifications' of Mass Media Use." *Et cetera* 23, no. 3 (September 1977).

Metz, Christian. *Film Language: A Semiotics of the Cinema.* New York: Oxford University Press, 1974.

———. *The Imaginary Signifier: Psychoanalysis and the Cinema.* Bloomington: Indiana University Press, 1982.

———. *Language and Cinema.* The Hague: Mouton, 1974.

Meyrowitz, Joshua. "Television and Interpersonal Behavior: Codes of Perception and Response." *Inter/Media: Interpersonal Communication in a Media World,* edited by Gary Gumpert and Robert Cathcart. New York: Oxford University Press, 1979.

Miller, Nancy K. "Emphasis Added: Plots and Plausibility in Women's Fiction." *PMLA* 96, no. 1 (January 1981).
———, ed. *The Poetics of Gender*. New York: Columbia University Press, 1986.
Mitchell, Juliet. *Women: The Longest Revolution.* New York: Pantheon, 1984.
Mitchell, W. J. T., ed. *The Politics of Interpretation*. Chicago: University of Chicago Press, 1983.
Mitroff, Ian I., and Warren Bennis. *The Unreality Industry: The Deliberate Manufacturing of Falsehood and What It Is Doing to Our Lives.* New York: Oxford University Press, 1993.
Modleski, Tania. *Loving with a Vengeance: Mass-Produced Fantasies for Women.* Hamden, Connecticut: Archon Books, 1982.
———, ed. *Studies in Entertainment: Critical Approaches to Mass Culture*. Bloomington: Indiana University Press, 1986.
———. "Time and Desire in the Woman's Film." *Cinema Journal,* 23, no. 3 (spring 1984).
Moretti, Franco. *Signs Taken for Wonders.* London: Verso, 1983.
Morley, David. *Family Television: Cultural Power and Domestic Leisure*. London: Comedia, 1986.
———. *Home Territories: Media, Mobility and Identity.* London: Routledge, 2000.
———. *The "Nationwide" Audience.* London: BFI, 1980.
———. *Television, Audiences and Cultural Studies.* London: Routledge, 1992.
Mukarovsky, Jan. "Two Studies in Dialogue." *The Word and Verbal Art.* New Haven, Conn.: Yale University Press, 1977.
Mulvey, Laura. "Afterthought on 'Visual Pleasure and Narrative Cinema' Inspired by *Duel in the Sun.*" *Framework* 15/16/17 (summer 1981).
———. "Notes on Sirk and Melodrama." *Movie* 25/26 (1976–1977).
———. "Visual Pleasure and Narrative Cinema." *Screen* 16, no. 3 (fall 1975).
Mumford, Laura Stempel. "AOL My Children: Meta-Discourse in the Cyber-Soap Community." Paper presented at Console-ing Passions Conference, Madison, Wisconsin, April 1996.
———. *Love and Ideology in the Afternoon: Soap Opera, Women, and Television Genre.* Bloomington: Indiana University Press, 1995.
Musil, Robert. *The Man Without Qualities.* New York: Capricorn Books, 1965 (1930).
Neale, Stephen. *Genre.* London: BFI, 1980.
———. "Melodrama and Tears." *Screen* 27, no. 16 (November/December, 1986).
Newcomb, Horace. *Television: The Critical View,* 5th edition. New York: Oxford University Press, 1994.
———. *TV: The Most Popular Art.* Garden City, N.Y.: Anchor Books, 1974.
New German Critique Editors. "Women and Film: A Discussion of Feminist Aesthetics." *New German Critique* 13 (winter 1977).
Nixon, Agnes. "Agnes Nixon Seminars at the Museum of Broadcasting." Transcript. New York: Museum of Television and Radio, January 1988.
———. "In Daytime TV the Golden Age Is Now." *Television Quarterly* (fall 1972).
Nochimson, Martha. *No End to Her: Soap Opera and the Female Subject.* Berkeley: University of California Press, 1993.

Nye, Russel. *The Unembarrassed Muse: The Popular Arts in America.* New York: Dial Press, 1970.

Oakley, Ann. *Woman's Work: The Housewife, Past and Present.* New York: Vintage Books, 1976.

Olsen, Tillie. *Silences.* New York: Delta, 1980.

Penley, Constance. "Feminism, Pschoanalysis, and the Study of Popular Culture." *Cultural Studies,* edited by Lawrence Grossbery, Cary Nelson, and Paula Treichler. New York and London: Routledge, 1992.

Petro, Patrice. "Criminality or Hysteria? Television and the Law." *Discourse* 10, no. 2 (spring/summer 1988).

Phillips, Irna. "Every Woman's Life Is a Soap Opera." *McCall's* (March 1965).

Phillips, Irna, and Janet Huckins. "Lonely Women." *Movie-Radio-Guide* 12, no. 6 (November 14–20, 1942).

Porter, Dennis. "Soap Time: Thoughts on a Commodity Art Form." *College English* 38, no. 8 (April 1977).

Propp, Vladimir. *Morphology of the Folk Tale.* Austin: University of Texas Press, 1968.

Rabinowitz, Lauren. "All My Computers: The Electronic World of Reception in Soap Opera Nets." Paper delivered at the Console-ing Passions Conference, Tucson, Arizona, April 1994.

———. "Soap Opera Bridal Fantasies." *Screen* 33, no. 3 (autumn 1992).

Radway, Janice A. *A Feeling for Books: The Book of the Month Club, Literary Taste, and Middle-Class Leisure.* Chapel Hill: University of North Carolina Press, 1997.

———. "Identifying Ideological Seams: Mass Culture, Analytical Method, and Political Practice." *Communication* 9 (1986).

———. *Reading the Romance: Women, Patriarchy and Popular Literature.* Chapel Hill: University of North Carolina Press, 1984.

Rapping, Elayne. "Daytime Utopias: If You Lived in Pine Valley, You'd Be Home." *Hop on Pop: The Politics and Pleasures of Popular Culture,* edited by Henry Jenkins, Tara McPherson, and Jane Shattuc. Durham, N.C.: Duke University Press, 2002.

———. *The Looking Glass World of Nonfiction TV.* Boston: South End Press, 1987.

Reiter, Rayna R., ed. *Toward an Anthropology of Women.* New York: Monthly Review Press, 1975.

Ricoeur, Paul. "Narrative Time." *Critical Inquiry* 7, no. 1 (winter 1980).

Riffaterre, Michael. *Fictional Truth.* Baltimore: Johns Hopkins University Press, 1990.

Rimmon-Kenan, Shlomith. "The Paradoxical Status of Repetition." *Poetics Today* 1, no. 4 (1980).

Robinson, Lillian S. *Sex, Class and Culture.* New York: Methuen, 1986.

Rosaldo, Michelle Zimbalist, and Louise Lamphere, eds. *Woman, Culture and Society.* Palo Alto, Calif.: Stanford University Press, 1974.

Rose, Brian. "Thickening the Plot." *Journal of Communication* 29, no. 4 (autumn 1979).

Rose, Jacqueline. *Sexuality in the Field of Vision.* London: New Left Books, 1986.

Rosen, Ruth. "Soap Operas: Search for Yesterday." *Watching Television,* edited by Todd Gitlin. New York: Pantheon, 1986.

Rouverol, Jean. *Writing for the Soaps*. Cincinnati: Writer's Digest Books, 1984.
Rowbotham, Sheila. *Woman's Consciousness, Man's World*. London: Penguin, 1973.
Said, Edward W. *Orientalism*. New York: Vintage Books, 1979.
Schemering, Christopher. *The Soap Opera Encyclopedia*. New York: Ballantine, 1985.
Scholes, Robert. "Narration and Narrativity in Film. *Film Theory and Criticism*, edited by Gerald Mast and Marshall Cohen. New York: Oxford University Press, 1985.
Schulz, Bruno. "Street of Crocodiles." *Street of Crocodiles*. New York: Penguin, 1977 (1934).
Seiter, Ellen. "Making Distinction in TV Audience Research: Case Study of a Troubling Interview." *Cultural Studies* 4, no. 1 (spring 1990).
———. "Men, Sex and Money in Recent Family Melodramas." *Journal of the University Film and Video Association* 35, no. 1 (winter 1983).
———. *The Promise of Melodrama: Recent Women's Films and Soap Operas*. Doctoral Dissertation, Northwestern University, 1981.
———. "The Role of the Woman Reader: Eco's Narrative Theory and Soap Operas." *Tabloid* 6 (1981).
———. *Television and New Media Audiences*. New York: Oxford University Press, 1999.
———. "'To Teach and To Sell': Irna Phillips and Her Sponsors, 1930–1954." *Journal of Film And Video* 41, no. 1 (spring 1989).
Seiter, Ellen, Hans Borchers, Gabriele Kreutzner, and Eva-Maria Warth, eds. *Remote Control: Television, Audiences and Cultural Power*. London: Routledge, 1989.
Shoham, S. Gíora. *Social Deviance*. New York: Gardner, 1976.
Sholle, David. "Reading the Audience, Reading Resistance: Prospects and Problems." *Journal of Film and Video* 43, no. 1/2 (spring/summer 1991).
Showalter, Elaine, ed. *The New Feminist Criticism: Essays on Women, Literature and Theory*. New York: Pantheon Books, 1985.
Simon, Ron, and Ellen O'Neill, eds. *Worlds Without End: The Art and History of the Soap Opera*. New York: Abrams/Museum of Television and Radio, 1997.
Slater, Philip. *The Pursuit of Loneliness*. New York: Beacon Press, 1970.
Smith, Barbara Herrnstein. *On the Margins of Discourse: The Relation of Literature to Language*. Chicago: University of Chicago Press, 1978.
Soap Opera Digest. 1981 to 1989.
Spigel, Lynn. "Detours in the Search for Tomorrow: Tania Modleski's *Loving with a Vengeance: Mass-Produced Fantasies for Women*." *Camera Obscura* 13/14 (spring/summer 1985).
———. *Make Room for TV: Television and the Family Ideal in Postwar America*. Chicago: University of Chicago Press, 1992.
Stallybrass, Peter, and Allon White. *The Politics and Poetics of Transgression*. Ithaca, N.Y.: Cornell University Press, 1986.
Stam, Robert, and Louise Spence. "Colonialism, Racism and Representation—An Introduction." *Screen* 24, no. 2 (March/April 1983).
Stedman, R. W. *The Serials: Suspense and Drama by Installment*. Norman: University of Oklahoma Press, 1977.

Steinberg, Cobbett. *TV Facts.* New York: Facts on File, 1980.

Sturken, Marita, and Lisa Cartwright. *Practices of Looking: An Introduction to Visual Culture.* New York: Oxford University Press, 2001.

Suleiman, Susan Rubin. *Authoritarian Fictions: The Ideological Novel As a Literary Genre.* New York: Columbia University Press, 1983.

Suleiman, Susan B., and Inge Crosman, eds. *The Reader in the Text: Essays on Audience and Interpretation.* (Princeton: Princeton University Press, 1980.

Sutherland, John C., and Shelly J. Siniawsky. "The Treatment and Resolution of Moral Violations on Soap Operas." *Journal of Communication* 32, no. 2 (spring 1982).

Thomas, Sari. *The Relationship Between Daytime Serials and Their Viewers.* Doctoral Dissertation, University of Pennsylvania, 1977.

———. "Some Problems of the Paradigm in Communications Theory." *Philosophy of the Social Sciences* 10 (1980).

Thompson, Kristen. *Breaking the Glass Armor: Neoformalist Film Analysis.* Princeton, N.J.: Princeton University Press, 1988.

Thorne, Barrie, with Marilyn Yalom, eds. *Rethinking the Family: Some Feminist Questions.* New York: Longman, 1982.

Thurber, James. "Soapland" [1948]. *The Beast in Me and Other Animals.* New York: Harcourt Brace Jovanovich, 1973.

Todorov, Tzvetan. *The Fantastic: A Structural Approach to a Literary Genre.* Ithaca, N.Y.: Cornell University Press, 1975.

———. *Introduction to Poetics.* Minneapolis: University of Minnesota Press, 1981.

Tompkins, Jane P., ed. *Reader Response Criticism: From Formalism to Post Structuralism.* Baltimore: Johns Hopkins University Press, 1980.

Tuchman, Gaye. *Making News: A Study in the Construction of Reality.* New York: The Free Press, 1978.

Turkle, Sherry. *Life on the Screen: Identity in the Age of the Internet.* New York: Touchstone, 1995.

TV Guide. 1981–1989.

Twitchell, James B. *Forbidden Partners: The Incest Taboo in Modern Culture.* New York: Columbia University Press, 1987.

Vance, Carole S., ed. *Pleasure and Danger: Exploring Female Sexuality.* Boston: Routledge & Kegan Paul, 1985.

Wakefield, Dan. *All Her Children.* New York: Avon, 1976.

Waldman, Diane. "Film Theory and the Gendered Spectator: The Female or the Feminist Reader?" *Camera Obscura* 18 (September 1988).

Walkerdine, Valerie. "Some Day My Prince Will Come." *Gender and Generation,* edited by Angela McRobbie and Mica Nava. London: MacMillan, 1984.

Warner, W. Lloyd, and Willian E. Henry. "The Radio Day Time Serial: A Symbolic Analysis." *Genetic Psychology Monographs* 37 (1948).

Webster, Steven. "Dialogue and Fiction in Ethnography." *Dialectical Anthropology* 7, no. 2 (November 1982).

Welter, Barbara. "The Cult of True Womanhood: 1820–1860." *American Quarterly* 17 (summer 1966).

White, Mimi. "Crossing Wavelengths: The Diegetic and Referential Imaginary of American Commercial Television." *Cinema Journal* 25, no. 2 (winter 1986).

———. *Tele-Advising: Therapeutic Discourses in American Television.* Chapel Hill: University of North Carolina Press, 1992.

Willett, John, ed. *Brecht on Theatre.* New York: Hill and Wang, 1977.

Williams, Raymond. "British Film History: New Perspectives." *British Cinema History,* edited by James Curran and Vincent Porter. London: Weidenfeld and Nicolson, 1983.

———. *Marxism and Literature.* London: Oxford University Press, 1977.

———. *Problems in Materialism and Culture.* London: Verso, 1980.

———. *Television: Technology and Cultural Form.* New York: Schocken, 1975.

Williamson, Judith. *Decoding Advertising: Ideology and Meaning in Advertising.* London: Marion Boyars, 1978.

———. "The Problems of Being Popular." *New Socialist* 41 (September 1986).

Willis, Susan. *A Primer for Daily Life.* New York: Routledge, 1991.

Wilson, Elizabeth, with Angela Weir. *Hidden Agendas: Theory, Politics, and Experience in the Women's Movement.* London: Tavistock, 1986.

Wolf, Christa. *The Quest for Christa T.* New York: Farrar, Straus & Giroux, 1970.

Zaretsky, Eli. *Capitalism, The Family and Personal Life.* New York: Harper & Row, 1976.

I am a part of all that I have met;
Yet all experience is an arch where-thro'
Gleams that untravell'd world, whose margin fades
Forever and forever when I move.
—Alfred, Lord Tennyson

Author's Note

Any work in progress as long as this one accumulates more than the usual number of debts. It is a great pleasure to thank the many who have helped. First and most of all, I want to express my appreciation to the women you have read about, the women who have given me so much of their time and their feelings. They have burst into my life, as I have into many of theirs. I frequently came away from our meetings acknowledging an appropriate sense of difference and a healthy sense of modesty. When I began in 1981, I may have thought my interest was intellectual and political. Over the years, however, I have come to realize that it is also emotional and social. I knew the words I was using were not mine alone and often felt a throng of readers looking over my shoulder as I wrote. Sometimes I questioned if my ideas were relevant to those whose lives I sought to celebrate. When it comes to conveying my gratitude, I am moved once more by how much this seems to be a collective endeavor.

Like many other studies, this one began as a modest inquiry and, at times, seemed like it was going to encompass the world. What you have before you contains the traces of several challenges, interruptions, and compromises. It reflects a process that was both dynamic and maddening. Yet those fading margins buoyed my days for many years.

I am neither a clever writer—nor a happy one. I owe a lot to the kind ones who stood by me along the way. Carl Lewis has always answered the phone when I needed to complain about something and somehow found time when I had work for him to read. Roald Hoffmann also interrupted his own writing to read mine. He never forgot to remind me to shorten my paragraphs (and to provide gifts of music and chocolate when I needed them most). Norma Spector and Karen Backstein carefully scrutinized parts of the text as well. My friend and intellectual companion, David Curtis, stepped in at the final moment to examine the manuscript. The depth and clarity of his perception, the generosity of his mind and spirit, and his impatience with pretension and too many commas deserve special notice. My tendency to lard my writing with digressions, glosses, and parenthetical observations must have driven David, Norma, Karen, Roald, and Carl crazy. If my syntax is accessible, it's probably thanks to the five of them.

Again and again over the years, I have been struck by how much scholarly writing is a cumulative process. I owe a debt of gratitude to many who have reflected on the issues that concern me. Stifled by conventional academic criticism that I felt was inappropriate to the subject of pleasure, a subject rich in hidden meanings, at times I felt I was walking a tightrope stretched over a void; other times, I looked down into a chasm in which Brueghelian figures struggling with similar matters frolicked.

I especially want to mention my teachers, official and unofficial, for inspiration and for introducing me to numerous others whose perspectives have, either in their acceptance or their rejection, formed the basis of ideas that you have read. For, as Roland Barthes has written, "the writer can only imitate a gesture that is always anterior, never original."[1] My work has benefited greatly from the scholarly examples of Annette Michelson and the late Jay Leyda (although this project has developed in a direction that neither of them could have anticipated).

This research started out as a dissertation project. Bob Sklar was a sharp and astute critic of my work in the early stages of development. If writers always have ideal readers, in those days I frequently found myself writing for Bill Simon and Fina Bathrick, imagining them laughing and replying with support. Faye Ginsburg stepped in at a later phase, read a chapter, and took time from her busy schedule to encourage me. Lynne Jackson's interest in my work sustained me in many a lonely moment and I have learned much from my talks with Steve Elworth. He read this work early on, was generous with his insights, and often seemed to know what it was really about. I would also like to thank Ien Ang. If, as I believe, thoughts come into being with the need to communicate them, then many of mine are indebted to our conversations and our letters. In the later stages, William Boddy, Becky Cole, Ron Simon, and Ellen O'Neill offered welcome suggestions. The talented, patient, and enthusiastic staff at Wesleyan University Press, particularly Lee Gibson, made my work enjoyable as they guided me through a few prickly problems. I always felt my book was in safe hands.

My colleagues at Sacred Heart University, especially Sid Gottlieb, Jeff Cain, Sandy Young, Jim Castonguay, Andrew Miller, and Greg Golda, have been a delightful font of fellowship and stimulating discussion. Besnik Hadjari provided superb technical support. I also wish to thank Fran Grodzinsky, my "ace informant" when it came to the Internet (although any blunders are all my own).

I thank the Graduate School of Arts and Science at New York University for a fellowship that supported me during nine months of writing. Sacred Heart granted me a sabbatical and a course reassignment that allowed me to work my research into book form. I am also grateful to subventions from the Office of the

University Seminars at Columbia University and the Department of Media Studies and Digital Culture, Sacred Heart University. Unaccountably, I sometimes felt the need to get away from home to write. I am indebted to the hospitality and congeniality of the Anderson Center for Interdisciplinary Studies, the Diaz-Fletcher family, Priscilla Hilton, and Jef Major-Westing.

I want to thank New York University, Goucher College, Hunter College, and Sacred Heart University for the opportunities to teach. For I am beholden to my students, especially those in Media Studies at Hunter and Sacred Heart, whose avid spectatorship and resistant scholarship forced me to shape and reshape my thoughts and language.

Audiences at various scholarly conferences and seminars have also offered helpful responses to drafts of parts of Chapters 3 and 4. Some of the material has appeared in *Cinema è Cinema,* vol. 10, nos. 35–36 (April, September 1983), *Quarterly Review of Film Studies,* vol. 9, no. 4 (fall 1984), *To Be Continued: Soap Operas Around the World,* Robert C. Allen, ed. (New York: Routledge, 1995), and *Worlds Without End: The Art and History of the Soap Opera,* Ron Simon and Ellen O'Neill, eds. (New York: Harry N. Abrams, Inc./Museum of Television and Radio, 1997). As they appear here, the arguments have been substantially revised and expanded. I would like to thank the editors of those books and journals for permission to reuse the material.

In many ways, this study was influenced by memories of a dinner that I had in the late seventies with David Garcia and his family. Their home had a complete set of Freud and a complete set of Marx—and no television set.

My family has shown extraordinary patience and keen interest through what must have seemed like inordinately slow progress. I am deeply grateful to my mother, Regina Heller, and her recently deceased mother, Rose Feigenbaum, two women whose quiet strength has always impressed me, and whose soap opera watching was part of my original curiosity. This book is a tribute to them.

And finally, a chance meeting with Paul Thek has meant more to my work than either of us could have realized that day. Much of the final chapter is infused with his memory.

Index

ABOUT THE AUTHOR

Louise Spence teaches Media Studies at Sacred Heart University. A graduate of New York University, she is the co-author of *Writing Himself into History: Oscar Micheaux, His Silent Films, and His Audiences.*